MULTIMEDIA INFORMATION COLLECTION IN DIGITAL LIBRARIES

MULTIMEDIA INFORMATION COLLECTION IN DIGITAL LIBRARIES

Editor
V. K. Suraj

ISHA

ISHA BOOKS
Delhi-110033

Multimedia Information Collection in Digital Libraries

Rs. 840

ISBN : 81-8205-242-4

Published in 2005 in India by
Isha Books
D-43, Prithviraj Road,
Adarsh Nagar, Delhi - 110033
e-mail : ishabooks@hotmail.com

Laser Typesetting at : Global Printers, New Delhi
Printed at : Chawla Offset Press, Delhi

Contents

Preface

In the information age, digital media have significantly impacted our lives and overloaded information systems worldwide. As the needs and expectations of library users change in the digital environment, libraries are trying to find the best ways to define their user communities, understand what they value, and evolve digital library collections and services to meet their demands. A digital library is, like a traditional library, a collection of books and reference materials. Unlike a traditional library, however, the collection of a digital library is, as you would expect, digital, and is usually served over the World Wide Web.

Digital libraries are large collections of multimedia information that are usually created with the purpose of supporting learning or knowledge acquisition. They have extended access to many types of collections from all points of the globe. These collections include film and video archives, news material, oral histories, museum images and digitized special collections. As more multimedia collections are digitised, there is a growing need for proactive digital design to assure access and interoperability without compromising the content of the collections. Subject areas range from digital image reference services; museums and web-based exhibits to the use of face recognition software for national security.

In this book an attempt has been made to synthesise all aspects of digital library collections. It enables the readers to understand the process of electronic dissemination of information, the emerging trends in digital libraries and the changing responsibilities of library professionals. The book will be useful to practising librarians, information scientists, teachers and students of library and information science and to those concerned with the digitisation of library resources.

Editor

1

Digital Libraries

Digital libraries are new, and investment in them is fraught with unknowns. Consequently, librarians and library directors are hungry for information about different institutional experiences, including what digital library investments are considered good, meaningful, and cost-effective, and what influences have helped shape successful digital library programmes.

Not all digital libraries focus primarily on digitally reformatting analog items in their collections and distributing them online. While possessing digitization capacity, focus principally on providing systems environments and infrastructure capable of managing digital assets as may be acquired or used within their host institution.

In the year 2000, digital conversion costs for member libraries ranged between $38,000 and $1,145,000; the average spending on all aspects of digital library programmes was $4,341,798 ($2,641,798 if the costs of acquiring access to commercial electronic content are excluded). Fewer than half of the digital libraries surveyed invest primarily in digital reformatting programmes. Most have oriented themselves toward the development of technical infrastructure and of various reference and other end-user services.

Llibrary Programmes

Llibrary programmes are initiated for different reasons, any one or more of which may be at work at a single institution. Most programmes derive from innovative thinking about the future role of libraries or the future role of the library in an extensively networked teaching and learning environment, but there are other motivations. The role of blue-sky planning may be particularly significant at institutions that entered the digital library business early and had few models to draw on.

Institutions that entered later could be imitative as well as creative. In this regard, it is worth noting that academic institutions compete at nearly every level: they compete for grant and philanthropic funding, good students, and respected faculty. Their libraries are not immune from competitive impulses, which also have a hand in initiating digital library investments. Thus, the progress of digital library programmes that are located at a library's peer institutions cannot be discounted as a powerful driver.

Digital library programmes that were developed as part of a campus-wide initiative to develop as a leader in the use of information technology; as a means of modernizing overall university services to attract better students; to keep up with the digital library programmes being developed at peer institutions; and as a commitment to the delivery of high-quality library services.

Most of the programmes are at some level deploying innovative technologies to deliver very traditional library services. For example, Harvard's Libraries Digital Initiative is preparing to collect and preserve scholarly and cultural outputs that happen to be in digital form, and to encourage their use in research and teaching. The digital library programme is supporting an institution that has a strong cross-disciplinary interest in theoretical and applied aspects of the performing arts. Michigan is supporting the development and conservation of out-of-copyright monograph and serial holdings and efforts to provide highly functional access to digital content.

Leadership and Ownership

Leadership is required at three levels: the political, the creative, and the executive. Political leadership may stem from the university librarian, as it has at Harvard, Virginia, Indiana, and NYU. Creative leadership, another important ingredient, comes from a number of sources. Creative leadership can also stem from an individual. At Virginia, the digital library programme owes a great deal to a single librarian who, in the 1980s, was already thinking deeply about what a twenty-first-century academic library should be.

The need for executive leadership is self-evident. No digital library programme, however well supported and envisioned, can develop without people who possess the appropriate technical, tactical, and even diplomatic skills. Programmes that otherwise had key elements in place, such as funding and mission orientation, were delayed to some extent until such leadership could be found.

Just as digital library leadership is required at several levels, ownership of the digital library programme needs to be felt widely across its host institution. This may be less important for the startup phase of a digital library programme than for its long-term operation. Foundling digital library initiatives seem to favor safe-haven environments where those involved can experiment without the operational demands made of other library units.

The reliance on digital library laboratories is apparent in both early- and late-starting programmes. At Michigan, the early programme involved a number of projects loosely coordinated by a programme director and fulfilling the evolving vision of the founding triumvirate. Crucially, the digital library programme was outside the library's normal management line: its director was responsible to the triumvirate.

The model of a digital library programme that is relatively autonomous in its early days is evident elsewhere with significant variation. Virginia cut its digital library teeth in experimental units that were outside the normal line of management—in the library's Electronic Text Center and, in the academic unit, the Institute for Advanced Technology in the Humanities (IATH), which is located in the main library. Through a series of digital library projects, staff (and through the staff, the library) gained competence in creating, managing, and distributing electronic information.

The Electronic Text Center was located in the library but was initially independent of other library departments and services. Even IATH reported directly to the associate provost for research and was thus removed to some extent from the "academic line." Virginia continued for some time to foster experimental efforts in relatively autonomous organizational units. Thus, as it sought to develop experience and capacity with new digital materials (e.g., images, statistical data), it opened new media centers that focused on the technical and other challenges that these materials introduced without being clouded by traditional library practices or even by practices that were growing up around the Electronic Text Center and IATH.

The Library Electronic Text Resource Service (LETRS) is an e-text center much like the one at Virginia. It is located in the library but is relatively autonomous of the traditional library departments. Digital Images Delivered Online (DIDO) was an early experiment that served faculty in the School of Fine Arts. In 1996, Indiana established the Digital Library Programme (DLP), which brought together these three projects. Through amalgamation, Indiana achieved economies and cross-fertilization at virtually every level, enabling a more coherent approach to research and development, selection and deployment of digital library technologies, and staff appointments. Amalgamation was not intended to bring the DLP into a more traditional library unit and thus out of its skunk-works environment. Organizationally, the DLP reports directly to the dean of libraries rather than up the normal operational chain. Moreover, the DLP is funded discretely, rather than from operational budgets that support traditional library services. Programmatically, initiatives are still mounted at least in part to build on digital library competencies as they accrue, to add staff to complement skills already in place, and to acquire technology as may be needed across the programme.

Trajectories at Harvard and the University of California differ from those at Indiana, reflecting the programmes' confederal nature and system-wide orientation. At Harvard, the digital library programme grew out of technical services developed on a system-wide basis, notably around shared cataloging needs. The CDL was instituted in parallel with a system-wide technical service, which it then subsumed. Although evolving from these more established services, digital library initiatives at CDL and Harvard also took on at least some of the attributes of the skunk works. Thus, while CDL made a point of launching at least one new operational service every six months, it fashioned numerous experimental initiatives and even established a small unit under a director for education and strategic innovation.

At Harvard, where the Library Digital Initiative was organizationally housed in the same unit that supplied system-wide technical services, the programme's emphasis on digital library infrastructure assumed a five-year development path during which time few infrastructural components became operational. The programme was seen as a highly practical applied research programme that would lead ultimately, but not immediately, to the development of operational systems.

The digital library's initial locus in experimental units a step or more outside the traditional management line was important. It created a space where experimentation could happen in a way that could not disappoint the service expectations of faculty and students, or even of other librarians. With few exceptions, institutionally based digital library programmes (as opposed to programmes such as those at Harvard and CDL, which operated at least in part on a system-wide basis) were challenged later to integrate their staff, work, and thinking about library collections and services into the mainstream of the library.

The need to promote digital library programmes was felt acutely by the programmes that were launched in the early 1990s. At that time, few of the agencies to which libraries had a natural or historic entrée were making any substantial investment in activities that we would today associate with the digital library. The National Science Foundation's (NSF's) DLI initiative changed the profile of digital library activities and the amount of federal dollars that might be available to support them.

The role of foundations was also important in kick-starting digital library initiatives. Here too, however, libraries were obliged to get themselves on the agencies' informal bidding lists and to make their case for being there. It would be interesting to know how many failed funding applications a digital library programme made on average before achieving its first success. Certainly, such failures were earning experiences that helped digital libraries focus their aims and build their technology expertise. These experiences also helped libraries learn to present their funding cases convincingly, in a language that was comprehensible to those outside the library community and in a way that demonstrated the broader significance of their institution's own efforts.

No amount of external grant funding, however, can replace the need for a substantial institutional commitment. Interestingly, as digital library programmes mature, reallocated library funding becomes more important, at once reflecting and contributing to the challenges of mainstreaming the digital library.

Characteristics

Because startup digital libraries are fundamentally

experimental, it is difficult to summarize what they do. They tend to set upon experimental tasks that reflect purely local circumstances and opportunities. Still, looking across a range of early initiatives, it is possible to get a feel for the startup digital library's practical orientation and for its rather severe limitations.

Very early programmes—those from the early to mid-1990s—are defined by the library's effort to harness the Internet to fulfill historic roles. Although innovative in many respects, these programmes may be best characterized as "old wine in new bottles." At least initially, the digital library exploits the Internet as an additional means of delivering traditional services, notably access to the library catalog and to some reference materials and scholarly journals.

Greater innovation is apparent from the mid-1990s—for example, in experimentation with digital reformatting. Surrounded with lofty rhetoric about universal access to all human knowledge, innovative scholarship and teaching, and national and international digital libraries, some startup programmes focused on providing online access to selected holdings. It is too soon to judge the results of these early initiatives. The risks involved for early adopters may have been so great that they were forced to exaggerate the claims for their work. Consequently, few of the earliest digitally reformatted collections stood a chance of meeting the expectations that grew up around them. Judged in light of initial expectations, the earliest online collections are, with notable exceptions

— too small to support more than very casual kinds of browsing

— too idiosyncratic to be integrated meaningfully into larger virtual collections

— too passive to maintain a user's interest for very long

Judged against more modest or realistic claims, however, early digital collections were remarkably successful, particularly since so many were developed as technical experiments rather than as means of redefining scholarship.

Killer Applications

The young digital library is also known for its quest for "killer applications." Like the Holy Grail, these killer apps were elusive and appeared to different seekers in very different places—in data and metadata formats, in network protocols, even in systems and system architectures. The logic of their appeal is simple enough. Digital libraries are complicated to build and hard to maintain. Complexity is compounded by the fact that few libraries have more than a handful of appropriately skilled research and development staff. The killer app was the silver-bullet solution that promised to propel the library into a networked age without undergoing the fundamental restructuring, staff retraining, and soul-searching mission reorientation that information technologies seem to have forced on virtually every other organization known to late twentieth-century society.

Competition

The young digital library is competitively disposed toward its peers. Competition is hardly new; research libraries have always vied for endowments, collections, and position. Where they are embedded within academic institutions, as so many are, they are part of a broader and possibly even more aggressive competitive dynamic. The competitive disposition is notable only among young digital libraries, because it runs contrary to the deep information and service sharing that network technologies permit.

Perhaps competition at this stage can be explained by the risk that early adopters embrace and by the need they feel to justify that risk in terms of demonstrable innovation. Whatever the cause, young digital libraries struggle to find distinctive furrows to plow. Some attach themselves to systems or standards that they hope will be codified in the ascendant. Others wed themselves to collections that will redefine or inform whole fields of inquiry. The competitive culture of online experimentation may help explain the slow progress of standards work into the mid- or late 1990s. Although few would question the need for standards, young digital libraries have difficulty agreeing on which standards—a question that is conceptually equivalent to "whose standards," and that, consequently, cannot easily be addressed on the true merits of any particular case.

The competitive dynamic is still apparent in startup digital libraries, and it may be intensified as unsettled space on the digital library frontier becomes more difficult to locate. Interestingly, fewer startup programmes appear to be staking their claims on a particular technology or practice. Instead, they are emphasizing service orientation (as at Carnegie Mellon, for example, which emphasizes user support services) and local collections and scholarship.

The competitive disposition of young digital libraries may also help explain the relatively slow, sometimes fractious progress of associations of digital libraries and of collaborative digital initiatives. There are, to be sure, interesting examples of fruitful information interchange and shared investigation, particularly in the development of metadata standards, e.g., the Text Encoding Initiative (TEI), Dublin Core, and Encoded Archival Description (EAD).

One can also point to early and successful information exchanges, notably the task forces, which still exist, sponsored by the Coalition for Networked Information. Still, the ubiquitous penetration of networked technologies creates opportunities for deeper forms of association and resource sharing (with collection development, for example) that have been left almost entirely unexplored. Constrained organizationally from pushing technologies to their logical extent, young digital libraries fell back on safer modes of cooperation in talking shops that explored new ideas and in shared cataloging activities. The former resulted in statements of principle. The latter extended the purview of shared cataloging to some nonbibliographic records (e.g., archival finding aids and descriptions of some digitally reformatted materials) and explored mechanisms for constructing virtual, as opposed to union catalog, databases.

The young digital library is, in summary, an immature, experimental organizational form. It explores new opportunities and gathers new competencies. It does this within the safe harbor of soft-money projects and other activities that are organizationally, financially, and even culturally removed from traditional library services.

Maturing Digital Library

The developmental trajectories of digital library programmes are as diverse as are their origins. However, common trends begin to emerge out of the experimental phases and into the mainstream of library collections and services. The digital library programme's drift into the library mainstream occurs at practical, technical, and organizational levels and requires new ways of thinking about how programmes are funded and promoted.

Characteristics

Practically speaking, the maturing digital library is transformed as the fruits of experimental efforts become apparent in operational online collections and services. Having acquired core competencies and technical understanding, the maturing digital library abandons the "build it and they will come" philosophy that characterized earlier approaches to collection development. It focuses instead on integrating digital materials into the library's collections and on developing (and supporting with core funding) the policies, technical capacities, and professional skills needed to sustain it.

Modular Systems Architecture

Maturing digital libraries are far less interested in killer apps than are young digital libraries. The maturing libraries view the digital library as a complex online service environment that is supported by local and global systems, each of which supplies specific functions and interrelates with others in a way that can be represented in a modular architectural schematic. The model is not only sophisticated but also practical and economical. It permits greater freedom in the selection of service components and enables the library to manage and respond to technical change with greater facility.

Relying on a modular systems architecture, the digital library can select a new authentication service, for example, or integrate a new authentication technology without re-engineering its entire service environment. It can concern itself primarily with the authentication system and the mechanism (the application programmeming interface [API]) through which that system communicates with others. This modular approach is fundamentally liberating, because it permits libraries to think creatively about how to build on services supplied by others. The extent to which libraries are able to realize any part of the grander vision, however, depends almost entirely on their ability to transcend their historic organizational independence and insularity.

Common Standards

The maturing digital library's approach to standards setting is shaped by nascent aspirations for a more deeply networked future. In brief, it becomes fashionable for digital libraries to lead from the rear with respect to the standards and practices they adopt, whether for their objects or their modular system components. That is, maturing digital libraries prefer to claim adherence to practices that are already vetted and endorsed by at least one peer institution, rather than to make bold claims for local innovations. This approach has become increasingly apparent. Following are the diverse array of essential digital library tools:

— a model for negotiating access to commercial journals and databases

— minimum requirements for digitally reformatted book and serial publications

— minimum requirements of a digital archival repository for electronic journals, and a data-encoding and transmission scheme that will serve as a means for conveying information about the structural, administrative, and technical characteristics of digital objects

As part of the maturation process, digital libraries transform interesting skunk-works projects into essential library infrastructure. At this stage, failures can no longer be written off as learning experiences gained at limited cost and subsidized with external or soft money. Attitudinal shifts also reflect changing understandings of digital collections and digital library architectures. Where online collections are concerned, maturing digital libraries recognize that they are unable, by themselves, to supply end-users with what they really want—enough online information to meet their specific and evolving information needs.

Consequently, they set a high premium on interoperability and on definition and adoption of the standards required to achieve it. The drift toward modular systems architecture is also responsible for new attitudes that favor adoption of more established standards, since systems modules (locally and globally arrayed) must interoperate at a fundamental level. Libraries at this stage demonstrate a desire to pool their collective uncertainties and to define, and then frame, a broad suite of practices as benchmarks in which they can all invest and upon which they can more safely and predictably build. Attempts to develop and codify digital library standards and best practices are tapping into this very fruitful seam.

Focus on the User

The maturing digital library also seems to rediscover users. Users do not figure much in the antecedent experimental phase. The library at that stage is experimenting with new technologies—a purely internal affair—or looking for additional means of giving users access to holdings catalogs, reference materials, and some journals—areas where users' needs are deemed to be well-known. As the integration of new technologies begins to transform the library and the possibilities for constructing innovative networked services, libraries see a pressing need to engage users and to reassess their interests and needs.

By the late 1990s, there was already evidence to suggest that the proliferation of Internet-based information was fundamentally altering the expectations, behaviors, and preferences of library users. Accordingly, the maturing digital library needs to know what users want from the networked library and what role users perceive for the library in a constellation of networked information and service providers. Some of the library associations that take the lead in quantifying traditional aspects of library use have been relatively slow to respond to this new and pressing need. The reasons for this are complicated.

To begin with, the metrics are complex and difficult to agree upon. The library associations that are so well suited to developing statistics for traditional library use are typically membership organizations that are driven by consensus, which, in this case, is difficult to engineer. Further, the measures themselves can potentially disrupt the organization by fundamentally altering the criteria by which it admits and excludes new members.

Some of the best analyses of user behavior and need take place at the grassroots level in what can only be described as a series of largely uncoordinated guerilla attacks that are mounted at the institutional level and by ad hoc and informal associations. Among the revelations emerging from these fragmented efforts is the extent to which users want to work in highly personalized and malleable online environments, that is, environments that present them with the information and services they actually need at any one time. The operational lessons for the library are twofold:

(1) users want seamless presentation of collections and services, irrespective of where, by whom, or in what format they are managed; and

(2) libraries should consider deploying user-profiling technologies that enable users to configure a networked information environment that meets their specific needs.

Both lessons, if taken seriously and reflected in new operational services, have revolutionary implications for the library. The first would integrate the library into a globally arrayed network of information services in a way that challenges its historic organizational insularity. The second potentially obscures from the user's view the library's importance as a portal to that global network, because chunks of the library's collections and services are removed from the library environment and placed into new contexts.

The maturing digital library takes very seriously its users' needs and interests through its support for a suite of activities that have become known as "e-scholarship." Although the phrase has a frustrating tendency to take on new meaning every time it is used, its definition usually includes initiatives that enable scholars to produce and disseminate "publications" with minimal intervention from third-party commercial publishers. Overall library interest in supporting innovative forms of scholarly communication (or e-scholarship) at this point perhaps has less to do with transforming scholarship than it does with a strategy to increase pressure on publishers, who have increased prices dramatically in the past 10 years, particularly in the sciences.

Technical and Organizational Integration

The changing practices associated with the maturing digital library have profound implications for how that library is sustained technically and organizationally and for the manner in which it is promoted. The quest for high-level modular architectures has already been mentioned. It is arguably the most common tendency that is evident among maturing digital library programmes. Interestingly, not all digital library programmes turn toward general technical solutions for the same reasons. At Indiana and Michigan, general technical solutions are sought for the economies they promise. Indiana, for example, is thinking hard about how to afford the technical development work it requires to integrate the diverse systems environments and data content in use across its various projects.

The problem had little to do with local expertise, which is amply available in seven full-time-equivalent staff members who contribute to the DLP through the library and its partners. Rather, it has to do with how—without completely disrupting the parallel projects where their services are required—skilled staff can be released to the tasks of specifying general technical requirements and investigating potential solutions. Michigan, an older programme, reached the same roadblock before Indiana did and for the same reasons. After several years of project work, Michigan found itself re-engineering its online distribution services each time it launched a new digital collection.

By late 1999, Michigan's Digital Library Production Service had launched a key project—to build an access system capable of providing user access to the numerous and heterogeneous digital objects that were being supplied through various digital reformatting and other content development initiatives. The fruits of that effort are available in its Digital Library Extension Service (DLXS) system. By mid-2002, Michigan was supplying support and software for that system to 27 digital library efforts around the world.

Virginia's quest for general technical solutions is more a response to users' needs than to economic forces. The media centers at Virginia have adopted their own range of approaches to the production, management, and distribution of the electronic information for which they were responsible, and each has an independent and highly distinctive online presence. The problem is that, from a user's perspective, the fragmentation of digital collections makes little sense. Virginia's notion of an online environment through which scholars can obtain high-quality information—irrespective of how, where, by whom, or in what format it is managed—required it to think hard about building a technical infrastructure that could be generalized and would be capable of supporting its heterogeneous collections.

The apparent importance to the maturing digital library of a general core infrastructure is only amplified by investigation into newer digital library programmes. The maturing digital library's quest for core technologies seems to bolster rather than to undermine its emphasis on applied research. Michigan, Virginia, Harvard, and CDL, for example, have obtained or are seeking permanent, base-budget funding for the research and development efforts that are focusing on the identification of core technology. They recognize that such research and development funding is essential to their programmes' successes, and that the programmes cannot be sustained exclusively, or even largely, on external funding and soft money. At Michigan, investment flows into the development of DLXS.

At Virginia, it is reflected in the Digital Library Research and Development Unit, established in 1999. At CDL, it is evident in the establishment of a small unit under a director for education and strategic innovation. Harvard is arguably the most interesting example. As a service to a confederation of largely independent library organizations, the Libraries Digital Initiative (LDI) did not launch as a series of independent projects. It began instead by building a common digital library infrastructure that would support Harvard libraries in their development and exploitation of digital collections. As it reaches the end of its first four years, the LDI has developed first-generation infrastructure. In its second phase, it will seek a means of ensuring that the infrastructure will be developed and maintained out of whatever base-budget funding is available to the programme.

The digital library's organizational integration into mainstream library services is another aspect of its maturation. In its startup phase, the programme may be relatively unknown to library staff. Interviewees at more than one institution noted how the programmes in their earliest phases were better known nationally than on campus or even within their host libraries. As digital library collections and services develop, their impacts are increasingly felt on local library staff. Reference staff find themselves fielding queries about digital library collections; catalogers consider descriptions for digital objects where once they focused exclusively on bibliographic materials; conservation officers find their work flow and priorities shaped to some extent by the progress of local digital reformatting activities.

The impacts do not flow in one direction only. Library staff members who are responsible for the development of print collections assert their perspective in setting priorities for digital collection development decisions. Bibliographic cataloging practices are considered as the library develops systems that allow users to search across collections, irrespective of their format and location. The hardware, network protocol, and systems choices that technical services make have implications for platform choices in the digital library. If the maturing digital library programme emerges out of the skunk works and into the mainstream of library services, it does so in part because the programme's work at some stage can neither be safely ignored by nor conducted in isolation from other library services.

Rationalization is encouraged by the library's relatively inelastic personnel budget. Simply put, digital library programmes are able to develop collections and services beyond their experimental phase only by organizing themselves so they may achieve an appropriate functional division of labor. At the very point when a digital library programme is ready to hire its second (possibly even its first) metadata librarian, for example, it may also be ready to think seriously about establishing a stronger liaison with the cataloging department.

Rationalization is most evident at institutions such as Michigan and Virginia, which have older digital library programmes. At Michigan, the programme that reported directly to its three founding partners from the library, the School of Information, and the campus computing service was incorporated into the library, and the programme's executive director was appointed as an associate director with responsibilities for IT services and electronic collections. This initial reorganization may have had more to do with changes in the personnel and priorities of the university's senior management than it did with any intrinsic need to rationalize digital library programmes.

Still, once implemented, this structure created opportunities for—and even required—further organizational adjustments. Once the programme was embedded within the library line, senior library management took pains to smooth its operation with existing library services. New money allocated to the library by a friendly university administration helped considerably in firming up infrastructure support and providing continuing funds for new programme development. The library also introduced a committee structure that maximized opportunities for cross-fertilization among library managers in traditional and nontraditional units.

By placing the Digital Library Services Division under the associate director, the digital library obtained representation on the library's senior management group—its executive council. From that perch it participated in thinking strategically and operationally about a broad array of library functions that interrelate with digital content, systems, and infrastructure. At the same time, managers responsible for those traditional functions helped think about and shape the digital library's future.

Virginia's experience of reorganization is not altogether different, though it was not quite as fundamental. Virginia's programme, unlike that of Michigan, was always represented in the library's senior management group through the deputy university librarian. One consequence is that the library's senior management had early opportunities to encourage the cross-fertilization of library staff in new and existing units. From an early date, the Electronic Text Center provided basic HTML instruction to library staff—offerings that were as popular as they were effective in giving those staff members insight into the opportunities, as well as the pitfalls, inherent in the online environment.

Virginia's staff-share programme was also effective in developing mutual understanding across library units and in supporting two-way transfers of professional skills. Structural reorganization, which came later, focused primarily on aligning effort at Virginia's media centers and on developing common services, such as digitization facilities and research and development units that they can share.

The DLF survey showed some evidence that consolidation of digital library activities is beginning to take place generally, at least with respect to the development of digital collections. For example, digital library staff members have a limited role in acquiring access to commercial electronic information. At 95 percent of the libraries responding to the DLF survey, that responsibility was vested in the subject bibliographers and other professional staff who were responsible for acquiring print materials. With respect to selecting materials from library holdings for digital reformatting, three-quarters of the survey respondents said that such responsibility was located largely, if not exclusively, in digital library departments and initiatives. Surprisingly, however, in half of those institutions, responsibility was shared with subject bibliographers—that is, with staff in traditional library services.

Reorganization of the maturing digital library has a number of practical implications. As staff members from outside the original skunk works become more involved in developing or supporting the use of digital library collections, the programme is at pains to document its practices in various process recommendations, including, for example, guidelines for standards implementation, flow control, and rights clearance. Indeed, the extent of this gray literature provides some measure of a programme's maturity. In the skunk works, processes and practices are in flux, and few are responsible for developing and implementing them.

As the digital library matures, its collections and services rely much more on professional staff who are distributed across the library and who will require access to such reference materials. Again, the influences flow in two directions. While the maturing digital library typically takes responsibility for practical and process guidelines, the library's senior management, assisted by staff from across the library, supplies the policy framework in which the programme's practices are applied. Early in the adolescent stage, for example, collection policies are revised so they can govern the selection of commercial electronic resources as well as bibliographic materials.

Later developments include preservation policies that take account of digital as well as bibliographic materials and policies that articulate the library's orientation toward intellectual property and the exercise of the fair-use exclusion with both digital and print materials. Regardless of whether the documentation guides or reflects evolving practices, it is significant. Its very existence recognizes initial thinking about how digital library activities fit into and help fulfill the library's overall collection and service goals. For this reason, it is an important milestone of the maturing digital library.

Institutions are differently positioned to effect the reorganization that is required to integrate digital initiatives into the fabric of the library. Staff development is a significant issue. However well suited professional librarians are to developing and maintaining high-quality digital libraries, they apply their skills differently in digital and traditional environments. Mastering different techniques requires training opportunities that all institutions are not equally positioned to supply. In addition, reorganization may require libraries to think anew about how, by whom, and in what combinations certain tasks are done. Here, too, there are numerous and substantial differences between institutions. Some lack the nimbleness and facility that is needed to effect such changes, which, at a fundamental level, will determine whether and at what pace a digital library programme will mature.

Marketing and Promotion

As a digital library grows, there are subtle shifts in the way it is promoted and presented to the world. Marketing is not unknown to startup programmes. Although the target audience is confined to key decision makers on campus (both inside and outside the library) and potential external funders, the marketing challenges in the early phase are important. At the University of California, it took years of committee work and a few well-placed champions to sell the CDL to key decision makers on the nine UC campuses and to the Office of the President. The case for Harvard's LDI was similarly made through committee work, although over a much shorter period of time. Michigan relied on a yearlong symposium.

As digital library programmes mature, they gain visibility through their online presence, their success in acquiring external funding, or their ability to attract regional, national, or even international acclaim. They rely as much as ever on effective promotions to senior managers and to external funders. They also find themselves having to appeal to new audiences: to their faculty and other patrons and to other library staff whose own work, as we have seen, is influenced by and contributes to the digital library. Faculty members have a substantial stake because the campus library supports their research and teaching. They also have very different needs with respect to library collections and services—needs that turn on discipline, age, and personal preference.

Adult Digital Library

The digital library is an organizational form that is in flux. It is much too soon to describe the adult programme with anything more certain than references to common trends and the challenges they reflect. It is not yet possible to identify any single programme that could comfortably describe itself at as fully grown or mature. It is becoming apparent that the adult digital library programme will no longer be organizationally or functionally distinct from the library as whole. When digital libraries mature, we will talk about libraries in a manner that assumes electronic information, computer technologies, and networked collections and services are as much a part of the infrastructure as book stacks and catalogs were for the traditional library.

Funding for Digitisation

Many believe that as the digital library becomes library infrastructure, the financial resources needed to maintain it will come from numerous budget lines rather than from one line that is earmarked for digitization. In the adult digital library, electronic resources will be acquired from general collection budgets, and digital preservation activities will be supported with general preservation funds. This integration makes sense at a number of levels. If a research library is concerned with collecting, maintaining, and ensuring access to cultural and scholarly information, then it will set priorities for collection, preservation, and access that take into consideration all the differently formatted information that comes under its purview.

These integrating tendencies are becoming apparent. Perpetual experimentation may also be a characteristic of the adult digital library. Interestingly, maturing digital libraries place more emphasis on research and development than do the most experimental startup facilities. In 2000, DLF member libraries on average spent 10 percent of their digital library budgets (more than $425,000) on research and development. This figure increases to 16 percent if the subscription and acquisition costs for commercial content (which average about $1,700,000 per institution) are not included as part of the digital library budget.

David Seaman stressed how the University of Virginia's digital library programme was constantly reinventing itself in a "virtuous" cycle that plowed evolving skills and capacities into the development of new collections or services and the growth around them of new library applications and user communities. Elsewhere, it became evident that digital libraries that had focused their efforts in one area—access systems and digitization at Michigan, the development of core infrastructure at Harvard—require permanent research and development effort to help them play catch-up in others as they develop elsewhere.

Deep Interdependency

Deep interdependency with off- and on-campus information organizations also characterizes mature digital libraries in an academic setting.

Off-Campus

The assumption that libraries will become more interdependent with information organizations off-campus is predicated on the logic of the network's development. Historically, the academic library brought together the information, people, and services necessary to organize, preserve, manage access to, and support the pedagogical and research use of scholarly and cultural information.The rapid penetration of network technology undermined the academic library's underpinnings—the foundation of its physical, cultural, organizational, financial, and professional form.

In a networked world, where access to information no longer requires proximity to the physical medium on which it is carried (e.g., printed paper, film), it no longer makes sense for academic libraries to develop research and teaching collections. This is not a question of whether libraries should preserve newspapers and other non-unique cultural artifacts—of course, they should. It is about whether it is economical, or even sensible, for every library to own, manage, and preserve those artifacts. In an extensively networked environment, one can access the information (on screen, on paper, and in other ways) that is carried by these materials without accessing the materials themselves. In a rational economic system, one might at a minimum envision the following:

- service points (academic libraries) managing access (online, print-on-demand, and other means)
- digital repositories (managing electronic corpora and ensuring they are available for different service points)
- print repositories that preserve the physical artifacts and make them available to scholars whose research requires that they handle the objects

One may also imagine a range of services essential to the operation of repositories and service points—services that include registries (or union catalogs) that record information about repository holdings (print and digital) and name-resolution services (assisting in the persistent identification of peripatetic digital files and physical artifacts). In this scenario, many academic libraries are able to relinquish functions having to do with the management of physical and digital materials without impinging on the collections and services they offer to their patrons. In fact, the collections and services they offer are greatly improved and extended as the library takes its place as part of a networked constellation of interdependent information collections and services.

The model that relies upon distributed provision of interlocking service functions works as well—or better, given the volume of information—for materials that are born digital (i.e., those that exist from the outset in a digital form, whether as databases, geospatial information, images, sound, video files, or mixed media applications). The model is being tried in the delivery of library reference services, but it is too soon to assess the result. There is evidence that the model's development need not be impeded by legal and business considerations such as those that may surround the distribution of copyrighted material.

One might argue that the library itself is the single greatest obstacle to a more distributed and economically rational provision of information services. It is difficult to cede to third parties responsibility for collections and services that have historically been provided in-house and upon which library patrons rely so heavily. It is especially difficult when those who are forced to consider such fundamental reorganization are encumbered with professional, cultural, and organizational baggage that defines a high-quality library as one that supports in a single place a very wide range of collections and services—a range so wide that it may now be beyond the reach of any single library.

On-Campus

Assumptions about adult digital libraries becoming more interdependent with information organizations on campus are also predicated upon the dynamic logic of the network's development and use. As the academic library develops into a service organization that supports access to scholarly information in all formats, to users both on- and off-campus, it requires a highly sophisticated technical infrastructure. Although circumstances vary across campuses, the library nowhere manages the sum total of that infrastructure, and it will never do so. Libraries rely on local campus networks that they do not build or manage. In many institutions, they provide access to electronic research and teaching resources but rely on campus units outside the library (e.g., academic computing services, instructional technology divisions, audiovisual departments) to support faculty and students in their use of these materials.

The fragmented organizational approach to information provision that exists on most large campuses harkens back to a prenetworked world when discrete information service functions were built on and delivered through distinctive technical platforms. In the early 1970s, campus telecommunications, mainframe computing, audiovisual departments, and libraries delivered discrete information services using very different technologies. In 2002, these discrete functions have migrated into a networked space where they are vastly more difficult to distinguish from one another, in part because they rely upon the same infrastructure. Convergence has also fostered competition as information organizations assert their claims against that portion of the university's resources that can be devoted to information management generally.

Interdepartmental Competition

Interdepartmental competition can impede provision of a new service where no single organization is able to assert a legitimate claim to that service. The best example may be the lack of coordination in the provision of digital archival repositories on campuses. Like corporate entities, universities produce an increasing amount of digital information, much of which has significant long-term value. That value, however, can be realized only if records are maintained. Databases of student records are a foundation upon which future fund-raising efforts may be built. Their value can be measured in financial terms. The value of other records is measured differently.

Electronic financial and administrative records, most of which have no print equivalent, need to be kept for accountability. Data produced as a by-product of research are a crucial part of the scientific record. Online course materials and a rapidly growing gray literature of pre-prints, working papers, and research data to which faculty and student Web sites contribute are an important part of the pedagogical and scholarly record.

At the same time, libraries perceived themselves as one of the few units on campus with an interest in preserving these materials. Therefore, the library may be positioned to stake a credible claim to some custodial role with respect the campus's digital information assets. The library may fulfill this role in cooperation with other units that have better capacity for providing some of the technological functions associated with large-scale data management and preservation. Some progress is clearly being made.

Instructional Technologies

Competition among campus information organizations has other effects that may impede the library in fulfilling important roles. Such effects are overwhelmingly apparent where the development and use of instructional technologies are concerned. Organizational location need not be a problem; in this case, however, it has resulted in the near-universal deployment of instructional technologies that do not integrate with the digital library. In many cases, instructional technologies or course management systems and digital libraries are being developed independently of one another.

Because of the distributed structure of IT on most campuses, this practice appears to be as true on campuses with well-developed digital library programmes as it is on those where such programmes are just getting under way.

The waste is excessive, even in good economic times. Bibliographic references that may be included with online course materials are not automatically hot-linked to the library's online catalog; in some instances, they cannot be linked. The digitally reformatted materials produced by the library, and the many more such materials produced at other libraries, museums, and archives, and to which most libraries now link through various means, are placed outside the pedagogical purview as it is defined online by instructional technologies. The digital library as a learning resource is therefore put at risk. Meanwhile, faculty and students work in isolation from a wealth of well-organized, high-quality information that is directly relevant to their learning and for which they have already paid, for example, through university and library spending.

Some libraries are beginning to realize how digital technologies might help reduce the costly and redundant management of print materials held by numbers of research libraries. Where libraries can reliably deliver access to online editions of scholarly journals (editions that evidence suggests faculty and students prefer anyway, they are beginning to be able to reduce redundant print copies while ensuring that at least some print editions are made persistently available. Some digital library programmes emphasize services over collection.

Library digitization programmes were driven initially by curatorial interests. They targeted unique special collections that research libraries owned. Today, an expanding dialog between libraries and scholars is allowing libraries to consider what online resources humanities scholars need. In the humanities, scholars investigate meaningful bodies of information and build ideas and conclusions from a context. Therefore, which collections are digitized will make a difference in how quickly online scholarship will grow. Research using digital resources is beginning to have an impact in the humanities, although it has not replaced the traditional critical mass of books and archives that scholars investigate.

Conversion of analog materials to digital is often confused as representing the sum total of what digital libraries do. Clearly, it is not. The digital library pioneers who led their organizations at an exciting and exploratory time created diverse programmes, but with synergies that hold promise through the application of network technologies. It is obvious that network technologies permit users to access information regardless of where information is located, but there are still significant obstacles to deep resource sharing, including the effect that competition among universities has on library cooperation.

Historically, libraries fulfilled diverse functions by acquiring and assembling collections, services, and professional staff in a single place. Access to the library and its professionals required proximity to them. The rapid development of network technologies has not eradicated the significance of the library as place and as owner of collections, but it has diminished and will continue to diminish it. Network technologies are forcing a fundamental transformation of the library and the university itself.

In the research library, achievements occurred precisely because these libraries were located in large and complicated environments. First, they existed within the framework of research and development that occurs on large campuses and were, in some instances, able to harness that expertise to their advantage through collaboration. Second, with significant budget, staff, and space, they were able to move discreetly some resources from traditional library activities into digital research and development. To do this, they needed to have a strong vision of the future that enabled them to push a largely process-driven environment into a research and development

Many libraries and archives have curbed their voracious appetites for acquisition and collecting in an effort to balance the breadth and depth of their holdings against long-term stewardship responsibilities. The change over from acid to alkaline paper in publishing and much desktop printing counts as a significant victory for preservation. Much remains to be done to preserve cultural, intellectual, and scholarly resources in traditional formats that form the foundation for humanities research and teaching.

Digital preservation raises challenges of a fundamentally different nature which are added to the problems of preserving traditional format materials. Digital preservation encompasses material that begins its life in digital form as well as material that is converted from traditional to digital formats. Recording media for digital materials are vulnerable to deterioration and catastrophic loss, and even under ideal conditions they are short lived relative to traditional format materials. Although archivists have been battling acid-based papers, thermo-fax, nitrate film, and other fragile media for decades, the threat posed by magnetic and optical media is qualitatively different. They are the first reusable media and they can deteriorate rapidly, making the time frame for decisions and actions to prevent loss is a matter of years, not decades.

More insidious and challenging than media deterioration is the problem of obsolescence in retrieval and playback technologies. Innovation in the computer hardware, storage, and software industries continues at a rapid pace, usually yeilding greater storage and processing capacities at lower cost. Devices, processes, and software for recording and storing information are being replaced with new products and methods on a regular three- to five-year cycle, driven primarily by market forces. Records created in digital form in the first instance and those converted retrospectively from paper or microfilm to digital form are equally vulnerable to technological obsolescence.

Another challenge is the absence of established standards, protocols, and proven methods for preserving digital information. With few exceptions, digital library research has focussed on architectures and systems for information organization and retrieval, presentation and visualization, and administration of intellectual property rights. The critical role of digital libraries and archives in ensuring the future accessibility of information with enduring value has taken a back seat to enhancing access to current and actively used materials. As a consequence, digital preservation remains largely experimental and replete with the risks associated with untested methods; and digital preservation requirements have not been factored into the architecture, resource allocation, or planning for digital libraries.

The two terms "mass storage" and "long-term preservation" embrace a contradiction in the current state of affairs of digital library development, representing a time bomb that threatens the long-term viability of this new type of library. New technologies for mass storage of digital information abound, yet the technologies and methods for long-term preservation of the vast and growing store of digital information lag far behind. Strategies, methods, and technologies for long-term preservation of digital information that already exist or are being discussed, designed, and developed today have yet to demonstrate the technological or economic feasibility of operating on a mass scale.

Preservation Requirements

In order to preserve digital materials on a scale commensurate with mass storage capabilities and in formats that are accessible and usable, it is necessary to articulate some basic requirements. There are two ways to examine digital preservation requirements: from the perspective of users of digital materials and from the view of libraries, archives, and other custodians who assume responsibility for their maintenance, preservation, and distribution. Libraries and archives will not accomplish their preservation missions if they do not satisfy the requirements of their users by preserving materials in formats that enable the types of analyses that users wish to perform. At the same time, libraries and archives are unlikely to be able to satisfy all requirements of all potential users primarily due to resource constraints. By making explicit preservation requirements from both the users' and custodians' perspectives, libraries and archives will be better able to integrate digital preservation into overall planning and resource allocation.

The potential uses of digital materials are varied, unpredictable, and almost endless. Any generalizations, even if restricted to one community of users such as humanities scholars, run the risk of overlooking and understating potential user needs. Precise requirements for presentation and analytical tools vary among disciplines, yet some basic requirements are likely to transcend fields and disciplines. The ability to establish the authenticity and integrity of a source is critical to users, whether it is generated by an individual, created in the conduct of institutional business, or produced through a formal publication process. Mechanisms that will enable users to establish authenticity require archives and libraries to store much more than the content of digital documents. Attributes such as formal document structures, metadata that document the maintenance and use history of the document, time and date stamps, and a series of references among documents are essential for determining authenticity and for understanding the provenance of sources and placing them in a larger context.

Networking and access to digital sources will change all dimensions the scholarly work process, including identifying sources, communicating with colleagues, interpreting and analyzing data, disseminating research findings, and teaching. If their projections are correct, digital preservation programmes must support a high degree of integration of source material into analytical processes by coupling research sources with the tools necessary to analyze them; by maintaining linkages between research results and the sources on which they are based; and by providing a means to incorporate primary sources into teaching. Users will seek documents that are easily retrieved and manipulated, transmittable, and transportable from a repository to the sites of research, presentation, and teaching. It seems safe to assume that humanities scholars will need the capability to search through and select relevant sources from large bodies of heterogenous materials, to compare sources to each other, and to view specific documents at high levels of granularity.

Digital preservation will add little value to the research process if it serves only as an alternative form of storage from which analog replicas are produced for use with conventional analytical methods. Preserving digital materials in formats that are reliable and usable, however, will require long-term maintenance of structural characteristics, descriptive metadata, and display, computational, and analytical capabilities that are very demanding of both mass storage and software for retrieval and interpretation. Digital preservation requirements may be expressed differently by archives, libraries, and other types of repositories that are struggling to meet escalating user expectations with limited financial and technical resources. Storage systems should be capable of handling digital information in a wide variety of formats, including text, data, graphics, video, and sound.

Digital storage is not only an alternative means for storing print formats because many types of digital objects do not have print equivalents and cannot be preserved in non-digital formats. Ideally, storage media will have a long life expectancy, a high degree of disaster resistance, sufficient durability to withstand regular use, and very large storage capacities. Conversion from analog to digital formats and migration to new generations of technology will be rapid, accurate, and inexpensive enough to permit very large scale transfers of heterogeneous materials. Storage space requirements will be minimal and not demand highly sensitive environmental controls. To make digital preservation affordable to the widest possible range of organizations and individuals, equipment, media, and maintenance costs must be modest.

Preservation Strategies

Most librarians and archivists have accepted the basic wisdom—for now at least—that digital preservation depends upon copying, not on the survival of the physical media. But copying, also referred to as "refreshing" or "migration" is more complex than simply transferring a stream of bits from old to new media or from one generation of systems to the next. Complex and expensive transformations of digital objects often are necessary to preserve digital materials so that they remain authentic representations of the original versions and useful sources for analysis and research.

Current methods for preserving digital materials do not fully support achieving these objectives. When faced with the responsibility for preserving digital materials, archives and libraries face a series of complex and difficult choices based on the format of the original materials, the anticipated uses for it, and the technical and financial resources available to invest in preservation initiatives. Probably the most commonly used preservation strategy is to transfer digital information from less stable magnetic and optical media by printing page images on paper or microfilm. It seems ironic that just as libraries and archives are discovering digital conversion as a cost-effective preservation method for certain deteriorating materials, much information that begins its life in electronic form is printed on paper or microfilm for safe, secure long-term storage.

Paper and microfilm have the additional advantage of requiring no special hardware or software for retrieval or viewing. Perhaps this explains why in many digital conversion projects, the digital images serve as a complement to rather than a replacement for the original hard copy materials. Another strategy for digital preservation is to preserve digital information in the simplest possible digital formats in order to minimize the requirements for sophisticated retrieval software.

Digital information can be transferred across successive generations of technology in a "software-independent" format as ASCII text files or as flat files with simple, uniform structures. Several data archives hold large collections of numerical data that were captured on punch cards in the 1950s or 1960s, migrated to two or three different magnetic tape formats, and now reside on optical media. As new media and storage formats were introduced, the data were migrated without any significant change in their logical structure. This approach has the distinct advantage of being universal and easy to implement. It is a cost-effective strategy for preserving digital information in those cases where retaining the content is paramount, but display, indexing, and computational characteristics are not critical. As long as the preservation community lacks more robust and cost-effective migration strategies, printing to paper or film and preserving flat files will remain the methods of last resort for many institutions and for certain formats of digital information.

Libraries and archives with large, complex, and diverse collections of digital materials are only beginning to test strategies that normalize various types of holdings by converting digital records from the great multiplicity of formats into a smaller, more manageable number of standard formats. A repository might accept textual documents only in one or a few commonly available commercial word processing formats or require that documents conform to standards like SGML. Databases might be stored in one or a few common formats or converted to a SQL (Structured Query Language) compliant format, while image files might conform to the tagged image file format (TIFF) with standard compression algorithms.

This approach has the advantage of preserving more of the display, dissemination, and computational characteristics of the original materials, while reducing the large variety of customized transformations that would otherwise be necessary to migrate material to future generations of technology. The strategy rests on the assumption that software products which are either compliant with widely adopted standards or are widely dispersed in the marketplace are less volatile than the software market as a whole. Most common commercial products today provide utilities for backward compatibility and for swapping documents, databases, and more complex objects between software systems. Although this strategy simplifies migration and may lower digital preservation costs by reducing the amount of customized reformatting needed as technology changes, it does not eliminate the need for regular migration of digital materials. Software and standards both continue to evolve and even repositories with structurally homogeneous holdings can expect to be required to migrate their digital materials periodically.

Current methods fall far short of what is required to preserve digital materials. All current preservation methods involve trade- offs between what is desirable from the standpoint of functionality, dependability, and cost and what is possible and affordable with current technologies and methods. Consequently, most repositories are coping by employing interim and less than desirable strategies, if they are addressing digital preservation issues at all. For example, the simplicity and universality of printing to paper or microfilm come at the expense of great losses in the functionality of digital information.

Migration strategies that involve reformatting of digital materials to a simple standard format usually eliminate the structure of documents and relationships imbedded in databases. Computation capabilities, graphic display, indexing, and other features often are lost, thus limiting future analytical potential. Normalization to standard formats is not always technically feasible and it usually is quite costly. Archives and libraries must also contend with entirely new forms of electronically-enabled discourse and new forms of artistic and cultural expression that do not have predecessors in the analog world. No current preservation method is adequate for preserving dynamic data objects from complex systems. There are no established conceptual models or technical processes for preserving multi-media works, interactive hyper-media, on-line dialogues, or many of the new electronic forms being created today. The archival requirements to preserve content, context, and structure and to maintain the capability to display, link, and manipulate digital objects only heighten their software dependency.

The preservation community is only beginning to explore possible alternatives to storing digital information in "software- independent" form. Rothenberg proposed an approach for maintaining the content of digital materials intact without losing the ability to retrieve meaning-rich sources. He recommended retaining the original document in its original format encapsulated in a virtual "envelope" that contains software instructions for retrieval, display, and processing of the message in the envelope. The envelopes would contain contextual information and the transformational history of each object. Execution of the instructions would rely on an archive of hardware and software emulators or on instructions in the envelope with specifications to construct emulators.

Important research is underway to define standards for data interchange that can support electronic commerce and satisfy business requirements in a variety of environments. A major research project at the University of Pittsburgh is defining metadata requirements for evidence that will support the need for integrity, authenticity, reliability, and archiving through standards for "metadata encapsulated objects". Archives, libraries, and other institutions with preservation responsibilities will benefit if systems are built to implement such metadata standards. Wide scale adoption of data and communication standards by the originators of digital information to support current business needs will also facilitate long-term preservation.

Standards initiatives that address business needs for the secure and reliable exchange of digital information among the current generation of systems will impose standardization and normalization of data that ultimately will facilitate migrations to new generations of technology. Yet to benefit fully from the synergy between business needs and preservation requirements we have to move beyond simply paying lip service to cultural heritage concerns and recognize that equally critical social goals, such as long-term genetic research, monitoring global environmental change, locating nuclear waste sites, and establishing property rights are also dependent on long-term access to reliable, electronic evidence.

Only a few libraries, archives, and other institutions have established digital preservation programmes, while most research and innovation comes from pilot projects and prototypes. Tested methods that have proven effective on a small scale in a limited number of repositories are not feasible for preservation of many of the types of digital materials that archives and libraries will confront in their preservation endeavors. The current state of digital preservation suggests several fruitful areas for research and development. There are four areas: storage media, migration, conversion, and management tools. These four domains are often mutually dependent and ultimately must to be integrated into an infrastructure for digital preservation.

Storage Media

The limited life of magnetic and optical media pose a significant problem, although this is not the primary limiting factor for digital preservation. Recent research on the longevity of magnetic media indicate a useful life span of 10 to 30 years if they are handled and stored properly. Some optical disk technologies promise life spans of up to 100 years. Most authorities argue that enhanced media longevity is of little value because current media outlast the software and devices needed to retrieve recorded information.

Nevertheless, improvements in the stability, capacity, and longevity of the base storage media are needed to drastically reduce the vulnerability of digital materials to loss and alteration and to lower storage costs. Ample research and experience provide evidence of what can go wrong with magnetic media as a result of binder degradation, magnetic particle instabilities, and substrate deformation. Optical media are susceptible to damage from high humidity, rapid and extreme temperature fluctuations, and contamination from airborne particulate matter. To prevent these problems, it is imperative to store magnetic and optical media under strict environmental controls that are not always available, affordable, or convenient.

Even modest improvements which produce storage media with larger per unit storage capacities and greater tolerance to variations in temperature and humidity will lower preservation costs by lessening the need for strict environmental controls, reducing the frequency with which digital media must be "refreshed" through recopying, and decreasing the number of storage units that must be handled. This raises the question, however, of whether research on incremental improvements in current storage technologies will benefit preservation in the long run or whether we should seek alternative approaches to digital storage that more adequately meet archival requirements. As a frame of reference it is worth remembering that microfilm, which is considered the only acceptable archival storage medium, lasts at least 300 years with minimal maintenance if stored properly.

High-Density Read-Only Memory (HD-ROM) technology that uses an ion beam to inscribe information on pins of stainless steel, iridium, or other materials. The HD-ROM is capable of storing 180 times more information than current CD-ROM technology at roughly one-half percent of CD-ROM costs. According to the release about this technology, the HD-ROM is impervious to material degradation and it requires no bit stream interpreter because the technology can describe in human-readable form all of the instructions needed to interpret the data (LANL Ion Beam Storage). Such an approach illustrates the potential for solutions built on entirely new storage technologies.

Migration

Better methods for migration of digital materials to new generations of hardware and software are much needed for digital preservation regardless of breakthroughs in mass storage technologies. Planning for migration is difficult because there is limited experience with the types of migrations needed to maintain access to complex digital objects over extended periods of time. When a custodian assumes responsibility for preserving a digital object it may be difficult to predict when migration will be necessary, how much reformatting will be needed, and how much migration will cost. There are no reliable or comprehensive data on costs associated with migrations, either for specific technologies and formats or for particular collections, and little research underway on methodologies that would reduce the costs and burdens of migration.

The preservation community as a whole would benefit tremendously from the development of backward compatibility paths that would be included as a standard feature of all software. Backward compatibility or migration paths would enable a new generation of software to "read" data from older systems without substantial reformatting and without loss of retrieval, display and computational capabilities. Although backward compatibility is increasingly common within software product lines, migration paths are not commonly provided between competing software products or for products that fail in the marketplace.

Stewards of digital material have a range of options for preserving digital information. One might preserve an exact replica of a digital record with complete display, retrieval, and computational functionality, or a representation of the record with only partial computation capabilities, or a surrogate for the record such as an abstract, summary, or aggregation. Detail or background noise might be dropped out intentionally through successive generations of migration, and custodians might change the format or storage media. Enhancements are technologically possible through clean-up, mark-up, and linkage, or by adding indexing and other features. These technological possibilities in turn impose serious new responsibilities to present digital materials to users in a way that allows them to determine the authenticity of the information and its relationship to the original record. Methods to document changes in digital objects during their life span need to be incorporated as an integral part of improved migration methods.

There are few well developed methods for preserving and migrating software so that it might be used to recreate digital documents that have the "look and feel" of the original sources. Maintaining repositories of obsolete hardware and software has been discussed periodically, but usually dismissed out of hand as too expensive and not demonstrably feasible. This approach deserves more serious consideration as a strategy for maintaining continuing access to certain types of digital materials. Feasibility studies and cost/benefit analyses should be conducted to determine the technological, economic, and commercial feasibility of maintaining selected legacy software systems and performing specialized migrations or, alternatively, of building and maintaining software emulators. Such an approach would support replay of original sources and contribute to the preservation of software as a significant cultural and intellectual resource in its own right.

Conversion

Faster, cheaper, and higher resolution conversion technologies are another critical element needed to make digital preservation feasible on a large scale. Most archivists and librarians accept the fact that we live in a hybrid environment where paper, microfilm, video, and magnetic and optical media need to interoperate in a more integrated and transparent manner. The vast majority of primary sources today still reside on paper and/or microfilm with little chance that we will see the mass conversion of existing archival and library holdings to digital formats. Research and planning for digital preservation must recognize that we will be dealing with conversion for a long time and that investments in improving capture rates, accuracy, resolution, and verification will have long-term benefits. Moreover, improvements in conversion technologies may support hybrid solutions to preservation and access problems by permitting repositories to store certain formats of digital material on stable media, such as microfilm, with on demand conversion to digital form for analysis and reuse. Efforts to capture and store descriptive mark-up on film for subsequent conversion are hampered by unacceptable error rates in OCR technology and cumbersome conversion processes (Giguere).

Development of Management Tools

A fourth area for research is in the development of management tools for digital libraries and archives that integrate descriptive control and maintenance with storage technologies. Dynamic digital objects, such as those found in hypertext systems, pose special management problems for both current and future retrieval and reuse. The boundaries of hypertext sources, like those found on the World Wide Web today, are difficult to ascertain because no single party or institution controls changes in the nodes and links that make hypertext objects live and highly responsive information resources. A high degree of volatility accompanies these objects because the contents of nodes change, the sites where information resources are stored change, and the links between nodes change, move, and vanish.

Some recent tools, such as the MOMspider (Multi- Owner Maintenance Spider) and Web:Lookout are capable of traversing a portion of the Web and noting maintenance problems such as broken links, moved documents, modified documents, and objects that have exceeded their expiration dates (Ackerman and Fielding). While tools such as these are useful for current maintenance, they do not address long-term preservation concerns. If further developed to address preservation problems, tools such as these have the potential to serve as filters, identify similar or identical objects, and monitor for maintenance problems.

Research and development of tools that would imbed more intelligence about the preservation status of digital material into the objects themselves would make monitoring and maintenance of large digital collections more automatic. Current methods for monitoring the physical status of digital materials are labor intensive, unreliable, and potentially damaging to the materials themselves. Recommended procedures for monitoring physical deterioration of magnetic tape, for example, involve reading a small sample of tapes periodically to determine whether any data losses have occurred (Eaton). The potential exists to build monitoring and reporting mechanisms into digital objects, storage systems, and network architectures that could support self- reporting of physical status and initiate automatic maintenance procedures.

Despite differences, some lessons from traditional preservation are transferable to the digital environment. In order to avoid commitments that far exceed available resources and costly rescue and restoration efforts, preservation must become an integral part of the planning, design, and resource allocation for digital libraries and archives. Integration of preservation requirements and methods with access and maintenance systems is essential to fully and efficiently support the processes of migration, regeneration, and documentation of the life of digital objects.

Planning for preservation must become an integral part of the design and management of digital libraries and archives. If left as an afterthought, there is little reason to believe that long-term preservation of digital information will be any more affordable than preservation of conventional formats has been.

3

Electronic Use in Libraries

The rapid ascent of multimedia technology over the last decade has brought about fundamental changes to computing, entertainment, and education. The exponential growth of multimedia technologies and applications has presented the computerized society with opportunities and challenges that in many cases are unprecedented. Nowhere is this impact felt more acutely than with information professionals. Multimedia applications have progressed to the point of sparking a fundamental paradigm shift in the very concept of information transfer and presentation.

Multimedia technologies face challenges as well. Any technology that enjoys such meteoric rise and rapid diffusion into the society from which it emerges cannot help but experience growing pains. As a result, the implementation of multimedia is hampered by questions of interoperability as many diverse vendors and producers attempt to lay claim to the market. It is stymied by its own rapid growth, with advances in multimedia leapfrogging, and being leapfrogged by, advances in hardware, storage, and bandwidth of the distributed networks that allow multimedia applications to be shared and utilized over telecommunications networks.

And the field of multimedia faces social challenges as well, as the technology progresses at a pace that the surrounding society has difficulty matching. As a result, many people, including some in the information field, have given up on understanding multimedia concepts and have turned their back on participating in the growth of the technology. In the case of information professionals, most particularly those professionals in the library and information science field, this is a critical error.

Traditionally, librarians have maintained jurisdiction over this process, keeping the library as we have known it a public entity, offering access to all, regardless of class or ability to pay. We may be witnessing a change to this tradition. More and more, private industry is entering the library business, not in the collection of books, but rather in the collection of digital information. While these entities often utilize librarians in their functions, the librarian's social role is being rendered subservient to the corporate policies of profit. This is a dangerous precedent.

The technologies that comprise the phenomenon of digital multimedia and the applications that employ those technologies are diverse, and end-user understanding and acceptance of these technologies and applications are equally varied. As the technology progresses, multimedia systems have become more and more ubiquitous and transparent. Indeed, many users today who would not identify themselves as someone having a use for multimedia technology or equipment are far more familiar with it than they believe; but they do not consider the applications for which they use multimedia to be "true multimedia." The very term has generated an aura of mystique to the non-digital professional.

Multimedia technology is loosely and generally defined as the combined use of several methods of sensory transmission, employed for the transmittal of information to a receiver. Under this definition, multimedia technology is old and widely used, comprising television, many printed materials, performance art, and many educational materials. All of these systems involve the use of multiple sensory formats to facilitate the transmittal of information.

It is in the digital age that the term multimedia has taken on the definition and level of prestige that it currently enjoys. The advent of digital technologies has increased multimedia capabilities and potential to unprecedented levels. Digital multimedia are defined as the processes of employing a variety of digital images, synchronized and perhaps embedded within one another, or within an application, to present and transmit information. This definition requires a further sub-definition, in that "images" may be taken to imply visual images. On the contrary, an "image" is defined as any type of digitized information. An image may be a sound, a picture, a representation, or a section of text.

In the recent past, multimedia technology has developed further with the rise of relatively inexpensive and high-bandwidth networking technologies. These means of mass communication over long distances gave multimedia systems the ability to escape the CD-ROM and become "distributed" among many end-users, in many locations, often operating on different platforms. Distributed multimedia, as a technology, deal with combining digital multimedia images and applications with computer-networking techniques. The result is a form of multimedia that is not confined to one computer or one storage medium, but rather may be transmitted, shared, and applied among large numbers of end-users over long distances in real time.

Distributed Multimedia

To date the World-Wide Web is the most prominent example of such distributed multimedia. The rise of distributed multimedia systems presents great opportunity for fields such as entertainment, education, health care, business, and the military. It also presents challenges in the areas of standardization and interoperability. Distributed multimedia systems are already being exploited, as evidenced by the rising popularity of the WWW, intranets, and multimedia groupware.

Hardware

Hardware may be defined as those physical components and peripherals that comprise a computer system. Hardware includes processor chips, memory chips, computer boards, information storage devices, networking devices, displays, input devices, and output devices. Today's digital multimedia applications require hardware platforms of increasing power and capabilities. Perhaps the most important hardware peripheral in the rise of consumer digital multimedia was the CD-ROM drive and the CD-ROM that is its storage medium.

Software

Software is defined as those programs and applications that run on computer systems. Multimedia software includes operating systems that run the multimedia platforms; drivers that control peripherals and I/O devices; applications; and data, which term includes the digital images that are combined to produce multimedia applications and presentations. Application programs can be used in a variety of ways to display, create, and edit digital images. These applications may support many digital-image formats, as in the case of Adobe Photoshop, or may be limited to one or a few proprietary formats, as with Apple QuickTime. Multiple formats exist for audio images, for static visual images, and for animated visual images.

Networks

Networks are defined as computers connected for the purposes of sharing information and/or applications. Networks can range in size from small peer-to-peer networks connecting only a few computers, to larger Local-Area Networks (LANs) that operate on client-server architectures, to Wide-Area Networks (WANs), large and geographically dispersed networks connecting thousands or even millions of computers, such as the Internet. These networks may consist of one network, or of networks of networks.

The primary definitions necessary to understand networking as it pertains to multimedia are bandwidth (data rate) and medium (the wiring used for data transmission.)

Bandwidth measures the rate at which data is transmitted through the network. It is often used as a gauge of speed in the network. As technology has advanced over recent decades, bandwidth of networks has increased. High bandwidth is needed to facilitate distributed multimedia systems due to the large amounts of data that must be transmitted in image files.

As a hardware term, medium refers to the physical means used for data transmission. Hardware media include copper wires, fiber-optic cables, and radio-frequency (RF) transmissions. The medium often directly affects bandwidth and is, therefore, important in the functioning of distributed multimedia systems.

Another pair of networking definitions concerns the difference between analog and digital signals. Analog signals are continuous. Digital signals are based on binary code and can have only two states, 0 and 1. Digital transmission is achieved over analog transmission lines by manipulating the analog signal, but some transmission media are strictly digital, such as fiber-optic cable and some RF transmissions (Kagan 168-70).

Many methodologies exist for increasing bandwidth in a transmission system, including multiplexing and packet-switching. These techniques are not essential for an understanding of distributed multimedia, but it is essential to understand that they are used to increase bandwidth, which in turn is essential to the functionality of distributed multimedia.

Networking also includes specific hardware and software applications. Network-hardware devices include the wiring previously discussed, as well as routers, bridges, modems, security firewalls, adapter cards, and connectors. Hardware may also include high-capacity computers to act as servers for networks, large mainframes designed to service client computers, relatively dumb network computers, or actual dumb terminals.

Software applications used in networking include those programs designed to allow the networked computers to operate in conjunction with one another. This type of software is referred to as groupware (e.g., Lotus Notes). In addition, the Internet--and specifically the World-Wide Web--utilizes its own software applications to facilitate communications between different computers. Protocols, such as HyperText Transfer Protocol (http), and File Transfer Protocol (FTP), while not software applications, are standards that allow communication and digital data to be transferred between computers. Programming languages, including Visual Basic, C++, Java, Perl, and HyperText Markup Language (HTML) allow the creation of applications that can be distributed over networked computer systems. Finally, applications such as Web browsers like Netscape, Apache, and Mosaic allow multimedia data to be accessed across the World-Wide Web. These types of distributed multimedia are computer-based.

Other forms of digital multimedia include satellite television, cable TV, and advanced features offered by telephone companies, such as video conferencing and telecommuting systems, which may or may not be computer-based. And there is always the transfer between end-users of binary image files that are then utilized through applications residing on the user's computer. While this form of distributed multimedia is neither real-time nor interactive, it is nonetheless distributed multimedia.

In recent years, there has been rapid development of multimedia systems and applications. A large part of the collections of libraries and information agencies are still in single-medium format (books, periodicals, audiocassettes, audio CDs, videocassettes, microforms, maps, etc.); but collection developers have recognized the usefulness of multimedia and have started collecting multimedia CDs, linking up to multimedia Web sites, and digitizing some of their own collections.

The introduction of multimedia has brought a number of problem issues, the solving of which will determine the level of future use of this new format. These issues include: the selection of multimedia products; the search for and retrieval of non-textual information; the cataloging of multimedia resources; metadata; copyright; licensing; costs; the migration of digital information; and the permanent preservation of digital resources.

Changes in Multimedia Technologies

Libraries and information agencies are using various technologies to offer access to electronic materials. CD-ROMs, dial-up online systems, the Internet, and tapes loaded on the library's computer are the most used current options. New technologies may make some of these options obsolete; but new technologies may also fail, never catching on because of insufficient consumer demand. CD-ROMs, which have been almost synonymous with interactive multimedia, are facing the fiercest competition. While videodiscs and laserdiscs have not been able to replace CD-ROMs, the new DVD (Digital Video Disc, or Digital Versatile Disk, depending [in part] on the user's marketing goals) technology is currently being advertised as the strongest contender among the next generation of optical media. The DVD technology may well replace CD-ROMs.

The disadvantages of CD-ROMs are the lack of storage space to accommodate large digital-video or interactive-multimedia applications and the absence of platform-independent publishing formats. At present, publishers have to upgrade their software every few months in order to revise and republish their products. While DVD technology does not automatically offer a more stable publishing format than CD-ROMs, it will provide higher delivery and storage capacities for applications demanding high capacity as well as the possibility of creating hybrid DVD-Internet applications.

DVD technology will also be able to deliver large amounts of information faster than the Internet at least as long as the bandwidth problems of the Internet networks remain. To make the transition easier for the users, DVD producers are making their DVD players capable of reading CD-ROMs. Whether DVD will actually become a long-lasting format depends on the ability to agree on standards, development of anticopy mechanisms, and the speed of further developments in imaging technology. New technologies will keep emerging because there seem always to be needs for more speed, greater ease of use, and more functions. Because of rapid change it is increasingly difficult for any collection developer to select products that will continue to be used for a long period of time.

Important materials will have to be converted from older digital formats to newer ones when the older techniques become obsolete. Such conversions can add significantly to the cost of the materials and force libraries and information agencies to follow technological developments closely. It will be more and more important for the producers to incorporate backwards compatibility of older products in the new technologies; or else they may find it hard to market their new products to hesitant users, which will make it hard to establish the new products.

The Internet is quickly changing from images and text to a more media-intensive Web of sound, video, animation, and virtual reality. As more and more sites add such features, and more and more end-users demand them, the Web will slow down considerably. For example, Slothouber's research demonstrates that as average file size increases, the maximum serving capacity (regardless of the server) decreases exponentially. According to him, when the file size increases from 5KB to just 80KB, the maximum server capacity would drop from about 35 hits per second to about 2 hits per second.

Real-time audio and video can easily fill an ISDN line. Larson states that an ISDN line can handle 5-10 concurrent RealAudio streams. Though a T1 line (capacity approximately 1.5 megabits/second) can manage up to 100 RealAudio streams simultaneously, it can handle only 12 simultaneous XingMPEG video streams at 30 frames per second. And, as we all know, the number of people using the Internet is constantly growing and thus adding to the load.

Improved compression techniques, faster modems, and network backbones with higher bandwidth (e.g., ATM, Fast Ethernet, fiber-optic gigabit networks) can help remove congestion. However, major network improvements are costly and take time. Until faster networks are in place, large-scale development and use of large multimedia files on the Internet will be limited.

Multimedia Collections and Research

The assumption behind a lot of the ongoing research on multimedia applications in libraries and information agencies is that the Internet will continue to be the most important medium to provide access to multimedia repositories. The advantages of the Internet are the low barrier to entry and the ease of publishing, with which other formats have not yet been able to compete. For any information agency planning to produce multimedia collections, the Internet can provide the most useful channel because the collection can be made accessible for many users.

Following are some examples of existing commercial and noncommercial multimedia collections and some of the research areas their developers are working on. A lot of work is being done to refine search and retrieval techniques, speech and image recognition, natural-language understanding, the presentation and summarization of search results, querying across heterogeneous systems, and ways to perform information-exchange transactions in a secure fashion.

The Columbia Digital Library Project

Columbia University is focusing on search and retrieval techniques for digital libraries. Their aim is to create an interface that allows the user to receive textual, image, video, or multimedia documents in response to a single query and that presents the results in a way that alleviates the problem of information overload. Examples of the university's projects are the Domain Independent Summarization Project and the COMPRESS Project.

The Domain Independent Summarization Project aims to develop concise but informative summaries for the presentation of search results so that relevant documents can be found more quickly. Summaries will be generated using complex statistical, semantic, and parsing techniques. Focus is on the combining of information into a meaningful utterance, identifying other data sources, and noting differences between sources.

The other project, COMPRESS (Columbia Multimedia Presentation System), aims at generating efficient techniques for the extraction, delivery, and presentation of information from heterogeneous knowledge repositories. The retrieved information will be presented in an automatically generated multimedia presentation that coordinates the available text, graphics, and speech on the subject.

University of Illinois at Urbana-Champaign - Digital Libraries Initiative

The aim of the Digital Libraries Initiative (DLI) project is to create a large indexed multiple-source collection of engineering and scientific information and to create enhanced search technology in order to access documents effectively. The DLI digital library consists of 18,000 searchable journal articles in SGML format from major scientific publishers. Users can search these using a search interface which the user can complement with his or her own terms with additional terms as suggested by subject thesaurus or co-occurrence lists on the screen.

The subject thesaurus is based on Inspec; the co-occurrence list is based on statistics about which terms occur together and how frequently. The searcher can sort through both lists and select potentially useful words from them. Research includes studies of the switching of vocabularies across subject domains by computing concept spaces on large document collections. This information will be used to develop automatic-indexing technology for the document content, and the protocols for concept spaces will be embedded as the infrastructure of a new network-information system. Multimedia semantic retrieval will be researched.

University of California, Santa Barbara - Project Alexandria

The goal of the Alexandria project is to create a digital library of geographic and spatially indexed information, from maps and images to multimedia. The aim is that users be able to access these different formats through the library's interface without having to know where the materials are actually located. Access is improved by adding metadata to all forms of data, whether remote-sensing images, digital-raster and vector-data sets, or videos. The user interface lets the user compose spatial search queries and retrieve holdings in various formats. Current research involves ways to make iteratively refined searches and save configurations for future use, ways to define the geographic search region on screen by inputting vector data, and ways to search by texture. Texture information has been extracted from images and put into a texture-template database that can be matched with textures extracted from the library holdings.

Carnegie Mellon University - Informedia Digital Video Library

The aim of CMU's Informedia Project is to establish a large online video library for use in education and training. As mere storage of the materials does not make the collection useful, a lot of the research concentrates on new technologies for the full-content search and retrieval of video materials. The research has been done in the fields of speech recognition, image understanding, and natural-language understanding in order to improve the organization of the materials and to create retrieval systems that can retrieve speech and video segments.

CMU started with a system in which a speech recognizer would transcribe the sound track of each video tape and image-understanding techniques would be used for segmenting video sequences. Transcripts and segment information were then stored in the retrieval system. Informedia permits the user to search the video collections intelligently. The remaining problems include finding ways to aid users in the identification of desired video when a search returns multiple objects, and ways to let users skim the videos to quickly locate sections of interest. Work is also being done on developing tools for the user to manipulate and reuse the video.

Another research area in which CMU is interested is the network accounting of copyright usage to enable owners of copyrighted materials to be compensated appropriately. The result has been an automatic generalized billing system, NetBill. NetBill relieves the Informedia Digital Library from having to be directly involved in handling payments and protects the privacy of the transaction through user IDs and encryption. The NetBill server maintains accounts for both consumers and merchants.

University of Michigan - Digital Library Project

The University of Michigan is using agent technology to make earth- and space-science materials available. The library is a distributed collection, with each document represented by different storage and retrieval mechanisms and different query languages. To manage queries across heterogeneous collections, the digital-library architecture is based on agents, software program modules for performing highly specialized tasks. For example, user-interface agents manage the interface that connects users to the digital library resources, suggest synonyms for given search terms, transform user queries in a form that search agents can interpret, maintain user profiles, customize presentation of query results, and manage the user's resources for payments.

Tasks are distributed to numerous agents to promote modularity and flexibility. Mediator agents transmit results, translate formats, monitor queries, and team up with other agents to accomplish tasks. Registry agents translate incoming requests into queries on the registry. The advantage of using agents is their modularity, which increases flexibility and incrementality. Services can be added, changed, or deleted without disturbing the overall system, which is important when dealing with a variety of different systems. Research includes integrating an agreement negotiation process with electronic payment and exchange protocols, bookkeeping, and security mechanisms.

Stanford University Digital Libraries Project

Stanford University focuses heavily on interoperability research. The goal of the Stanford Digital Library project is to develop a single integrated library including a variety of heterogeneous repositories ranging from personal information collections to conventional library collections and scientists' data collections. The project aims for high-level protocols that could enable users to navigate the information space in a consistent way.

Tools created at Stanford include the InfoBus protocol, which allows the user to search remote databases using the protocol of the local system. Proxies act as interpreters between the InfoBus protocol and the native protocol. The InfoBus shields users from the details of accessing diverse sources.

Another tool, SenseMaker, helps users find information from multiple search services by allowing them to "make sense" out of their search results by looking at them through multiple views (author, subject, title, location, etc.) and by offering a range of ways to limit or expand a search. For example, users may bundle together results from the same site or results with similar titles. SenseMaker also employs several high-level duplicate detection strategies the user can choose from.

Elsevier's Electronic Subscriptions

In 1993 Elsevier started the Tulip Project, an experiment in providing page images of 45 science journals to 8 American universities. After two years of experimentation, Elsevier started delivering page images cover-to-cover from all its more than 1100 journals. OCLC provides the retrieval software (database builder and search engine Newton) and the graphical interface. Full text is provided as an ASCII file; bibliographic information, as structured SGML-tagged text. Customers can get a license for unlimited use or pay for individual articles.

ProQuest Digital Dissertations (UMI)

UMI is developing a digital library of doctoral dissertations and masters' theses that will consist of dissertations and theses submitted electronically, as well as of dissertations converted from paper-based format. The conversion from analog format to Adobe PDF (Portable Document Format) will start with 1997 titles, and by the end of this year, UMI is planning to have 45,000 titles in digital format. The library will be accessible on the Internet and later through ProQuest Direct, UMI's online information system. Institutions submitting dissertations and theses will have free access to the materials they have submitted and to the most current three months of citations and abstracts. Individuals and institutions can order the full text online using Dissertation Express.

Corbis

Corbis is a privately-held company, founded by Bill Gates in 1989. Its mission is to become the world's premier provider of high-quality digital content, beginning with still imagery and expanding in the future into other media. Including the Bettmann Collection, the archive contains millions of digital images on a range of subjects from science and technology to history. Corbis acquires rights to images through non-exclusive licensing, commissioning assignment photography, and outright purchase. The images are available for licensing through the company's Web site and the company's CD-ROM.

To prevent unauthorized use, the images on Corbis Web site are encoded with a watermark that shows when the image is reproduced without authorization. Client-service representatives provide technology consulting to the company's clients. Future expansion plans include additional formats (e.g., full-motion video, audio, graphics, and film) and new delivery systems, such as interactive television.

SuperJournal Project

SuperJournal is a British collaborative project among some 20 publishers, leading British universities, and their libraries. The project aims to develop some 50 peer-reviewed multimedia journals in key areas of the sciences and social sciences: e.g., molecular genetics and proteins, polymer physics, communication and cultural studies, political science, and computer graphics. The journals will then be delivered to participating user communities using the JANET and SuperJANET networks. (JANET is an academic and research network that links universities, colleges and research organizations throughout Great Britain and Northern Ireland. SuperJANET adds to JANET a broadband environment with advanced networking technologies such as ATM, SDH, and SMDS.) The broadband environment of SuperJANET allows the display of 3-D graphics, simulations to illustrate new techniques, videos, animation, and sound recordings, as well as statistical databases. Standard formats (SGML, PDF, HTML, and GIF) will be used. The interface allows users not only to view but also to manipulate multimedia documents.

Selection Criteria for Multimedia Technologies

Libraries and information agencies wanting to obtain multimedia resources face a far more challenging task than they did obtaining materials in non-electronic times. Traditionally, libraries owned the materials to which they provided access. Today, they are also providing access to remote materials. Assessing electronic materials entails using new criteria that collection developers did not use when selecting mainly among print materials: e.g., cost of searching or downloading, training, preservation costs, special equipment needed to use the material, search capabilities, and future accessibility. Moreover, the cost will be more difficult to assess than that of printed materials, for the costs for electronic materials are usually less predictable, depending on equipment costs, search time, amount of downloading or printing, preservation costs, etc.

Therefore, multimedia may not be the best choice for every kind of material. The information professional will choose from among a variety of formats (print, CD-ROM, DVD, Internet, microform, etc.) the one most appropriate for each purpose. To do this the selector must take into account a lot of different factors: e.g.,

— Contents and organization of information

— Quality of production

— Cost (including the cost of searching, downloading, printing, and preservation)

— If an Internet resource is selected, can it be expected to remain free?

— Do all the formats have the same information? How far back in time do they go? Is the coverage really what vendor says it is?

— If images are important, which format handles them best?

— Will the visuals date quickly?

— Does viewing, reading, or listening to the materials require special equipment, software, or plug-ins?

— Which format has the most current information? How often is it updated?

Multimedia formats add to the already wide range of information formats. As the same information may be found in different packages, it will be harder for collection developers to avoid duplication. Some duplication may be necessary to provide users their materials in a format with which they are comfortable. Therefore, it seems unlikely that multimedia would replace books, for example.

On the contrary, libraries that have digital collections have noticed that the use of their print collections has increased rather than decreased since they have become digital. Yet it is likely that the preference for electronic media will grow as libraries and information agencies start getting users who have been surrounded by computers all their lives and who may actually prefer to obtain their information online.

The two main selection issues for multimedia are cost and longevity. While the barrier for providing access to free or low-cost multimedia is low, the costlier the product is, the more difficult it is to select multimedia over a considerably cheaper product in traditional format. As long as multimedia technology changes rapidly, the price level is by no means fixed, which makes the selection even harder. The other issue, longevity, is a concern because rapidly developing technology shortens product life and at the same time increases the need for reformatting or migrations, adding to future costs.

Most resources on the Internet are free, and libraries and information agencies provide links to them. The downside of Internet links is that their maintenance requires more effort. Libraries that have incorporated the Internet in their selection policy have had to find answers to questions such as the following regarding selection from the Internet:

— Which types of Internet resources will the library select?

— Will access be provided to whole servers and everything in them, or only to title-level resources?

— Will out-of-date sites be removed? Will topical sites be mounted only for short durations?

— When (if ever) should the resource be downloaded and stored locally?

— Should an incomplete resource be selected?

As libraries and information agencies start incorporating multimedia resources into their collections, the question arises how to make the useful resources available to the users. There are three basic ways in which access to documents can be improved: First, to improve searching with search engines, producers of the resources can add metadata, i.e., information about the information in the resource, to the documents. Second, libraries and information agencies can catalog and set pointers to selected information resources. Third, search engines can be improved so that searchers can find the desired information faster.

Metadata consist of elements that can help the user choose the resource more quickly during an Internet search: e.g., topic, title, author, publisher, date, genre, format (e.g., PostScript, PDF, Windows file), version (e.g., high-resolution image, medium-quality image, thumbnail), source, language, coverage, rights and permissions, and last update. Each piece of information within a document that might be used on its own should have its own metadata so that the item can be accessed independently.

Efficient use of multimedia will depend on how soon and in how great detail metadata will incorporate video, sound, and animation. Developments in metadata enable the design of more capable search engines, allowing the users more opportunities to limit their search. Several different metadata projects are underway (TEI, Dublin Core, URC, IAFA, MARC, etc.), and as yet there is little consensus on the complexity level of semantic structure needed in metadata.

Interoperability between different systems and better search aids can be achieved only if sufficient agreement can be reached on the semantic structures. The University of California, Berkeley is one of the universities working on the construction of such content standards. While the semantic structure has not been agreed upon, there is a widely accepted general standard for constructing syntax and conventions for naming the elements of documents: Standard Generalized Markup Language (SGML). For the encoders of metadata it is important that the standard not become obsolete. The users of SGML are fairly confident that the metadata created in SGML-based documents will not become obsolete soon, for several reasons:

(1) SGML is widely accepted by software producers, various industries, the government, publishers, and library and information scientists;

(2) SGML is independent of proprietary hardware or software; and

(3) it is possible to create software that will work with any compliant Document Type Definition (DTD), i.e., with any markup language following SGML rules

Accessibility to documents can also be created by creating pointers to them or by cataloging them. Many libraries, computing centers, corporations, and individuals have employed various systems to organize link collections.

Relatively few libraries and information agencies have incorporated Internet links in their public-access catalogs.

While cataloging of electronic materials on CD-ROM or diskette has been regarded as worthwhile, cataloging Internet resources has been a controversial issue. The supporters of cataloging have pointed out that at present the Internet search tools are not always efficient in RESETlocating fast what the user wants to find. The opponents, in turn, contend that too many resources on the Internet either disappear or change location frequently, making it hard for the maintainer to keep the links updated.

Nevertheless, some 231 participants took part in the OCLC Internet Cataloguing project from October 1994 through June 1996, creating nearly 9,000 MARC records for selected Internet resources. Although the project has formally concluded, OCLC is planning to maintain InterCat as a learning resource for improved description practices.

Another OCLC initiative, NetFirst, was introduced in 1995 and currently contains over 60,000 records authoritative for all types of Internet resources. Unlike InterCat, NetFirst does not have full MARC records. Each record contains classification numbers, LC subject headings, and a short abstract. The sites are selected following the NetFirst Collection Development Policy. As one solution to the problem of changing location, the Internet Engineering Taskforce (IETF) has been working on developing a Uniform Resource Name (URN).

A URN would be a unique 'persistent' identification for a resource; it would be independent of the location and would utilize the resource's metadata. Examples of URNs are Persistent URLs (PURLs) and handles. There are also link-checking programs that help to identify broken links and moved or modified documents, e.g., MOMspider, Doctor HTML, and WebWatch. To fight the problem of the rapid disappearance of much Web-based information, the Internet Archive started archiving WWW documents in 1996 to make them available for future research when they are no longer available from their original source.

At present, the archive is not a complete archive of the whole Web because the crawler software used to collect sites does not have access to all file formats. Moreover, it may take some time before it will capture monthly—let alone weekly or daily—changes in Websites. The first round took almost a year to complete, and updates are planned to take place every few months. This schedule means that a lot of pages still disappear faster than they can be stored. More efforts like this will probably follow as the intellectual property issues involving archives are clarified. Access to multimedia will improve in the future, which will increase the usefulness of multimedia and its demand.

As long as licensing procedures remain as complex as they are now, libraries wanting to produce multimedia are most likely to rely on their own sources and the public domain and to use copyrighted sources only if they qualify for fair use.

Digitization has been seen as a way to secure the information stored in deteriorating formats and to reduce the need for building storage space. So far, converting large parts of a collection into digitized format has not been economical and projects have been limited to older materials that are out of copyright. Thus, a large amount of the digitized material consists of older works that are not heavily used.

Digitization of newer copyrighted material can be costly. A frequently cited example is IBM's spending over $1 million on clearing rights for its commemorative Columbus CD-ROM, only $10,000 of which went to rights holders. The rest was spent on administrative and legal costs. Cooperation between commercial and noncommercial organizations may be something to consider to ensure good-quality products. Examples of such cooperation include the Multimedia Dictionary of Modern & Contemporary Art, The Gothic Cathedrals of Europe, and Mount Olympos: Myth History and Poetry. All these are co-produced by several commercial and non-commercial organizations from different European countries.

Pressure for economical use of funds may lead to further nationwide coordination on digitization efforts, so that duplication can be reduced and selection of materials to be preserved can be made easier. For example, the Research Libraries Group (RLG) is investigating methods to include information about current or future digitization projects in bibliographic records. Clearly, a simpler negotiation system has to be developed before any large-scale digitization can take place. With smaller administrative costs, digitization of copyrighted material may become economical on a larger scale, especially if:

— institutions will share digital collections
— sharing digital collections decreases need for full traditional libraries at the local level
— use will increase with electronic access
— the long-term value of digital collections will exceed the maintenance and delivery costs
— the capture is rich enough to be useful over time.

Although the storage and copying costs are decreasing, the rapid development of technology and lack of clear standards may increase preservation costs if the preservation requires migrating the digitized materials from one generation of computer technology to the next or from one configuration to another. It is relatively easy to migrate ASCII-text files; but unless standards can be established, multiple formats may involve more complex, expensive, and frequent transformations. The success of multimedia archiving will depend on the identification of systems and standards that will reduce or make it easier to migrate multimedia materials or that will be able to read data from created with older systems with minimal reformatting. Therefore it is important for librarians and information scientists to be involved in digitizing efforts and in standardization issues.

Copyright Issues

In the electronic era, copyright issues constitute a big concern for producers, publishers, and those whose work is included in multimedia products. It is relatively easy for anyone to copy digitized works or digitize print materials and post them on the Internet, where they are freely accessible to the whole world. Therefore, as long as there is no efficient way to control the distribution of copyrighted materials, producers will hesitate to put their high-quality work on the Internet.

Efforts are underway to create tools that prevent illegal copying—or at least make it difficult—and that have the capability of performing transactions needed to give producers the compensation that according to the copyright legislation belongs to them. For example, companies have developed so-called trusted systems that can sell digital works and can allow or not allow copying, transport, or editing according to the terms and conditions specified by the publisher.

Techniques developed to prevent the pirating of intellectual property include watermarking, steganography, "dongle", and flickering. The first two, watermarking and steganography, involve a concealed special code within the digital object, which does not prevent copying but can be used to track illegal copies. The dongle is a device that must be installed on the machine in order for the software to work. Flickering is a technique in which random bits are added to the backgrounds of a digital object; these then appear as garbage if screen dumps are captured but can be read and viewed on the screen. There are still problems with these techniques. For instance, watermarks may be easily removed, and the current technology does not provide fast enough flickering and small enough dots for the flickering technique.

The emergence of such systems will make it possible to charge the users directly, which may mean that in the future there will be fewer materials available for free. It remains to be seen to what extent these systems will overcome the challenges of guaranteeing confidentiality, authenticity, and integrity of data in all circumstances. Users need to feel confident that their transactions and usage patterns will remain secure and confidential, even when someone tries to tamper with the system or something unexpected occurs. They also need to be able to trace the ultimate creator of the product and the history of changes made to the product.

For libraries and information agencies the consequences of introducing systems that can enforce copyright and possibly charge for the use of the material are that (1) decisions will have to be made as to what extent costs will be passed onto customers, and (2) ways will have to be found to enable fair use (i.e., the use of copyrighted material without the copyright owner's permission for certain specific uses such as teaching, research, news reporting, or criticism). If the copyright owners are given arbitrary control over the use of their work, there is a danger that the world would be moving from an age favoring fair use with little control over illegal copying to an era favoring the owners' rights with little concern for users' rights.

The role of librarians and information agents should be to help define fair use in the electronic area, in order to ensure that fair use will apply to all information formats. Librarians are already participating in The Conference on Fair Use (CONFU), which was convened by The Working Group on Intellectual Property Rights to bring together copyright owners, publishers, educators, and librarians to develop guidelines for fair uses.

Librarians and information scientists need to follow closely any copyright proposals because they can seriously affect the way information can be used. Multimedia technologies are faced with complex and cumbersome licensing practices, as different products (e.g., books, music, movies) are subject to different copyright applications. Licensing fees add to the production costs and often limit the choices of a producer who wants to keep costs at a reasonable level in order to be able to sell the product. If a simpler copyright negotiating solution can be found, producers can produce and make available a wider range of multimedia products at lower prices.

Compulsory licensing—i.e., a system in which the copyright owner would be required to license his or her work even if he or she does not want to do so—would be the most practical solution, in that it would simplify the copyright-negotiation process and thus make multimedia production more attractive. On the other hand, any such system would be hard to implement because of valuation difficulties. These are caused by such differences as varying quality, length, or the amount of value the copyrighted item brings to the total production.

Future of Multimedia for Image Formats

This section presents a general overview of multimedia standards for image formats. Attention is given to defining image formats, providing a brief history of the development of image standards, and providing a general discussion of current and future trends. Hardware used in graphics development will be discussed, as there is a direct connection between the evolutionary tracks of graphics hardware and software.

Two organizations need to be noted at the outset: ISO and ANSI. They are organizations involved in the creation of national and international agreements on standards in formats. The International Organization for Standardization (ISO) is a worldwide federation of national standards bodies from some 100 countries, one from each country. ANSI is the American National Standards Institute, a member of ISO. ISO is a nongovernmental organization established in 1947. The mission of ISO is to promote the development of standardization and related activities in the world, in the context of facilitating the international exchange of goods and services, and to develop cooperation in the spheres of intellectual, scientific, technological and economic activity.

The American National Standards Institute has served for 78 years in its capacity as administrator and coordinator of the voluntary standardization system in the private sector in the United States. Founded in 1918 by five engineering societies and three government agencies, the Institute remains a private, nonprofit membership organization supported by a diverse constituency of private and public sector organizations. The digital image has its origins in the desktop-publishing world, where images and pictures are an important part of the market. The use of images has evolved through their use in television, movies, photography, and the Internet. Recent developments in computergenerated graphics are increasingly seen in special effects for the small screen. Their relatively inexpensive nature has made them popular for effects in everything from science fiction to commercial advertising.

The push for standards in image formats greatly increased as thinking was directed at creating and cataloging collections and archives of photographs and paintings. The need for standards also increases as the use of graphics software becomes more commonplace in various media (both electronic and print). The best format in which to preserve an image is still a debatable topic, but recent developments in storage capacity may eliminate the worry of file size in creating a graphic file.

In 1985 that advances in technology allowed the concepts of cataloguing and collecting graphic images to become a reality. Further rapid advances occurred during 1990 to 1993. These advances have made it economical to digitize photographs and paintings. The origins of scanners can be traced to their development in 1985-1986 for the desktop-publishing market. Initially, the software developed for the hardware was able to control for brightness and contrast and could select between only two modes, "line art" and "halftone". The image files could then be saved in several file formats common to the desktop-publishing market. There were many limitations compared to the scanners and software available today. The number of scanners available at present has increased, and their prices have dropped. There are hand-held scanners, flatbed scanners, and several assorted page-feed scanners. A hybrid is the combination printer, copier, and scanner developed by HewlettPackard.

New devices include cameras, video capture cards, and specialized imaging devices such as are used in hospitals for high-resolution scans of the human body. Image use on the Internet has been another reason for seeking a standard in image formats. The field has been driven partially by the large size of graphics files and the impact that transferring such large files over the Internet can have on download times as well as on general Internet traffic. Recent developments in increasing bandwidth and increasing modem speeds may render such concerns moot. The search for an acceptable image format may revert to seeking formats that provide the best quality rather than formats that compress files substantially without sacrificing "too much" detail.

In traversing the land of digital images, we have provided some definitions and explanations of terms used in the field. The types of image files seem a good place to start. The standards provided by organizations such as ISO and ANSI will be more coherent after some clarity is brought to the plethora of acronyms and abbreviations in multimedia. Although image files can be print or pictures that can be produced through printers or fax machines, computer graphics are specific to those images that will be produced and displayed on a computer monitor that can display graphic as well as alphanumeric data.

A computergraphics system basically consists of a computer to store and manipulate images, a display screen, various input and output devices, and a graphics software package, i.e., a program that enables a computer to process graphic images by means of mathematical language. These programs enable the computer to draw, color, shade, and manipulate the images held in its memory. At present, the four most commonly used graphics formats are GIF, JPEG, TIFF and BMP; a new graphic format is currently entering the field, PNG. There are some that have become de facto standards; for example, JPEG is considered the most economical use of image compression for use in Web page construction.

TIFF is the format used in manipulating images. BMP files are known to Microsoft Windows users as this is the format used for desktop backgrounds, as well as the default file format in the Windows Paint program. GIF is a format originally developed by CompuServe to enable compression of large image files. It has also known widespread use despite its proprietary nature, even though CompuServe has at times seemed to indicate that it might try to restrict the use of GIF outside of CompuServe itself.

Following are definitions of various digital-image formats, taken from the Internet and other sources:

— *JPEG Joint Photographers Experts Group.* The title refers to the committee that was charged with developing this standard. As this title might suggest, JPEG compression is designed for use on photographs and other highly detailed multicolored images. JPEG also permits you storage of 24-bit images, which means that it will accommodate over 16.7 million different colors

— *GIF Graphic Interchange Format.* This is perhaps the most common type of graphic format found on the Web and represents the background image or texture on most Web pages. GIF is a compressed file format that relies on LZW (Lempel-Zev-Welch) compression to create very small files. For this reason, GIF formatting works best with images that contain large areas of similarly colored pixels. It is an 8bit file format, which means that it has a very limited color palette. Each pixel in a GIF image can represent one of up to 256 distinct colors. Because of this limitation to only 256 colors, the GIF format may not be the most appropriate choice for highly detailed color files.

— *TIFF Tagged Image/Interchange File Format*. This file-storage format is implemented on a wide array of computer systems and is the preferred file format of some of the most popular graphics software programs.

— *BMP Bitmap Format*. An image created from a series of bits and bytes that form pixels. Each pixel can vary in color or gray-scale value. Also known as a raster image.

— *PNG Portable Network Graphics*. PNG provides a patent-free replacement for GIF and can also replace many common uses of TIFF. Indexed-color, grayscale, and true-color images are supported, in addition to an optional alpha channel. Sample depths range from 1 to 16 bits.

Scanners and Related Hardware

Recent trends in the marketplace have brought the price of scanners down to an affordable level. A modestly performing scanner can be bought now for a little under $200, while high-end scanners provide powerful tools and accessories. With growing demand for scanned images in documents and on World-Wide Web pages, the time to buy a personal scanner has never been better. Until recently, a fullpage, flatbed color scanner was priced beyond the reach of most personal computer users. Unless you were unusually affluent, or had a professional graphics use to justify spending the $1,500 to $4,000 that a decent scanner cost, it was hard to justify buying your own scanner. Small, handheld, black-and-white scanners and pagefed scanners are cheaper, but less satisfactory in terms of ease of use and image quality. In the last year, scanners with extremely impressive feature sets have come to sell for $450 to $750. Personal scanners, it would seem, are set to become widely popular among even ordinary computer folk.

Ironically, just when scanners are becoming cheap enough to be a viable choice for many PC and Mac users, other imagecapture alternatives are also vying for the attention of buyers. Digital cameras, which are also now appearing in the $450-750 range, and videocapture cards, which begin at even lower prices, have certain advantages over flatbed scanners, although they also come with some severe limitations. In comparing the two technologies, digital cameras and scanners, we consider two issues: flexibility and resolution.

Most current lowcost, flatbed scanners can digitize an image laid onto their scanning surface at up to 600 pixels per inch (ppi), with a scanning area of about 21.5 by 28 centimeters (8.5 by 11 inches). This means images can be scanned into your computer with as many 5100x6600 (or 33,660,000) pixels, with a file size of up to 100 MB, assuming the user has a computer with enough RAM and hard-drive space to handle such a job. By comparison, most digital cameras and videocapture cards are limited to image resolutions of 640x480 pixels or less; and these cameras and cards make image files that, when compressed, are measured in tens of kilobytes, not tens of megabytes. They can also capture images instantly, while a flatbed scanner can take from several seconds to many minutes to complete a scan. And unlike flatbed scanners, cameras can capture images of three-dimensional (3-D) objects as well as artwork. Many computer users are satisfied with pictures that look good when displayed on the computer screen, even if they do not have enough detail for commercial printing processes.

A Hewlett-Packard company document claims that "one of the key participants in bringing scanner technology to the consumer market" has been HewlettPackard, whose ScanJet products (particularly the ScanJet 4p) have helped to change the way consumers look at these products. The ScanJet 4p was introduced in March 1997 as a lowcost color scanner "offering business customers professional image quality with pointandshoot simplicity." You can find the 4p for under $700 these days.

HP put more into the product than just a low price. The company spent a lot of time on the software that goes with it--an area where many lowcost scanners had fallen down in the past. And it did not skimp on the base hardware-the ScanJet 4p is a 24bit color and 8bit grayscale scanner that offers 1,200 dots per inch (dpi) in highresolution mode and 300 dpi optical resolution for optical character recognition (OCR) work.

According to HP, scanners have been huge beneficiaries of the fact that, while the "paperless office" idea has never really taken off in a big way, paper is not always the most effective way to share information within a large company. In a brief document, the company says scanners are quickly emerging as a key enabler of electronic distribution of paperbased documents in the office and beyond.

A desktop scanner or network scanner allows business professionals to scan paperbased documents, manage them effectively, and distribute them in a timely fashion. Users can share and distribute information easily by scanning directly to their email or PC fax applications, the company document explains. HP also says that the growing popularity of faxmodems and email is driving the acceptance of "scannerenabled" document distribution in offices of all sizes. HP says the workgroup (and by extension, the intranet) concept has been instrumental in bringing electronic document distribution to business offices, and should produce a huge market potential for scanners.

Although the electroniccommunications market is exploding, millions of PC users still receive a lot of paperbased information that they need to share with colleagues. Scanners can be used to help users optimize paperbased information, regardless of its original form. To meet the information needs of today's business professionals, HP is expanding and enhancing its family of scanners to enable rapid sharing, filing and communication of paperbased documents throughout and beyond an enterprise.

Document imaging utilizes digital scanners to generate a digital representation of a document page. An image scanner divides the page into minute picture areas called pixels and produces an array of binary digits, each representing the brightness of a pixel. The resulting stream of bits is enhanced and compressed by a device called an image controller and is stored on a magnetic or optical medium. A large storage capacity is required, because it takes about 45,000 bytes to store a typical compressed text page of 2,500 characters and as much as 1,000,000 bytes to store a page containing an image. Aside from document imaging applications, digital scanning is used for transmission of documents via facsimile, in satellite photography, and in other applications.

An image scanner digitizes an entire document page for storage and displays it as an image. In itself, it does not recognize characters and words of text. Text processing and other software techniques, therefore, cannot linguistically manipulate the stored material. When such manipulation is desired, a software program performs the optical-character-recognition (OCR) function by converting each optically scanned character into an electric signal and comparing it with the internally stored representation of an alphabet of characters, so as to select from it the one that matches the scanned character most closely or to reject it as an unidentifiable token. The more sophisticated of presentday OCR programs distinguish shapes, sizes, and pitch of symbolsincluding handwritingand learn from experience. A universal optical-character-recognition machine is not available, however, for even a single alphabet.

Future Trends

Multimedia and Hypermedia Experts Group (MHEG) is another group of specialists created by ISO, the International Standards Organization. This group was charged with the task of creating a standard method of storage, exchange, and display of multimedia presentations. MHEG version 5, the current work item for the group, was created in November 1994. It has been a DIS (Draft International Standard) since December 1995, and was due to be promoted to the status of full international standard in July 1996. Its basic goals are:

— To provide a simple but useful, easy-to-implement framework for multimedia applications using minimal system resources

— To define a digital final form for presentations, which may be used for exchanging presentations between different machines regardless of make or platform

— To provide extensibility; i.e., the system should be expandable and customizable with additional application specific code, though this may make the presentation platform-dependent.

The WorldWide Web Consortium has endorsed PNG as a replacement for the GIF files currently in use at most Web sites. These socalled "Ping" files are as much as 30 percent smaller than GIF files, so they load faster in a browser. The article continues, "Native support for PNG files is included in Internet Explorer 4.0, but Netscape has so far chosen to handle PNG files via a free plugin called PNG Live. Version 2.0 of that plugin has just been released, although it supports only the Communicator platform."

Greg Reolofs, a Web Consortium member who maintains a Web site dedicated to PNG, said he expects to see a big changeover to the new format. "I think that the browsers are essentially the sole gating factor here," he said, "and once Internet Explorer and Netscape Communicator are both out in release form and replacing the 3.0 versions, I think you'll see a large migration."

Chris Lilly, the Web Consortium's technical leader for graphics, said there is no good reason to stay with the GIF file format. The faster transfers that come from the smaller file size under PNG, users will also perceive an additional speed increase from the way PNG handles interlacing—a technique for making graphics files gradually come into focus in your browser as they load. If you have an interlaced PNG, you will start seeing a recognizable image when only one-sixty-fourth of data has come in, whereas with GIF, you have to wait until an eighth of the data has come in, he said. "Also, GIF gives you full resolution horizontally and only one-eighth of your resolution vertically, so text is not readable until at least half of the data has come in. With PNG the text is readable with 10 to 12 percent of the data."

Implications

New standards including MPEG II and hardware such as the DVD will guide the future development of digital imaging. JPG and GIF are still the most used formats on the Internet for Web graphics, with PNG a rising star on the image-formats horizon. Graphics-software manufacturer formats, using TIFF and proprietary file formats, push the use of older and familiar formats. The battle over formats, like the battle over operating systems for computers, may ultimately be won by the demand of cross-platform flexibility. This would render the differing file formats interchangeable, eliminating the need for graphics software to convert one file format to another. The growing use of graphic and image technology is being driven by the increasing variety of uses to which these technologies can be applied.

A good example of this growing use is to be found in New Zealand. Recently installed computer-imaging technology is enhancing the conservation of, and access to, the wealth of pictorial material held by the Alexander Turnbull Library of the National Library of New Zealand (NLNZ). The Turnbull Library, which houses the NLNZ's heritage collections, contains some 800,000 accessible photographs, 50,000 drawings and prints, and 50,000 maps, as well as newspapers, serials, cartoons, posters, and music.

In what would seem unbelievable to the original photographers with their glass plates, imaging technology is taking the faces and scenes of times gone by, scanning them, transforming them into digital data, and printing them out in a variety of high-quality formats. Publication or reference-quality reproductions are available as digital photographic prints, laser photocopies, or overhead transparencies, or in digital form on SyQuest cartridge or disk.

One of the great things about this new technology is that it has a significant role to play in conserving the Turnbull Library's valuable materials, many of which are unique and irreplaceable. Before the Turnbull Library established its Image Services department, producing copies of images often involved sending originals outside the Library. Now they can be reproduced within their own controlled environment, making fragile or large items more accessible and reducing the risk of damage or loss. Image Services is currently reproducing 200 to 250 images a week and is about to start a collection of stored digital images, including the materials most vulnerable to decay. Because the images are stored digitally, quick and repeated access can be made to the documents without repeated handling of the originals..

Within a year Image Services plans to offer options for digital output made available on CD-ROM. By late 1997 access will be possible via PCs in schools, local libraries, and homes. At that time, online users should be able to scroll through a selection of thumbnail sized-images of the Alexander Turnbull Library's collections and place an electronic order for a printed copy if desired.

The future seems to be headed in the direction of the digital picture. The recent ruling to have U.S. television become digital High Definition Television by the year 2006 is the latest trend in the evolution of digital-imaging technology. Increasingly, the move toward cheaper storage devices and faster telecommunication lines will resolve the issues of file size and download time, and the focus will be on the substance of the picture instead of its delivery mode. The implications for the future in digital-image formats seem to be toward an ultimate divorce, for the consumer, from having to make the choice between resolution and speed. Digital images, audio, and video will eventually blend into a seamless multimedia experience.

Open Standards

As we have seen, the use of multimedia opens up new possibilities for user experiences with media. However, a haphazard approach to dealing with multimedia will ultimately be destructive to that new form. Before we can determine methods of classifying, cataloging, or accessing multimedia, we must first agree upon the formats in which multimedia materials are to be created. If we do not, then multiple formats will continue to exist, with disastrous sideeffects: e.g., higher cost of maintenance, multiple and contradictory versions of materials, and the needless cost of the acquisition of the same content in different formats.

The idea of "Open Standards" within digital-media formats comes from the efforts of standards-creation bodies to plan digital systems that are flexible and able to operate together. These systems are known as "open systems." There are three types of open system, or three criteria by which the openness of a system or standard is judged:

"If a system supports the exchange of information among various components of similar levels, then it supports 'interoperability'. If a subsystem . . . can be moved from one environment to another, then it is said to be 'portable'. An 'integrated' set of applications . . . provides a consistent user interface."

Thus, an open standard supports these traits to one degree or another: interoperability between systems, portability between platforms, and integration of user interfaces. The extent to which a standard could be considered "open" can be determined by the level of compliance it has with each of these traits. As a simple example, we could consider an image browser created by a corporation for viewing or converting image formats. An interoperable image browser would allow a user access to many common image formats found on the Internet and on the browser's native platform.

If that image browser were portable, it might run on a Windows machine as well as a Macintosh or Unix machine. Finally, an integrated image browser would use the types of interface elements used throughout the rest of the user's system in a consistent manner. Very few formats or systems meet all three of these criteria equally or fully. We will find that one of the most important new multimedia standards, HTML, comes close to meeting each of these. The HTML standard has had to adapt to the desires of multimedia creators, and yet it has retained its cross-platform interoperability, as well as its basic rules of interface or interaction.

There are two types of standard which are widely recognized as influential within organizations and user communities. These are "de jure standards" and "de facto standards."

De jure standards are those which have been determined and specified by standards-creation organizations, and which are then set forth as a proposed standard for adoption by the user community. HTML is an example of this type of standard.

De facto standards are those which are created by a corporation or other entity and end up becoming the standard simply through their wide-range adoption throughout user communities by trial and error or commanding market share. Adobe's PDF format for printable digital documents is an example of a de facto standard; the Windows operating system is another.

It is possible for de jure standards to be widely agreed upon and used by various user communities. This is considered the ideal situation, as it usually allows for the greatest openness; as you may have guessed, HTML is a good example of this happening; it is, however, quite uncommon for any standard to truly gain acceptance as broadly and openly as HTML and the Web.

We can trace the history of progress in digital-media standards through these phases of computing: batch computing with mainframes; timesharing; proprietary networks; personal computing; networked computing; and distributed computing. It is important to remember that the first de jure standards came out of the need for diverse systems to interoperate with each other as they began sharing information across the Internet. Proprietary standards, some of which are now de facto standards, arose out of the movement to offer proprietary alternatives to the Internet in the form of proprietary networks, and also out of the need for personal computer makers to competewith one another as they sought market share and usership.

As these worlds have collided—as personal computers have met the Internet and as businesses have begun to use the Internet as a normal arm of commerce—, the boundaries between these types of standards have blurred. We, as information and media specialists, must understand the differences between these types of standards, and must be able to judge which types are most likely to serve the long-term needs of traditional libraries and forward-thinking organizations.

For an example of a success story—both in terms of widespread use as well as in terms of the openness of its standards—, we shall take a close look at the World-Wide Web, as contrasted with the traditional carrier of multimedia content: the CD-ROM. For years, the standard format for multimedia works and presentations was the CD-ROM. Capable of holding more than 600MB of data, it made a convenient format for large presentations. However, it did have some disadvantages.

For one, users needed to be equipped with CD-ROM drives in their computers in order to use multimedia CD-ROMs. Another problem was the lack of interoperability: while the same presentation could be made in different formats (usually the two most common home computer formats, PC and Macintosh), it was not possible for different computers to view exactly the same presentation and version; they had to view versions geared towards their particular platform.

The World-Wide Web was and remains simple in principle. The basic concept is: If there is a resource somewhere, and we can uniquely address it, then we can display and interlink it by pointing to it. In its simplest form, a network is a cluster of computers, with one computer acting as a server to provide network services such as file transfer, email, and document printing to the client computers of that network.

By allowing any of these resources to be accessed through reference to a unique location, the Web created of the Internet seems as connected and seamless-appearing a system (remember the goal of "integration") as the world of communication has ever seen. Thus the HyperText Transfer Protocol (HTTP) and the Uniform Resource Locator (URL) were born. And, subtly, online multimedia uses began.

At first, these uses hardly resembled multimedia. Whereas multimedia include full-motion video, high-resolution graphics, and sound, the early Web had none of these. However, the stage had been set for these changes. So long as a resource could be labeled and pointed to, all one had to wait for was the requisite speeds and capacities of the transfer media. And these speeds and capacities have caught up. The World-Wide Web as a modern fulfillment of the promises of widespread multimedia use.

Future Trends

The explosive growth of the Internet is the most exciting development for multimedia since the introduction of the CD-ROM. In 1993, the potential audience for multimedia was the million people who had personal computers equipped with CD-ROM drives. This widespread use is, to be sure, extremely important, as the messages of multimedia become increasingly global. Additionally, the relative ease with which an individual can place information on the Web renews the possibilities of low-cost and high-audience self-publishing. And more and more large companies and multimedia teams are stretching the tools of the Web to create classy and sophisticated multimedia presentations as well. It seems as though the Web could turn out as a win-win situation: empowerment for the individual as well as for the creative team with vision and resources.

An important factor in the Web's success has been that it unites each of the three ideals of open systems:

— *Interoperability*—The URL allows diverse (or, technically, "heterogeneous") systems to access each other seamlessly and without failure; Unix machines can share media with PCs who are sharing media with Macintoshes, etcetera.

— *Portability*—A cluster of HTML files can be (and often is) uprooted and moved as a whole from one server to another. While the old URLs in existence will no longer access the pages, the pages will work, in themselves. All that is needed to suggest complete seamlessness is a command placed at the old URL that automatically forwards the browser to the new location.

— *Integration*—This is one of the most difficult tasks of open systems. However, the Web's metaphor of following links forwards and backwards, deeper and shallower, holds throughout the system. In addition, new conventions—such as the Home Page, with which a user creates a personalized resource—have developed and hold across all platforms and access communities on the Web.

Given these successes, the only ingredient needed for a truly revolutionary form of multimedia would be very widespread use. While the need for expensive equipment to view the more detailed or multimedia-like aspects of the Web remains a challenge, the basic structure of the Web is accessible to someone with a text-alone browser. In addition, the Web and its conduit, the Internet, show no signs of slowing in their rapid growth.

Technically, a "host" is a machine which is hooked up to the Internet full time, constantly serving (or, allowing access to) Web pages and routing email messages. Given this widespread access, we would do well to learn to work with the Web as a native environment, whether we are considering cataloging needs or the organization of resources. It is felt by the multimedia community that soon technological hurdles will be nonexistent and that the quality of the machines which we use to access the Web will increase dramatically.

In a few years, multimedia computers will be an anachronism. All computers will readily integrate images, sounds, and motion video—and this capability will be built onto the motherboard as an essential part of what a computer is. Already, these computers are connected to the Internet for worldwide real-time sharing of high-quality images, sounds, and video. As the Internet becomes used for commerce and as more individuals find their way there, we need to familiarize ourselves with all types of multimedia formats, and to be able to form value judgements on the effectiveness and expected longevity of each of these possible formats.

Longevity

There are several reasons for the judgments on the longevity of multimedia formats matter today more than ever before.

The Library and Preservation of the Cultural Record

The economy is now based on a vast system of knowledge

created by the merging of technologies, information, and media. In the past, knowledge systems were in the domain of information services managers and information scientists (otherwise known as librarians) whose professions weren't highly esteemed because of their focus on organizing data, rather than creating it. . . . Information architecture, the meaningful organization of information, is becoming an important discipline because it concentrates on deciphering data and giving it shape within the complex structures behind the computer screen.

Longevity of Mission-Critical Data

Longevity is affected by the format in which the information is encoded and entrusted to future generations. Certainly, given the pace at which means of information delivery and access are changing, we cannot plan which formats will be readable or even useful a generation hence; however, we can continually err on the side of openness, as defined by the three criteria of interoperability, portability, and integration. The term corporations use for information that is of vital importance today and of long-term value to the archives of the organization is "Mission-Critical Data."

While many organizations are forced to view only the bottom line when deciding on standards and formats for support, we need continually to judge the possible options and to explain the advantages of openness in relation to the importance of these mission-critical data.

Types of Multimedia Standards

Sound

There are several different formats for electronic sound and music being used in multimedia today. "A sound file's format," writes Tay Vaughn, "is simply a recognized methodology for organizing the digitized sound's data bits and bytes into a data file." One of the oldest, yet also one of the most flexible, is the MIDI format. Vaughn continues, "MIDI (Musical Instrument Digital Interface) is a communications standard developed in the early 1980s for electronic musical instruments and computers. . . . MIDI provides a protocol for passing detailed descriptions of a musical score, such as the notes, sequences of notes, and what instrument will play these notes. But MIDI data is not digitized sound; it is a shorthand representation of music stored in numeric form."

Thus, when a small MIDI file is downloaded and played through a sequencer or program set up to render MIDI sounds and music, it will come out much as the creator intended, in a very small file size. This only works if the downloading user is equipped to play back MIDI files accurately. Otherwise, the music might sound completely different from what the creator intended. Indeed, a user can even make MIDI music different by intention.

Another possibility for digital music, one being used more and more, is simply digitizing the analog signal of sound into a format which is faithful to the original recording, but which is far larger in size. In contrast to MIDI data, digital audio data is the actual representation of a sound, stored in the form of thousands of individual numbers (called samples). The digital data represent the instantaneous amplitude (or loudness) of a sound at discrete slices of time. Because it is not device dependent, digital audio sounds the same every time it is played. But that consistency comes at a price: large data storage files."

In the past, MIDI formats were used to save precious memory space in multimedia works. However, as the capacities of home computers improve and space issues are no longer of such great concern, digital recordings are coming into widespread use. As a final learning aid, we provide a table of common sound formats, as they might be encountered on the Web. The MIME type is a convention for denoting different media types.

Images

Images are covered in detail in the section on "Multimedia Standards in Image Formats" and will not be treated extensively here. The one aspect of images we touch upon here is the difference between bitmapped images and vector-drawn images. As Tay Vaughn notes: "A bitmap is a simple information matrix describing the individual dots that are the smallest elements of resolution on a computer screen or other display or printing device." Thus, when an image is taken and broken into a component description that can be rendered pixel by pixel, we find a bitmapped image. This would be analogous to the digital format for sound, insofar as an analog signal is translated into a series of ones and zeroes.

As might be expected, there is likewise a format for digital images that works by defining a mathematical range or scope to be rendered; and although the final rendering, if displayed on a screen, must be pixellated, its definition or description is not. Originally, this method produced what were known as "vector-drawn" images. These were mathematically described images, which were then rendered for display. Vaughn explains that a vector is a line that is described by the location of its two endpoints.

Today, similar techniques are used for three-dimensional (3-D) rendering; these are often called "wireframes," but the principle is the same. 3-D imaging is still in its infancy, in terms of what is possible on the Web though not yet accessible to many.

Video

Video, like 3-D imagery, is fairly new to the Web, although it has been in multimedia for some time. "Standards and formats for digital text, imagery, and sound are well established and familiar," notes Vaughn. "But video is the most recent addition to the elements of multimedia. And it is still being refined as transport, storage, compression, and display technologies take shape in laboratories and in the marketplace."

One of the most common forms of digital video found in traditional multimedia is QuickTime, a format developed by Apple Computers. QuickTime is similar to Adobe's PDF format in that it is a copyrighted and proprietary format, whose evolution will continue to be determined by Apple. However, Apple has been more lenient with licensing QuickTime and with encoding systems from third parties than has Adobe, partly because Apple has been around longer and so can afford to be more open without sacrificing its widespread use within multimedia.

One open video format that is also in widespread use is the MPEG video format. MPEG stands for "Moving Picture Experts Group" (compare with JPEG); the MPEG format was designed to allow for inexpensive and accessible digital video of fairly high quality. "The MPEG standard has been developed by the Moving Picture Experts Group. . . . MPEG1 and MPEG2 are the current standards. Using MPEG1, you can deliver 1.2 Mbps (megabits per second) of video and 250Kbps (kilobits per second) of two- channel stereo audio using CD-ROM technology. MPEG2, a completely different system from MPEG1, requires higher data rates (3 to 15 Mbps) but delivers higher image resolution, picture quality, interlaced video formats, multi-resolution scalability, and multichannel audio features."

While MPEG video takes up more memory than QuickTime video, MPEG formats have the advantage of being established and open standards. Recent modifications to the QuickTime format and its players point to a very near future in which QuickTime-ready playback and recording systems can read and translate between QuickTime and the MPEG format with little trouble.

We live in a time of rapid change and opportunity. As librarians and information scientists learn to speak to the issues animating the growth of the Internet and the multimedia fusion it foreshadows, they will become more and more respected by the organizations and access communities that seek guidance through tangle of information. One important fact to remember is that it was never imagined, when the Web was developed in theory, that so much would be asked of it in practice. The remarkable growth of the World Wide Web is stressing the 'old' designs for displaying text on computers. Indeed, while marked up text files (HTML documents) remain at the foundation of Web activity, when you visit a well-designed site you often discover graphic images, animations, and interactive work-arounds contrived to avoid displaying text. The neat paragraphs, indented lists, and formats for which HTML was originally intended are evolving into multimedia documents, not text documents, and the HTML method and standard is consequently suffering great stress. As features, tags, plug-ins, and special scripts are tacked onto or embedded into HTML to satisfy the demands for multimedia interfaces, at some point HTML will need to be redesigned from the ground up—as a multimedia delivery tool, not just a text display tool with assorted attachments.

Indeed, moves have already been made to do similar things. The extensions made to browser capabilities and markup language by Netscape and Microsoft are well known. When Netscape realized that commercial entities would pay money for the ability to place elegant or detailed imagery on the Web, Netscape responded with HTML tags that could do some basic layout. The process continued when Microsoft duplicated all of those extensions in its own browser, and then added more. While the Web was not designed with all of this in mind, it was nevertheless designed to be extensible.

Vaughn's prognosis—that HTML would have to be re-designed from the ground up—ignores the fact that media and formats, once created, seldom disappear entirely, but rather shrink in their utilization until they occupy a suitable niche. While in five years HTML may not be expected to carry the many forms of media now being created, it will nevertheless form a respected and utilitarian component of whatever infrastructure someday emerges to replace it.

The World-Wide Web Consortium (W3C), the body that determines formats for the Web, has already released a working specification for what it is calling "XML" or Extensible Markup Language, version 1.0. This should allow various protocols to be extended and shared openly and freely, in much the way that the initial HTML specifications allowed. More on XML, and the work of the W3C, can be found at the Web page of the Consortium.

The Web's move towards increased interoperability comes none too soon, from the perspective of the field of library and information science. We will need to learn to support and organize the digital media that are chosen by the growing marketplace as de facto standards, even while viewing those formats and media with attention to their openness, and thus their longevity. As various corporate interests battle for corners of digital turf, the LIS professions, as a culture, run the risk of losing access to media and their messages, even before our field can adapt to new ways of organizing them.

Java

Java is a programming language that has great implications for the future and longevity of information. Java operates much like any other programming language, with the very significant difference that programs written in Java can be used on any platform for which there is a "Java Virtual Machine," or JVM. In essence, the JVM rests on a native computer and interprets the Java programs; the Java programs only interact with the JVM, and think of it as the machine. The face of the JVM that runs Java is identical from platform to platform; the face of the JVM that connects with each platform differs, but the end result is the same: programs written for Java on the Mac will run on Java for the PC, and vice-versa. This is a tremendous leap, and its importance has not been lost on the telecommunications community; nor should it be lost on ours.

New User Interfaces

Consistent interfaces will become more and more important. That something will become consistent is not in question. Whether that interface will be useable, clear, comprehensive, and friendly is very much in question.

Search Engines

A search engine is a program that searches through given data sets and attempts to match keywords of the query to related documents. Ideally, it uncovers relevant material quickly and accurately. In the context of the World-Wide Web, the term "search engine" is most often used to describe search forms produced and maintained by a particular organization. Once provided with user information, the programs explore various databases of HTML documents, which have been indexed either manually or automatically. Each engine uses slightly different strategies and searches potentially different collections of information within documents. The traditional methods enable search engines to examine lists of already existing URLs, such as server lists, "What's New" pages, and other heavily trafficked sites on the Web.

But effective searching is dependent on the search engine's intimate knowledge of the Web's resources. In other words, what has not been found and recorded already will not be retrieved by even the most sophisticated search engines. So, the questions of whether data have already been acknowledged through some form of indexing, and of which particular data are searched, become as significant as how the search is performed. Most indexing services also permit authors to make manual submissions of documents, which will then most likely be queued and visited by a robot.

However, the resulting information retrieved by today's search engines typically seems to be significantly less than what a searcher often believes is actually out there: less than hoped for in both relevance and quantity. That is, results fail to generate a comprehensive list of all existing HTML documents related to one's search, and today's user confidence toward the effectiveness of search engines tends to reflect this.

There are over 100 known search engines active on the Internet today. As mentioned, they evaluate data, and compare them with the query string, using some kind of logic-based system (e.g., Boolean). Most are designed to accept some level of tailoring or "customization", in case the user wants to aim a search at a more specifically defined set of documents. Yahoo, for example, has a seldom used "options" button that allows a user to be far more specific in his or her search parameters than would otherwise be possible during a standard Yahoo query.

The understanding and use of appropriate modifiers (+, _, " ") can also greatly increase the power of an ordinary search engine, though this feature is unsupported by many of today's search programs. In response to the typically poor number and types of hits attained through traditional search engines, a number of Web indexing projects have begun, typically falling into one of two groups: meta-indexes or spider-generated index pages. Meta-indexes are also known as meta-search tools. Two representatives of the meta-index type are Dogpile and Savvy.

Meta-indexes are unusual in that they submit the keywords of the search to a multitude of other, traditional search engines. These meta-search tools operate as facilitators, distributing the search and attempting to match the query to the most relevant hits of multiple search engines at the same time. Redundant hits are generally filtered out, and results are provided along with the name of the particular company that actually retrieved them. Thus both the scope and accuracy of the findings typically far exceed those of any single engine search. These may well be the super-search engines of the future.

Spiders and Robots

The inventory of the Web is getting larger and more heavily charted as automation plays an increasingly more significant role in resource discovery. Web spiders (sometimes referred to as robots, walkers, wanderers, or worms) are programs that inspect Web documents and take some action in response to them, usually adding them to a pool of other searchable documents or constructing a path from hyperlinks that the spider identifies within a given document.

A spider or robot is a program that automatically traverses the Web's hypertext structure by first retrieving a single document, and then recursively retrieving all documents that the retrieved document refers or links to. Typical Web browsers (e.g., Netscape) are not considered robots because they are limited to being operated by a human, and do not automatically retrieve referenced documents (other than inline images). The names, "spider," "robot," etc., while perhaps appealing, may be misleading, as these terms give the false impression that the robot itself moves, while the term "worm" tends to imply that the robot multiplies itself like a virus. As a result of these misconceptions, these automated resource discoverers have received undue, uninformed criticism. In reality however, these robots are implemented as a single software system that retrieves information from remote sites using standard Web protocols, and the only tangible problem they potentially pose is in adding to network congestion. WebCrawler is a commercial example of a robot- or spider-based search engine.

The true value of spiders will be in the eventual automated construction of up-to-date virtual neighborhoods of documents, which a spider constructs through methodical exploration of the Web's textual resources, and whose momentum is fueled by the Web's inherent connectivity. The growth of the Web is such that it defies the ability of any but a single-purpose server, which does not yet exist, to construct a complete full-text index.

Development plans for spiders involve eventual domain-specific Web index construction, using domain profiles to identify documents and then organize these into local neighborhoods. Advanced spiders currently not only review the textual content of Web sites but also note the file names of any images or sounds they encounter. This use of remote-indexing programs represents the approaching standard for resource discovery on the Web. Subsequently, the resulting growth of search-tool capabilities dependent on a greater level of indexing than now exists promises to bring a new confidence in the accuracy of search engines' results and to help reduce both the time and frustration level associated with searching the Web.

The growth of the Web is beginning to elude even the most earnest attempts to catalog it—even on a purely textual level. As mentioned above, resource discovery has been greatly enhanced through the widespread use of Web-crawling robots, programs that automatically traverse the Web, inventorying varying aspects of document content as they go. As a result of this sudden increase in recorded data, search engines must cover more ground in order to conduct a thorough search. New search technology, of the type mentioned earlier, called meta-search tools, routes queries through many search engines simultaneously.

Images on the Web are also cataloged by robots, but classification is still dependent only on file name, and not necessarily on the picture's content or theme. However, actual image-processing techniques, along with object- or pattern-recognition techniques, are improving quickly. The construction of a complete, fulltext index of the Web once depended on authors or visitors of a given URL to manually report and record a given page's content. This can now be augmented by robots and spiders, which attempt to do the charting for us. Sounds and images, however, continue to elude comprehensive cataloging attempts in all ways but by file name. Specific attributes (e.g., .AIFF or .GIF) can be used in association with other key words for search purposes, but such searches are hardly comprehensive.

In the future, broader bandwidth and growth in the amount of electronic information available will increase the use of electronic resources, including multimedia. The amount of high-quality materials will increase as digital libraries, universities, publishers, museums and individual authors put more materials into electronic formats. Some of it will be available only for a fee, as payment systems develop that enable cost-effective handling of transactions. Information professionals will have to decide whether to pass on some, any, or no cost, to the users. Thus students should be made aware of some of the questions concerning fees for services in public and academic libraries.

4

Digital Archiving

The late twentieth century saw the beginning of the age of digital information in corporate archives, the creative arts, financial markets, medical information, and scholarship, among other venues. How the United States chooses to preserve and manage its digital information affects core issues in key industries—from medical textbook publishing to entertainment and to future scholarship in science, technology, and the arts and humanities.

Formal 30-minute interviews and shorter conversations and e-mail exchanges were conducted with individuals who represent a range of interests and organizations across publishing, film, entertainment, news, electronic books, computer science, libraries, corporate research, nonprofit organizations, professional and trade associations, and academe. Information gained from the interviews was complemented by six "environmental scans" that were intended to provide baseline information for concerned groups outside the library, preservation, and archival communities. Their intent was to define the basic issues while illuminating the concerns brought by the library, preservation, and archival communities. Not surprisingly, there is a range of opinion and emphasis placed on different issues across communities.

Born Digital

The scope of the effort was defined to encompass material that is "born digital," that is, objects that have been created in digital form rather than converted from analog to digital. This distinction, however, was not consistently useful to interviewees or to the writers. Historic film or news footage may be embedded in a newly created digital educational project. Re-release of entertainment products partly or wholly in digital form, either as new editions of older works or as reused elements in an otherwise-new work, further blurs the distinction. The production process itself is not hermetically sealed analog or digital.

Even on the Web, many sites offer digitized versions of print works; for this reason, archiving the Web itself can be seen as encompassing both born-digital and digitized materials. One publishing executive argued that "digital" should be thought of as a medium in which content was both created and made accessible to the public. However, another publisher cautioned that the distinction between "digitized" and "born digital" is very important because it relates to the concept of completeness, and that accompanying that concept are notions of "copies," "versions," and other ideas critical to managing works and their associated rights.

Several people inside and outside the library community urged planners to consider the scope of the effort carefully, including such factors as what was selected for the collection (even if it were a single collection), its longevity (10, 100, or 1,000 years), and its purpose (preservation, limited access, or public access). From a practical point of view, given the sizes of the resources, selection seems particularly important in film, television, and the Web. The Web is complicated by the fact that only part of it is publicly accessible and by unresolved issues over rights. It is not clear, for example, that a Web site may be "harvested" for purposes of preservation without the knowledge and permission of the various rights holders. (In the case of an interactive Web site, the range of potential rights holders extends well beyond those involved in its creation.)

Several people in both the technical and the arts communities urged attention to "ephemera" as well as to "published" works (the definition of "publication" is being contested). A number of respondents in film, television, and sound noted that again, the distinction between publication and ephemera is blurred. For example, a historic radio broadcast that is captured by the listener may contain aural information that reflects its relatively poor reception at the time; retaining that quality goes to the traditional mandate of preserving the experience, which might not be reflected in the script or in a studio recording.

Similarly, only a very small percentage of the material shot is actually used in the commercial release of a film, yet digital video disc (DVD) releases have provided new life for outtakes and other associated production materials. The relative utility of material changes over the cultural life of a film or a performance; the first public release does not necessarily capture all of its aesthetic or future scholarly value. There is a substantial economic incentive, since enhancing a DVD release is one strategy for combating piracy.

The notion of scope also surfaced at the level of the artifact or item. Discussions of Web sites, e-books, e-journals, and digital television make clear the difficulty of drawing boundaries among these items. Within the Web itself are emerging distinctions between the "surface" Web and the "deep" Web. E-books and e-journals download content from the Web to their respective formats and include hyperlinks to the Web for ancillary augmentation. The advent of interactive television also invites new forms of multimedia that combine resources built for the Web with those created for broadcasting in digital form.

Moreover, an item that appears seamless to the user is frequently a composite document. Formats as well understood as electronic scholarly journals are built as multimedia objects in which the constituent elements may include text, images, animation, or advertisements, each of which may be encoded in a different format. Finally, several people from the arts communities emphasized the importance of collecting the version of the object that the creator (e.g., the director of a film) considered final in the format that he or she considered final.

There are complexities to notions of "authorship"; many of these are not new to digital but are magnified by the circumstances under which digital products may be distributed and used. These complexities are related to the complicated intellectual property considerations that surround digital information. Even in a format as carefully studied as is that of electronic scholarly journals, creation and deposit can involve numerous stakeholders, and the number of interested parties multiplies in sound, television, and film, in which individuals and entities have traditionally had rights in the processes of creation and distribution.

Frank Romano points out that the e-books world is witnessing changes in traditional roles and functions; for example, writers can self-publish and thus become distributors, while software companies can behave like publishers. Similar shifts and realignments can be seen in some metadata discussions, where, as Peter Lyman notes, both computer scientists and librarians are putting forth different yet overlapping views of how the systems might work.

Technical Issues

The issues, which include technical obsolescence and standards, metadata, information security, and the overall architecture of the system, are by no means discrete. For example, standards affect creation as well as preservation. As one scholar of film and new media pointed out, the evolution of his organization's Web site represented a patchwork of changing and evolving standards. Several writers pointed out that the issue is not only making sure that bits survive but also ensuring the preservation of a technical environment that will permit future retrieval of the information, the work as envisioned by the author or creator, and the experience of the user.

The longevity of the storage medium was a consistent concern, as was signal degradation and software obsolescence. One technical expert urged that degradation be compared with the process by which a photograph ages. The image fades; the medium on which the image is printed also disintegrates. There are methods for error detection; however, at some point, there is concern that the integrity of the digital object is compromised. One solution is migration from one medium to another.

However, there are discussions over whether to use sampling/compression strategies (particularly if the object is made available in, for example, Joint Photographic Experts Group [JPEG] or Motion Picture Experts Group [MPEG] format), the extent to which migrating the information introduces errors if the data are resampled, and the implications of migrating formats for version control and integrity. When a digital work is migrated (e.g., from MPEGn to MPEGn+1), perhaps in very short order given the rapid development of the technology, what is the original work? In the case of recorded sound, for example, would improvements to fidelity resulting from more sophisticated software technology compromise the integrity of the original, since it is no longer truly the artist's treatment of a work and misrepresents the recording technology of the time?

At least one technical expert did not consider this to be a serious problem but did acknowledge that the rules for the successive formats must be retained. For film and television, this has resulted in attention to selection and collection policies inside traditional libraries as well as other organizations and has highlighted the importance of metadata as a management tool.

Playback

Playback—usually associated with the equipment or software that enables users to re-create the performance of a film, for example—was seen to be a particular problem for e-books as well as for digitally recorded sound and film. For example, certain early tapes are no longer accessible because the equipment to read them no longer exists or is hard to find. Playback affects any effort to enable future users to re-create the work (however defined) as it was originally experienced. Issues associated with playback can be expanded to operating systems, browsers, and so on. Solutions vary from emulation to maintaining collections of relevant hardware and software so that an archive or archiving system of digital content can imply preservation of certain kinds of equipment as well. Particularly for e-books, where so much of the design is predicated on screen size, re-creating the experience for future users implies access to the device that was intended to display the content.

Rapid Obsolescence

The rapid obsolescence of some formats, as well as the plethora of standards, was widely considered to be a barrier both to creation and to preservation. Those who had opinions on open versus proprietary standards favored the former because they were believed to facilitate management of the archive and its content. This applies to a broad range of issues, from operating systems to markup language, compression, and fonts.

Information Security

Before September 11, 2001, few people consulted had strong opinions on information security, but those who did thought that it was important as a guarantor of trust. One technical expert did not see the information security needs of an archive as being different from its general needs, or that, for example, the mission of the archive added a layer of concern. Another technical expert cautioned that "security" means a number of things in this context, including robustness and safety of the storage, privacy, and copyright control.

With respect to confidentiality and privacy, several people noted different dimensions and concerns that arise when the procedures associated with managing the archive go digital. One example that was offered was the information typically provided on copyright registration concerning the authors, who might use a pseudonym or who might wish to keep their own addresses, or the addresses of their agents, from general use. There are overlaps between this kind of information and the information included in metadata. At least one person cautioned against excessive restriction, arguing that too many restrictions inhibit accountability.

Storage Architecture

Those who addressed technical issues tended to favor distributed rather than centralized systems, because the former would accommodate a high degree of "local" variation within shared protocols. There were also calls for interoperability, which would make it possible for information to be shared across platforms and among vendors.

Metadata

Metadata, or "data about data," are simultaneously a standard, a management and access tool, and a feature of the system architecture. For example, whether the metadata are bundled into the content or are maintained separately is a question that is being discussed with respect to several formats. This is a matter that affects approaches to interoperability as well as system design. Wactlar and Christel illustrating the range of academic and commercial interests that have become involved in defining metadata. The metadata discussions reveal the different visions of archiving as embodied by the library and computer science communities.

Intellectual Property Rights Management

Few failed to identify intellectual property rights (IPR) management and fair use as key issues. The complexity of this set of issues varies across media. Thus, questions of international law hang heavily over the Web and any products that are distributed through the Web, while changing perceptions of who is or is not a public figure and the layered rights associated with recorded sound, film, and television figure prominently in discussions of those formats.

While there was near unanimity on the importance of managing intellectual property responsibly, no voices called for some version of complete lockout. Indeed, one representative from a major company with interests in several areas thought that the most important issues were both protection of intellectual property rights and ease of use (with appropriate accommodation for potential users with special needs). There was widespread acknowledgment of the need to find a balance between the economic needs of the creators and distributors and the legitimate uses of the works, but there was a range of opinion as to what that meant. Some suggested ways to handle management of intellectual property "behind the scenes" through technological means, which could be coupled with pricing that discouraged inappropriate use. Other proposals revolved around ways to use time, such as restricting access on the basis of estimates of time during which the owner expected to extract the economic value. However, product cycles of reuse would complicate that approach.

Several people felt that existing laws were sufficient: what is required, they maintained, is appropriate enforcement. Others believed that there was a need to clarify the law. Given that the Web is an international phenomenon, attention to international law is particularly important. The terms such as "copy," "publication," "performance," and "public figure," whose definitions were once widely agreed on, had become subject to discussion. Still others pointed to misperceptions that were clouding the discussion in several contradictory ways: people think that information in digital form has both more value (those who tended to inflate the costs for permissions) and far less value (those who thought information should be free) than does information in analog form. Finally, a number of people, particularly in the film and entertainment industries, noted that the inflamed environment in which the discussions are taking place makes reasonable attempts at compromise very difficult.

Several people pointed out that copyright as a mechanism, which had arisen in the context of print, had already begun to fray under the stress of its application to media other than text, and that it was becoming increasingly unwieldy. For example, in film, the multiplicity of rights and permissions that affect distribution and reuse of material had derailed educational projects because it was simply impossible to unravel the layers. Recorded sound has similar layers of rights. Finally, ambiguity over the law is itself becoming a barrier.

Academic Data Archiving

Academic data archives selectively develop, maintain, and encourage re-use of unique data resources which are of interest to particular end-using communities and which are drawn from a wide variety of depositors. These resources have typically been electronic texts or datasets but are increasingly extending to other data types (e.g. digital images, sound, film, and GIS). Like the digitisers, the academic data archives are influenced by the information needs of the end user communities that they serve. Unlike the digitisers, the academic data archives tend on the whole to serve relatively small or at least well defined end-user communities whose members have a relatively deep and sophisticated understanding of the data and their uses.

Another difference is that academic data archives exert less influence than the digitisers over how data are created. In this respect, they are closer to the institutional archives and, like the institutional archives, will attempt to influence data creators in both formal and informal ways. Unlike the institutional archives, the academic data archives rely more for their collections on voluntary and/or non-exclusive rather than on statutory deposit, - a feature which tends to minimise the direct influence they may have over depositors behaviour as data creators. Accordingly, academic data archives will typically devote resources to enriching deposited data to ensure they are maximally useful to and usable by end users.

Data Creation

Academic data archives are as eager as institutional archives to influence the behaviour of data creators and for the same reason. How data are created will determine how, whether, and at what cost they can be preserved. The academic data archive's influence over data creators, however, is less than that exercised by the institutional archive. Academic data archives rely largely for their collections upon voluntary deposit by data creators who may not be subject to any standards regime other than research criteria,. Nor are data creators ideally positioned to implement such standards retrospectively since they typically offer their data to an academic data archive after their active interest in those data has ceased.

The academic data archives' influence over data creators is therefore largely informal. It tends to be exercised crucially through their relationships with funding agencies (which can recommend the standards and best practices identified by the academic archives) or through a range of informational and instructional activities. The latter will typically seek to raise awareness about the long-term research and educational value of data resources created in the course of research, and about the importance of standards best practice in data creation in terms which appeal to the data creators' self interest.

Data Acquisition

Academic data archives are highly selective in their accessions and use both content and technical criteria to maximise their holdings' re-use value to a particular end-user community. Content criteria are shaped by the archives':

— formal and informal assessment of what data resources end users require and seek actively to accession these where they exist;

— formal and informal assessment of research and teaching trends - academic data archives will attempt to predict the emergence of such trends and develop collections of data which can support them;

— interest in developing special collections - such collections may fill gaps in the archives holdings or supplement existing holdings to create a critical mass of material focusing on particular topics or themes.

The development of special collections may entail more active recruitment of relevant data resources, or, funding permitting, the development or enrichment of such data resources by the archive. Technical criteria help to determine whether and how and at what cost a data resource may be used by others and preserved by the archive over the longer term. In general, the academic data archive will give preference to data resources which conform to a suite of specified technical and documentation standards chosen to reflect the kind of data being accessioned (electronic texts are formatted and documented differently than digital images), and the information requirements of end-using communities.

Significantly, academic data archives will not necessarily reject data resources which promise long-term secondary use value but fail to meet preferred technical criteria. Rather, the archive will define a strategy whereby such a resource may be accessioned and, funding permitting, appropriately enriched, transformed, or improved. The academic data archive's interest in secondary analysis for research or re-use in teaching also influences the accession process. Documentation supplied with deposited data will be verified against the data themselves and, where deemed appropriate, improved or enriched to standard in order to facilitate its secondary use.

The Oxford Text Archive, for example, will ensure that electronic texts within its collections are accompanied by an SGML header conforming to the Text Encoding Initiative's specifications and to in-house cataloguing practices. The Data Archive similarly will prepare comparable catalogue records for its data resources, and ensure that data resources are accompanied with user-supplied codebooks and other documentation. In some case s, the Data Archive will also prepare user packs offering guidance in the use of particularly complex data resources which are in high demand.

Similarly the academic data archive may intervene in the data's structure. The Oxford Text Archive prefers the use of TEI-conformant SGML and will undertake to introduce this encoding where possible for resources in its collections. The Data Archive principally accessions alphanumeric data in a range of tabular or list-like formats but prefers to store data in the SPSS file format owing to the ease with which the SPSS software may be used to produce subsets and to write data into a variety of different formats as may be required for delivery to end users. Where possible it will transform data resources into the SPSS file format upon accession.

De-selection is not usually an issue for the academic data archive although version control is, particularly where the archive holds data resources which are either periodically amended or updated by their creators or subject to further development in the course of their secondary use. Where deposited resources are superseded by newer versions, older versions will be maintained though their distribution may be restricted. It is important to note that version control adds a level of administrative complexity

Data Management

Data management in the academic data archive reflects its dual emphasis on secondary use and long-term storage, and are contingent upon what kinds of data an archive caters to and the end-user scenarios it wishes to support.

Data Structures

The academic data archive is likely to hold copies of its holdings in different formats and reformat accessioned data accordingly. Such formats may include:

— that in which the data are deposited;

— that considered most appropriate for the data's archival management;

— that considered most suitable for distribution to end users.

Inevitably, reformatting adds a cost to the academic data archive which will be considered when a data resource is evaluated for accession. That cost can be reduced substantially where data creators can be encouraged to deposit data in approved formats, though there are severe limits on the extent to which the adoption of such formats can be encouraged. The Data Archive's collections currently consist primarily of alphanumeric data stored in tabular or list-like formats and delivered to end-users on a range of portable magnetic media and by ftp, and in a range of different formats. The Archive accordingly accessions appropriately documented data in any number of formats.

It prefers SPSS file formats as a management format, however, owing to its flexibility, and may convert accessioned data into that format. Additional copies of the data in different formats will be created in response to user demand. Thus, a data resource deposited as a SAS export file may be stored as a SAS export file (the accession format) and co pied at accession into an SPSS export file format (the management format). Where a user requests the data resource as a SIR file, it may be reformatted as required for distribution and a copy of the SIR file may be stored against future requests for the data in that format.

The Oxford Text Archive accessions electronic texts as ASCII files employing a range of different mark-up (encoding) schemes and conventions. Preferring TEI-conformant SGML, it will where possible impose a light SGML encoding onto all deposits, storing the original file as deposited, and the SGML-encoded version. Texts are distributed as SGML-encoded files but may in some circumstances be transformed or re-encoded as appropriate to their use with particular application software (e.g. HTML-aware browsers).

Data Storage

As with the institutional archives data storage scenarios reflect the data distribution ones that the academic data archives wishes to support. On-line storage is paramount for Internet access, but also for frequently requested resources which are distributed on portable media.

Data Documentation and Description

Given its orientation toward secondary analysis, the academic data archive stresses the use of richly descriptive documentation which may be considered at several levels:

— a brief catalogue record with which users will be able to locate a resource and to decide whether it warrants further investigation;

— more richly descriptive information about the resource's contents, context, creation, provenance, and structure, and about the terms and conditions of its use which may enable the user to determine whether or not the resource is worth acquiring for a particular research or teaching purpose;

— supplementary information as and where required to enable the user to mount and analyse or use the resource for their own purposes (e.g. code books for variables used in a database, information about any sampling strategies used to create a resource, etc.).

In some cases, for example, with an SGML-encoded electronic text, all of the above information is contained within a single electronic record or record component (in this case, within the SGML header). In others, it may be available in electronic and printed documents (for example, with a social science database for which a catalogue record exists independently of a detailed study description and codebook) which may be stored independently of the data themselves.

Depositors are best suited to the supply of required documentation. Consequently, the academic data archive will encourage them to document their data by providing detailed guide-lines and professional assistance. Despite this pro-active approach, experience suggests once more the limits to depositors' compliance with archive approved standards. Preparing documentation which is appropriate and sufficiently detailed for secondary analysis and for preservation, accordingly tends to involve both depositor s and archive staff and frequently has substantial resource implications for the academic data archive. These resource implications are typically considered by the academic data archive when evaluating a data resource for possible accession.

Data Preservation

Academic data archives demonstrate a preference for data migration as a preservation strategy; a fact reflected in the technical criteria and preferred data standards against which potential deposits are evaluated and which depositors are encourage d to adopt. Preservation procedures reflect the infrastructure and technologies available to the archive and vary substantially. In the best case, preservation procedures reflect those used by the data banks and the institutional archives. In the worst case, they rely upon more minimalist practices which extend no further than regular back-ups of data stored on-line.

Remote Management

Academic data archives' collections may have physical and virtual holdings. Physical holdings are those for which the archive is the principal managing service. Virtual components are those which are available from the archive but which are managed off site Virtual holdings may be mirrored at the archive but have a primary archival home at another organisation. The Data Archive, for example, distributes data rèsources which are held by the Inter-University Consortium for Political and Social Research (ICPSR) in the US. The first time an ICPSR data resource is distributed by the Data Archive, a copy of that resource may be kept by the archive against subsequent user demand. Despite its holding a mirror copy, the ICPSR retains primary curatorial responsibility over that resource.

Virtual holdings may also be managed entirely off-site though references to them made available to them through the academic data archive's catalogue. Typically, remote data management relies upon agreements between the academic data archive and third-party data managers. Those agreements will seek to assure the academic data archive that remotely managed data conform to minimum level content and technical requirements as normally applied by the archive in selection of its own physical holdings. They will also seek assurance that the data are maintained and distributed in a manner which conforms to and fulfills the archives' own data management and us e strategies.

Data Use

Academic data archives typically make information about their holdings available through [on-line] catalogues, and may adopt one or several of the following data distribution scenarios:

— data resources may be accessed and manipulated over the Internet via Telnet sessions or World Wide Web browsers;

— data resources may be distributed to end users over the Internet via ftp (File Transfer Protocol);

— data resources may be distributed to end users on a predefined range of portable magnetic media.

However they are made available, the re-use of data resources within the academic data archive will be contingent upon a number of factors including their relevance (content), quality, structure, and documentation. As we have seen, the academic data archive strives to enhance the usefulness of its holdings by being highly selective about what resources it acquires and by enriching deposited resources (e.g. by enhancing their documentation, or by reformatting their structure). The academic data archive may also seek to improve and enhance the usefulness of its holdings by influencing the behaviour of individuals and organisations which are responsible for the creation of potentially depositable resources, raising awareness about the benefits to be had from secondary use and of the crucial importance of appropriate standards and best practices in the creation of re-usable data resources.

The academic data archive may play a similarly active role amongst potential user communities, raising awareness about the benefits which accrue from secondary analysis, and providing guidance to best practice in its conduct. With regard to support, the academic data archives, like the institutional ones, focus their attention on their two principal (and potentially overlapping) user communities including depositors and users, respectively. Both are supported with documentation which may be available on-line and/or in printed form.

Depositors are typically supplied with detailed information about the deposit process (including detailed information about the evaluation criteria employed by the archive and the data formats an d documentation standards that it either prefers or requires), and about the terms and conditions under which data are deposited. Depositors are also encouraged to access and adopt those technical and documentation standards which are promoted by the archive in order to support its dual aims of preservation and use.

Users will, at a minimum, have access to information about the archive, its holdings, and about procedures for and terms and conditions applying to access to the archive's holdings.

Rights Management

The academic data archive acts as an intermediary between depositors and users, and will use inter-related depositors licences and user agreements to ensure that any restrictive terms and conditions imposed by depositors upon are adhered to by bona fide users. Given their emphasis on secondary use, there will be a strong emphasis in the licensing on protecting the moral rights, academic integrity regulation citation of the resource, and the impartiality of data creations and funding agencies, than may occur elsewhere. For resources derived from censuses, social surveys, or other government sources, measures to protect the confidentiality of individuals and institutions will also be required.

Academic data archives may also be reluctant to accession resources whose re-use at least for personal and educational purposes, is severely restricted, and to distribute resources to individuals and institutions which cannot prove their bona fides as educational users. Their pre-eminent reliance upon voluntary deposit, however, may have an opposite effect, encouraging academic data archives to restrict or at least guard access very closely using a range of authentication and other mechanisms, so as not to deter depositors from offering their data in the first place.

Copyright Issues in Digital Archiving

The collection and long-term preservation of digital content pose challenges to the intellectual property regime within which libraries and archives are accustomed to working. How to achieve an appropriate balance between copyright owners and users is a topic of ongoing debate in legal and policy circles. The purpose of an archive (e.g., to ensure preservation or to provide an easy and convenient means of access), its subject matter, and the manner in which it will acquire copies, as well as who will have access to the archive, from where, and under what conditions, are all factors critical to determining the copyright implications for works to be included in it.

A "copyright" exists in any original work of authorship fixed in a tangible medium. That medium can be almost anything, including paper, computer disk, clay, canvas, and so on. For a work to be "original," it must meet two qualifications:

A copyright provides not just a single right, but a bundle of rights that can be exploited or licensed separately or together. The economic rights embraced within a copyright include the following:

The reproduction right (the right to make copies): For purposes of the reproduction right, a "copy" of a work is any form in which the work is fixed and from which it can be perceived, reproduced, or communicated, either directly or with the aid of a machine. Courts have held that even the reproduction created in the short-term memory (RAM) of a computer when a program is loaded for use qualifies as a copy.6

The right to create adaptations, or derivative works. A "derivative work" is a work that is based on a copyrighted work, but contains new material that is original in the copyright sense. For example, the movie Gone With the Wind is a derivative work of the book by Margaret Mitchell. "Version" is not a term of art in copyright law. If a new version consists merely of the same work in a new form—such as a book or photograph that has been scanned to create a digital version—then it is a reproduction of the work. However, if new copyrightable authorship is added, then it is a derivative work. For example, Windows 2000 is a derivative work based on Windows 98.

The right to distribute copies of the work to the public. The distribution right is limited by the "first sale doctrine," which provides that the owner of a particular copy of a copyrighted work may sell or transfer that copy. In other words, the copyright owner, after the first sale of a copy, cannot control the subsequent disposition of that copy. Making copies of a work available for public downloading over an electronic network qualifies as a public distribution. However, neither the courts nor the Copyright Office has yet endorsed a "digital first sale doctrine" to allow users to retransmit digital copies over the Internet.

The right to perform the work publicly. To "perform" a work means to recite, render, play, dance, or act it, with or without the aid of a machine. Thus, a live concert is a performance of a musical composition, as is the playing of a CD on which the composition is recorded. The right to display the work publicly. To perform or display a work "publicly" means to perform or display it anywhere that is open to the public or anywhere that a "substantial number of persons outside of a normal circle of a family and its social acquaintances is gathered." Transmitting a performance or display to such a place also makes it public. It does not matter whether members of the public receive the performance at the same time or different times, at the same place or different places.

The law distinguishes between ownership of a copy of a work (even the original copy, if there is only one) and ownership of the copyright rights. A museum that acquires a painting does not thereby automatically acquire the right to reproduce it. Libraries and archives commonly receive donations of manuscripts or letters, but they generally own only the physical copies and not the copyright rights.Not all rights attach to all works. For example, some works, such as sculpture, are not capable of being performed. Other works—notably musical compositions and sound recordings of musical compositions—have rights that are limited in certain respects.

For example, reproduction of musical compositions in copies of sound recordings is governed by a compulsory license that sets the rate at which the copyright owner must be paid. Sound recordings, for historical reasons, long had no right of public performance, and they now enjoy only a limited performance right in the case of digital audio transmissions. Even though works can be converted into mere 1's and 0's when digitized, they generally retain their fundamental character. In other words, if the digitized work is a computer program, it is subject to the privilege the law provides to owners of copies of computer programs to make archival copies.

Copyright Exceptions

Copyright rights are not absolute; they are subject to a number of limiting principles and exceptions. Those principles most relevant to the creation of a digital archive are as follows:

— The exception for certain archival and other copying by libraries and archives in section 108 of the Copyright Act. Libraries and archives are permitted to make up to three copies of an unpublished copyrighted work "solely for purposes of preservation and security or for deposit for research use in another library or archives." The work must be currently in the collections of the library or archives, and any copy made in digital format may not be made available to the public in that format outside the library premises.

— Libraries and archives may also make up to three copies of a published work to replace a work in their collections that is damaged, deteriorating, or lost, or whose format has become obsolete, if the library determines that an unused replacement cannot be obtained at a fair price. Copies in digital format, like those of unpublished works, may not be made available to the public outside the library premises.

— Even if copying a work is not expressly allowed by section 108, it may still be permitted under the fair-use doctrine. However, the privileges under section 108 do not supersede any contractual obligations a library may have with respect to a work that it wishes to copy.

Fair use is the copyright exception with which people are often most familiar. Whether a use is "fair" depends on the facts of a particular case. Four factors must be evaluated when such decisions are made. The first factor is the purpose and character of the use. Among the considerations is whether the use is for commercial or for nonprofit educational purposes. Works that transform the original by adding new creative authorship are more likely to be considered fair use than those that do not; however, even a reproduction can be considered a fair use in some circumstances. The second factor is the nature of the copyrighted work.

The scope of fair use is generally broader for fact-based works than it is for fanciful works, and broader for published works than for unpublished ones.20 The third fair use factor is the amount and substantiality of the portion used. Generally, the more that is taken, the less likely it is to be fair use, but there are situations in which making complete copies is considered fair. The fourth factor is the effect on the potential market for or value of the copyrighted work. A use that supplants the market for the original is unlikely to qualify as fair.

Certain uses are favored in the statute; they include criticism, comment, news reporting, teaching (including multiple copies for classroom use), scholarship, and research. A nonprofit digital archive for scholarly or research use, for example, would be favored by the law. However, favored uses are not automatically deemed fair, and other uses are not automatically deemed unfair. The four factors discussed earlier must be evaluated in each case.

Some users become frustrated because there is no magic formula to determine whether a use is fair. However, the same flexibility that sometimes makes it difficult to predict whether a use will be considered fair also allows the statute to evolve through case law with new circumstances and new types of uses. A statute that provided greater certainty would inevitably be more rigid.

Section 117 allows the owner of a copy of a computer program to make an archival copy of that program. This section, however, applies only to computer programs, not to all works in digital form.

As discussed in section 3, the first sale doctrine prevents the copyright owner from controlling the disposition of a particular copy of a work after the initial sale or transfer of that copy. The first sale doctrine enables, for example, library lending and marketing in used books.

Copyright Requirements

Those who are not specialists in the field tend to confuse two processes: registration of copyright and mandatory deposit of copyright-protected works (discussed in the next section). A copyright owner is not required to register his or her copyright or to use a copyright notice in order to establish or maintain copyright in a work. This fact is often misunderstood, particularly by people using the Internet, who sometimes assume that if there is no copyright notice, a work is in the public domain.

Copyright owners are required to register their copyrights before filing an infringement suit, if the work is of U.S. origin. The law contains incentives designed to motivate copyright owners to file a timely registration; however, many copyright owners choose not to register for a variety of reasons. In any case, one should not assume that the Copyright Office has a record of all copyright-protected works.

Mandatory Deposit

Some works—large databases, for example—are no longer distributed in complete copies in a portable medium such as a book or CD-ROM. Instead, the end users license access to the database through the Internet and generally download and print only the portion of the database relevant to their research. Whether and how the mandatory deposit provisions should be applied to works distributed in this manner, and to Web sites generally, is far from clear. For example:

- To what extent can such works be considered published, if not all of the work is available for downloading in copies?
- What if material is available to a limited group, with restrictions, and thus constitutes a "limited publication" that is technically considered unpublished under copyright law?
- How can the deposit copy of a Web site be defined, when Web site boundaries are so amorphous?
- If the work is distributed only with technological security measures, can LC demand it in a different form?
- What is the legal effect of the license agreements that frequently accompany works available online?

Copyright Ownership

The human creator of a work is generally the author and initial owner of copyright. Copyright rights can be transferred, either separately or together. For example, someone can transfer the right to reproduce a work without transferring the right to create a derivative work. A transfer of copyright ownership, including the grant of an exclusive license, must be in writing and signed by the grantor. Nonexclusive licenses need not be in writing, but frequently are.

A copyright license can span a very long period of time. Complicated issues can arise when new forms of exploitation are developed during the license term. Usually, the grantor will claim she or he did not intend to include the new rights in the license, and the grantee will claim the opposite.

The process can be complicated and sometimes frustrating. The Copyright Office registration and renewal records are usually a good place to start. Registration and renewal of copyrights used to be mandatory, so registration records for older works are more likely to be complete than are those for newer works. However, even if the copyright is registered, rights may have changed hands subsequent to registration. It is also possible to obtain information from the copyright notice (no longer mandatory but still commonly used) or other materials associated with the work. Other records in the Copyright Office may be helpful. For example, the copyright law provides for recordation in the Copyright Office of transfers related to copyright.

To perfect a security interest in a copyrighted work or to ensure that the first transferee will prevail over a second transferee of the same interest, a license or assignment must be recorded in the Copyright Office in a timely fashion. Not all copyright owners record their agreements; it is most commonly done for works of significant commercial value.

Some users are reluctant to use anything without clear rights, but others will engage in risk assessment. For example, if the work is to be used in a database from which it can be removed promptly if there is a complaint, the user may decide to take the risk. If, by contrast, the work is a short story that is to be the basis of a new screenplay and motion picture, and the investment could be lost if the copyright owner learned of and objected to the project, the user may decide the risk is too great and choose not to proceed.

Unpublished Works

A work is "published" when copies are distributed to the public by sale or other transfer of ownership or by rental, lease, or lending. Publicly performing or displaying a work does not constitute publication. The law makes a number of distinctions between published and unpublished works. The most significant distinction in this context relates to the treatment of published and unpublished copies for purposes of preservation under section 108 and fair use.

The scope of fair use is narrower for unpublished works than for published works, although the fact that a work is unpublished does not itself bar fair use. The unpublished nature of the manuscript of President Ford's memoirs was a significant factor in the U.S. Supreme Court's decision that The Nation was liable for copyright infringement in publishing excerpts of those memoirs.

Digital Millennium Copyright Act

The Digital Millennium Copyright Act (DMCA) prohibits the act of circumventing a technological measure that "effectively controls access" to a work protected by copyright. Technological access controls are mechanisms such as passwords or encryption that prevent viewing or listening to a work without authorization.

The law also contains two provisions that prohibit trafficking in devices that circumvent technological measures of protection. The first provision is aimed at devices and services that circumvent access controls. Specifically, it prohibits manufacturing, importing, offering to the public, or providing or otherwise trafficking in technologies, products, or services

— that are primarily designed or produced to circumvent a technological measure that effectively controls access to a copyrighted work;

— that have only limited commercially significant purpose or use other than to circumvent such controls; or

— that are marketed for use in circumventing such controls.

The second, similarly worded provision is a prohibition against trafficking in devices or services to circumvent rights controls. Technological rights controls are mechanisms that restrict copying the work or playing it in a particular environment without authorization. There is no prohibition on the act of circumventing rights controls. Legislators believed if copies made as a consequence of circumventing rights controls were excused by copyright exceptions or privileges, there should be no liability for the circumvention. If, on the other hand, such copies are infringing, the rights holder has a claim under the copyright law.

There are a number of exceptions to the ban on circumventing access controls and a few exceptions to the antitrafficking ban. There is no exception for archiving, nor is there a general "fair use"-type exception written into the statute. The law does, however, include an administrative procedure for creating new exceptions. The DMCA could affect archiving in a couple of ways.

First, the law would prohibit an archive from circumventing technological access controls to obtain access to copyrighted works. However, should a situation arise in which that archive has legally defensible reasons for seeking to archive materials to which it has no authorized access, it could seek an exception pursuant to the rule-making procedure discussed above.

The second potential problem is the DMCA's ban on the circulation of circumvention devices. Even where a library or archive has valid access to a work, that work may be protected by a copy control. Circumventing the copy control would not violate the DMCA (its permissibility would be judged separately under the Copyright Act); however, a library or archive may not have the means readily available to make that copy because of the antitrafficking provision. It is possible that a digital archive could develop the expertise to circumvent technological controls where necessary. Moreover, it may also be possible to engage expert assistance: the law would appear to allow someone to offer circumvention services whose primary purpose and effect would be to facilitate permissible library archiving. The implications of the DMCA for archiving activities warrant further study.

International Issues

At least three categories of international issues must be considered in planning a digital archive. First, international treaties place certain constraints on the United States' ability to create exceptions to copyright protection or to impose requirements on copyright owners. Second, legal and logistical uncertainties could make it difficult for a copyright owner to obtain redress for copyright infringements committed abroad. These uncertainties should be considered in deciding which works should be included in the digital archive and from where they will be accessible. Third, a digital archive that permits online access outside the United States could itself be vulnerable to suit by foreign copyright owners whose works are included.

Limitations

Through a series of copyright treaties with other countries, United States nationals have the benefit of copyright laws in many foreign countries, and nationals of many foreign countries have the benefit of U.S. laws. The principal international copyright treaty is the Berne Convention for the Protection of Literary and Artistic Works. In 1996, a new international copyright treaty was negotiated under the auspices of the World Intellectual Property Organization (WIPO). Known as the WIPO Copyright Treaty, it addresses issues raised by new technologies. Many countries are amending their laws to comply with the treaty.

These treaties generally provide for two things: (1) national treatment, and (2) minimum standards of protection. "National treatment" means that when a U.S. citizen sues in another country—Germany, for example—he or she will be treated as a German citizen, with the benefit of German laws. Those laws will likely be similar to U.S. laws in many respects, because of the minimum standards imposed by the treaties. However, there are still likely to be differences, especially in areas related to new technologies, where international treaties and national laws sometimes have a difficult time keeping pace with technological developments.

There are many standards for copyright protection imposed on treaty members. The principal ones that could be implicated by a digital archive are the prohibition on "formalities," the limitation on exceptions to copyright rights, and the prohibition on compulsory licensing. Article 5(2) of the Berne Convention provides that the "enjoyment and exercise" of copyright rights "shall not be subject to any formality." Prohibited formalities include such things as mandatory copyright notice or registration. Mandatory deposit is permitted, provided it is not a condition of copyright protection.

Article 9(2) of the Berne Convention provides that countries may allow for exceptions to the author's exclusive right of reproduction "in certain special cases, provided that such reproduction does not conflict with a normal exploitation of the work and does not unreasonably prejudice the legitimate interests of the author." The WIPO Copyright Treaty extends this limitation to all rights provided by that treaty or by the Berne Convention, not just the reproduction right.

Compulsory licenses "obviously run counter to the whole basis of the [Berne] Convention, which is that the rights conferred under it are the author's exclusive rights which he can dispose of as he wishes." A compulsory license reduces the author's freedom to license (or not) to a mere right of remuneration. The Berne Convention expressly recognizes compulsory licenses only in two cases: (1) broadcasting, and (2) recordings of musical compositions.

It is certainly possible to create a digital archive without violating any U.S. treaty obligations; however, such an action could not be premised on a requirement for deposit or notice linked to copyright protection. Likewise, such action could not be premised on an exception to copyright rights that would jeopardize the normal exploitation of a work, harm the author's legitimate interests, or subject works to a broad compulsory license.

Potential Difficulties

It is assumed, for purposes of discussing this point and the next, that the archive would be located in the United States but accessible online in other countries, and that users outside the United States could download and reproduce works without authorization. Such an archive could increase copyright owners' exposure to economic harm from infringement. The logistics of bringing a suit based on an infringement that takes place in another country can be daunting. First, it is difficult and costly to sue in another country. Second, even though national treatment is the rule, there may be significant differences among copyright laws of various nations, particularly in areas of new technology. Third, even in the unlikely case that the copyright owner were able to obtain personal jurisdiction over the defendant in the United States, a U.S. court might be reluctant to adjudicate a case involving an interpretation of a foreign country's laws.

Finally, the archive itself could be exposed to infringement suits if it were accessible outside the United States. Foreign copyright owners whose works were included in the archive might sue if their works were made accessible in countries where such use is infringing. A court outside the United States could apply the law of a country (its own or a third country) that regards placing a copyrighted work on a publicly accessible network without authorization to be an infringement.

5

Library Collections

Information is of little long-term use if it is not preserved and made accessible through indexing or cataloging. At the same time, much of what has been collected and made accessible by libraries and archives admittedly receives little or no use. This leads some to argue that investments in preserving so much material that has so little demonstrated use are a waste of resources.

There is ongoing tension between how much information is produced and how much can be acquired, preserved, and made accessible in meaningful ways. There is tension between those who think we should collect as broadly as possible to expand our research base and those who think too much information can impede one's ability to find meaningful information. And there is always the question of who should be bearing the burden of whatever preservation society deems necessary.

Although information overload is not a new problem, the introduction of digital technology onto campuses and into research libraries has fundamentally altered the information landscape and created problems for scholars and students that have potentially serious ramifications. The creation and dissemination of digital resources are creating new models of service and access, such as licensing rather than owning essential intellectual assets. The mutability of digital documents is redefining what constitutes a text. Moreover, the conversion of texts into searchable texts is resulting in increased interdisciplinary research, as researchers in one field serendipitously find resources that had heretofore been confined (in print) to another field.

Accompanying the trend toward networked information are others that at first seem paradoxical. For example, at the very time that more material is made available online and retrievable any time, anywhere, there is increased attention among scholars to original, unreformatted materials and an increased appreciation for the material aspects of these sources. There are eruptions of public outcry when material losses in libraries and archives are discovered. Scholars demand increasing attention to an ever-expanding range of candidates for preservation, but library budgets simply cannot support those demands.

Preservation has thus become an unfunded mandate, the more pernicious for often being implicit. Academic institutions have learned the huge costs of penny-wise facilities management and deferred maintenance. It is reasonable to fear that libraries are incurring future costs by deferring preservation. There is, however, a crucial difference between deferring maintenance costs and deferring expenses for preservation. When we do not allocate sufficient funds for preservation, we face the probability that significant resources will be lost forever. Library collections are among the most valued of a research institution's intellectual and cultural assets—assets that form a crucial part of what might be called "public goods." Unfortunately, with library collections, as with other public goods, many of those who make claim to their use are not prepared to take responsibility for their well-being.

Preservation is a critical part of good stewardship of the intellectual and cultural heritage. Its chief challenges at the turn of the twenty-first century are fourfold:

Quantity: Because of the relentless growth of research libraries and their collections, an immense number of research items demand resources to remain accessible. In 1999, the 121 member libraries of the Association of Research Libraries (ARL) in US, reported owning a total of 462,965,204 volumes. The three greatest periods of growth for research libraries occurred after World War I, after World War II, and during the 1990s. A look at 12 representative public university libraries during this period reveals a typical growth pattern. In 1907, these libraries held an average of 107,425 volumes. By 1961, that number had grown to 1,772,831, and by 1995, the average number of volumes per library was 5,334,620.

Stability of Media: Library collections exist in a variety of physical formats, all of which are vulnerable to some degree. As the rate of information production has increased, storage media have become more compact and efficient. However, miniaturization comes at the expense of stability and longevity. With the exception of preservation-quality microfilm, the new media of the twentieth century are more fragile than those of the nineteenth, including the infamous wood-pulp paper that has been known to deteriorate into flakes over time.

The media invented in the last 150 years to capture light and sound are generally extremely fragile, dependent on machines for playback, and subject to rapid technological obsolescence. For example, the wax cylinders on which are inscribed the earliest known recorded voices of Native Americans are susceptible to mold, heat, scratching, skin oils, and other physical trauma. Moreover, they are dependent on playback equipment for which no replacement parts are manufactured and that few technicians are able to repair. Nonetheless, the information on them is invaluable and should be saved for future generations.

Economics: Since 1993, preservation budgets in ARL libraries have remained flat. The number of staff assigned to preservation is at a 10-year low. At the same time, the demand for access to original materials has grown, especially for access to those materials in special formats that often are at greatest risk from physical handling or environmental stress. Meanwhile, although the technology for reformatting for access has greatly improved, the funding for preservation continues to decrease. More money now goes to digital reformatting of items to provide access than to microfilming to preserve the low-use brittle books that are rotting on shelves.

Unknown and Unfixed Values of Artifacts: The most difficult challenge for libraries is deciding how to set priorities for preservation. As long as the claim on preservation resources exceeds the available funds, it will be necessary to select which materials will get treatment and which will not. The choices are made in the context of changing perceptions of value and the fluid dynamics of intellectual inquiry. The recent elevation of nineteenth-century popular imprints and ephemera to a status of high research value poses an exemplary challenge. Providing access to those items, which are often at high risk from embrittlement and routine physical handling, has put great strain on library resources. Knowing that the intellectual interests and research methodologies of scholars will change over time, research institutions have collected "just in case" there is a demand in the future, rather than "just in time" for current demand.

Research libraries and archives are full of items that have not been consulted in decades, if ever, and for which future demand is unpredictable, yet which make their claim for preservation attention. Despite the enormous collections of printed materials that have been amassed, entire categories of primary sources have disappeared before collecting institutions and their users understood their value. A notorious example of such neglect is the fact that 80 percent of all silent films made in the United States are gone without a trace. Fifty percent of films made in the nitrate era have also perished. Among those extant, a significant portion are not well preserved. Given that the materials that have vanished were not well documented at the time of their creation, the full extent of this loss will never be known.

Scholars and librarians have common interests in the collection-building process. Although scholars are routinely, and often intimately, engaged with librarians in the acquisitions and use phases of collection building, they are usually exposed only to specific aspects of preservation activities, such as testifying to the value of a collection proposed for preservation microfilming. Rarely do scholars have the opportunity to view the preservation function as a whole. Recent vigorous debates in the scholarly community and in the public arena about the value of saving books and newspapers as artifacts, in addition to preserving their content through reformatting and extending access through digitization, have raised questions about the involvement of scholars in these decisions. Do scholars know what happens to original materials after preservation treatment? Do they participate in decision making about the disposition of original materials after preservation treatment or reformatting?

Artifact

The word "artifact" can be confusing because it masks a number of unexamined assumptions. In academic parlance, "artifact" can refer to a physical object, a primary record, or a physical object that constitutes a primary record. An artifact will be defined as an information resource in which the information is recorded on a physical medium, such as a photograph or a book, and in which the information value of the resource adheres not only in the text or content but also in the object itself. In other words, artifacts are things that have intrinsic value as objects, independent of their informational content.

In recent years, scholars have identified an increasing number of library items that have research value as physical objects, above and beyond the information recorded in them. The Modern Language Association (MLA) has been concerned that the technologies of reproduction, such as photocopying, microfilming, and digital scanning, are becoming so good, so readily available, and so serviceable for many research and teaching purposes, that the importance of the underlying original might be devalued. To call attention to the dangers inherent in ignoring the fate of physical collections, the association created a committee to consider the issue. This group defined an artifact or primary record as "a physical object produced or used at the particular past time that one is concerned with in a given instance".

Nicholson Baker recently alleged that libraries' poor stewardship of books and serials has resulted in the loss of many resources of artifactual value. He further asserted that it is the responsibility of libraries in general and of certain large libraries in particular to collect masses of primary source materials and preserve them in their artifactual form. Yet he, too, failed to address the crucial matters of who would bear the responsibility for setting priorities, who would assume the custodial burden of these comprehensive collections, and who would fund these activities.

An increasing number of library collections are being promoted, as it were, to resources of artifactual, not just informational, value. Given the nature of contemporary scholarship and its wide-ranging interest in material and popular culture, this trend makes perfect sense. Regrettably, libraries have never had sufficient funds to collect and preserve everything of potential research value. Thus, for libraries, this expansive view of artifactual value presents problems that are not primarily theoretical, but eminently practical.

Preservation

The library preservation community has agreed on certain cardinal features of physical objects that warrant preservation in their original formats. These features are:

— age

— evidential value

— aesthetic value

— scarcity

— associational value

— market value

— exhibition value

Objective criteria or established practice determine many of these features, and the criteria vary little among libraries. They are, in short, best practice. These items are often crucially important for research and teaching; at the same time, there is little debate about their value as physical objects. Moreover, their disposition after reformatting is not an issue. Despite their importance to research collections and their rightful demand on preservation resources, their value is not seriously contested in the libraries that have responsibility for them. The value of the artifact for research purposes—as opposed to its monetary value or exhibition value—is chiefly evidentiary. An artifact is of evidential value because it testifies to the extent the information in it is original, faithful, fixed, or stable.

Originality: An original manifestation of a book, photograph, or recorded performance is valuable because through it a scholar may come closer to uncovering the original intent of the creator or the publisher or both. When a copy yields insufficient information about that intent, access to the original may be needed. Reformatting and copying information are analogous to translation from one language to another. Depending on the source and the target language, as well as the skill, care, and cultural biases of the translator, something inalienable to the original is always lost. A good translation, like good recopying, is one that loses the least amount of original content and intent.

Fidelity: The physical artifact is useful, and at times essential, in establishing the authenticity of an item. In other words, it has forensic value. There are internal clues in a document that give evidence of authenticity. Among these are the accuracy and appropriateness of the content. A newspaper dated 1901 that contains listings of television broadcasts, for example, is unlikely to be authentic. In addition, the external information contained in a physical manifestation provides clues of authenticity and integrity. Erasure marks on a sheet of paper, splices in a film, dried white erasure fluid on property maps—all these are physical clues to the integrity of the object and, hence, the authenticity of the information recorded in it.

Fixity: The content of the artifact when it was first produced constitutes the text (in the case of textual materials) or the document (in the case of a photograph or an opera performance). If one is holding a fifteenth-generation fax, one cannot guarantee that the full content of the original is conveyed except by comparing it with the original, which has fixed the content by recording it at one instant in time. One of the wonders of mass reproduction of text is the way in which replication by machine en masse tended to stabilize texts that had previously been somewhat fluid. Recent humanities scholarship, however, has done much to undermine the notion of even mass printings producing a stable version or versions of various texts, and the digital realm is eroding further the concept of the fixed content of a published item.

Stability: The persistence of an object over time leads to the stable and continuous accessibility of the information contained in it. Documents whose physical substrate changes over time themselves change. Film that gets spliced and repaired loses content; digital files that get reformatted into a newer version of a software program change; photographic images printed or displayed in various manners shift tone. When one looks at a 30-year-old image of a woman in a red coat that has been printed on paper that fades and at a contemporary image made from the same negative that has been made into a slide and is being projected on a screen, chances are that the coat will appear as a different shade of red in each image. The content or value of that red is not stable, and it is difficult to efface mentally the effects of age and reformatting and to determine whether the original color of the coat was scarlet or crimson.

Some artifacts are valuable for research because the format itself is the subject of investigation. Original bindings carry evidence of print history, just as original daguerreotypes carry evidence of an early imaging technology. Bindings can also testify to the economic status of the intended reader (inexpensive as opposed to expensive presentations, for example). In these cases, the object itself is the primary source of interest.

Also of value to the research process is the physical encounter between the researcher and the object—an encounter that can help prime the scholar's imaginative and analytical skills. While this factor is highly subjective and difficult to quantify, many scholars claim it has had, at least at some stage of their careers, an irreplaceable heuristic value. A medievalist who has never worked directly from manuscripts is at a disadvantage, just as a biographer of Thomas Jefferson who has worked exclusively from the printed editions of his letters may be said to work at one critical remove from his or her subject. Nevertheless, given the toll that physical handling takes on all types of materials, surrogates can be judiciously used by those who have a familiarity with original source materials and that, from the perspectives of preservation and convenience of access, surrogates are often preferable.

Determining Value Frameworks

Questions about the nature of the artifact have caused scholars and library professionals to realize that, even for the early part of the nineteenth century, much more information of potential research value exists in traditional formats such as paper and image than had previously been recognized. Consequently, the process of redefining what constitutes an artifact must be done not only for new media but also for a considerable body of information from the 1800s. The fragility of paper-based materials printed since 1850, especially newspapers, has been a concern for some time. Because newsprint is so fragile, preserving one or more instances of all imprints of newspapers poses enormous technical as well as financial challenges.

More recently, there has been a growing awareness of other kinds of artifacts from the nineteenth and early twentieth centuries that also require the attention of preservationists. These include materials that serve as primary evidence of popular culture, ranging from baseball cards to ladies' magazines to dime novels to political posters. Scholars, archivists, and librarians have always assumed a hierarchy in collections. The artifact or original document was the item initially collected and accessioned. When it was prized for some unique aspect of its material or historical existence (e.g., a first edition, a holograph manuscript, a signed author's copy, or a presentation copy of a work), the artifact was given priority for preservation.

Absent that uniqueness, a lower level of care might be given, and a lost or damaged copy might be replaced by one whose physical manifestations were quite different (e.g., a photocopy or a reprint). The value of the unique artifact could be defined variously as "historically important," "rare," "associational," and so on. In each instance, however, there was an individual material object that someone had once defined as valuable enough to retain.

The Achilles' heel of traditional definitions of the artifact lay in the value judgment that determined artifactual status in the first instance. What were the grounds for deciding in favor of one object and against another? How can libraries cope with the fact that the value of the artifact is never quite the same to different researchers? While one scholar will seek certain information from the item, scholars from other disciplines will require different kinds of data that may involve a wholly different way of handling the object. Can one say that these users are even seeing the same object?

Scholars and others who use artifacts may think of them in the aggregate as unified objects; however, when they interrogate the artifact for their research, they tend to focus on parts rather than the whole. One may define the artifact as a series of multiple discrete components—handwriting, watermarks, marginalia, splices, evidence of use—each potentially a focal point for scholars and others, depending on what they are studying. From the standpoint of usage, people normally analyze discrete sets of information contained within an artifact. The fact that artifacts are complex and that they lend themselves to a variety of intellectual endeavors means that one must think of them in terms of their parts, and not just as wholes. One way to think of the artifact, then, would be as a multiplicity of informational sets, including the material form of the object and its contextual history, where known.

One element of the artifact's complexity is the fact that scholars from different fields will perceive and use it in different ways. A first edition of a novel by Charles Dickens will be used very differently by a historian of Victorian England researching the economics of the book trade, a literary scholar concerned with different versions of the work, an art historian interested in Victorian book illustration, a textual historian interested in layout, and a historian of bookmaking. Each will consult the same artifact for a different kind of information, and none may notice the information sought by the others. Similarly, photographs of the Civil War by Alexander Gardner can be used to study the battles; the public's reception of the war in the North; the history of clothing, medicine, or gender; or even the medium of photography. Which subject interest and methodology would require use of the original? Which could make do with copy prints? Which could make use only of the original photographs in their original presentation portfolios? Which would be enhanced by access to the images through digital delivery, which could then be manipulated to magnify details?

The possibility of proposing a contextual definition of the artifact as follows:

— An artifact is a physical object produced at some time in the past, and attesting to a given set of practices, thinking, and ways of viewing the world, and whose importance will be defined by present and future needs and use. The value of the artifact is strongly influenced, but not completely determined, by its rare or unique features.

— The artifact conveys historical consciousness in different ways, depending on who studies it and for what purpose. Much of the information conveyed by an artifact does not require the presence of the physical object. Surrogates of the object (e.g., photographs, photocopies, and digital versions) may convey much of the information stored by the artifact. Indeed, for many purposes, a high-quality surrogate may convey this information better than does the original. The surrogate may enable access and use that would otherwise be impossible; for example, it allows a user to view an object that is physically distant, to enhance images, or to perform full-text searches. Surrogates do not obviate some scholars' need to consult the object itself; however, in many instances, a surrogate can serve scholarly needs as well as, or better than, does the artifact itself.

— The artifact matters. It matters very much. Nevertheless, in a time when artifacts are abundant and resources scarce, the scholarly and library communities are called to rethink the status of the artifact in terms of its content and material form. Acknowledging that every aspect of an artifact yields information that will be of use to some scholar or other, we nonetheless need to assess the relative importance of the different aspects of an artifact pragmatically. Scholars and library professionals jointly face issues such as the following.

— First, within the timeframe of the last 200 years, what constitutes an artifact worth retaining? The answer is not obvious in the case of nineteenth-century material artifacts: baseball manuals or railway timetables have not traditionally been viewed as important cultural documents, although they probably would be today. The question becomes truly perplexing in the case of media that are dependent on playback equipment, from recorded sound to moving images, in which the concepts of original or unique, stable or fixed, may not even apply.

— A second question concerns resources and priorities. This imperative may be spelled out as the "how, who, and when" of artifact preservation. In other words, accepting the reality that resources for preservation are limited, and assuming some common, gross-level understanding of the value of artifacts, how (in what form) are they to be preserved, by whom, and when (or how often)? Are all libraries or archives to be held responsible for collecting and preserving the same categories of artifacts? How much redundancy of preservation is necessary? How much can libraries afford? Redundant collections serve as insurance policies for preserving and making accessible information in a physical format. This is even true for digital information, which can be cloned and shipped around the globe almost instantaneously, yet is highly fragile if no one assumes archiving responsibility for the data.

In the case of digital information, given the high costs of building and maintaining information technological infrastructures, the same degrees of redundancy that we see for print may be neither desirable nor feasible. If and when digital files become the default mode for access—even for materials such as journal articles or encyclopedias, which were originally physical artifacts—what are the implications for duplicative collections of physical artifacts?

The point is not to determine whether baseball manuals and railway timetables from the nineteenth century, for example, are of sufficient artifactual value to justify the expense of collecting and preserving them. Rather, it is to set priorities in the face of financial constraints that too often mean, practically speaking, that if one decides to collect and preserve one kind of artifact, resources for other kinds will be insufficient.

The issue is not to evaluate the artifact per se to determine what survives and what does not. The scholarly community has no more of a claim to the wisdom of the ages than does the library community. The issue is to identify productive methods for interrogating the individual artifact that would, in a climate of finite resources, inform decisions about whether and how to preserve it. Such methods would help ensure survival of the greatest number of artifacts by intelligent analysis and careful consideration among knowledgeable and committed communities.

There is no single method of engaging primary sources, nor is there one overriding set of priorities—text over image, manuscript over map, English language over non-English—that will meet the needs of present or future research. But how do scholars, librarians, and archivists work together to prevent the kinds of losses that we can now regret in leisure—local newspapers, silent films, early television broadcasts, among others? Some past initiatives have brought together the scholarly, archival, and libraries communities to propose preservation and collection guidelines.

In the 1990s, the American Historical Association, the ARL, and the MLA created a task force on the preservation of the artifact to document preservation challenges and inform scholars about the need to collaborate with libraries to address them. These efforts have effectively addressed specific problems. However, most of the collaborations between scholars and librarians have been either locally based or designed to address only specific areas of concern, and they have focused largely on print materials.

American scholarship has historically relied on a decentralized network of libraries, archives, historical societies, and museums to collect, preserve, and make accessible the intellectual and cultural resources that form the basis of academic inquiry. This decentralized and largely uncoordinated approach is unlikely to change, despite the resulting losses of artifacts that have occurred. However, new preservation and information technologies promise to offer cost-effective means to prevent or slow physical deterioration and to keep the research community well informed about what others in the community are doing to preserve their holdings. These technologies will be successful to the extent that the research community is committed to identifying preservation challenges and to lobbying for financial resources—from provosts and foundations to federal agencies—to address them.

Strategies for collaboration will depend on the use of new information technologies to share crucial information about the status of various collections. They will also depend on the continued engagement of scholars, librarians, and archivists to deploy those technologies in meeting their responsibilities to the well-being of the intellectual and cultural assets whose benefits they enjoy.

Changing Features of the Artifact

Research library collections are primarily made up of printed matter: books, serials, journals, and newspapers. Even with the rapid growth of machine-readable and electronic resources, 85 to 90 percent of the acquisitions budgets of libraries still goes toward the purchase of printed matter. Humanities and social science scholars rely heavily on print journals for scholarly communication and so do scientists. Those who work within the print regime rely on a series of conventions about documents and their relationship to their physical manifestation that may be so familiar that they are invisible. These conventions bear mentioning, however, because many of them do not operate in realms of audiovisual and digital resources.

Among the many consequences of the adoption of printing technology, several became fixtures in the print landscape. They are

— the creation of a comparatively fixed and stable text
— the concept of authorship and of intellectual property inhering in authorship
— easy duplication and wide dissemination of texts, especially after the introduction of high-volume presses in the nineteenth century
— the notion of fungibility of informational content (also a result of mass-market publishing)

While texts copied by hand were intended to replicate their sources, they did not do so precisely or completely. With the advent of printing, it became possible to produce nearly identical copies in large numbers. This great increase in the accuracy of reproduction was crucial in the development of scientific and technical literature, and especially so in the reproduction of illustrations. While there certainly have been variations between printings, and even among copies from the same press run, the presumption that authorship and content were, in principle, stable and fixed, took hold, with significant consequences.

In an information economy, much now depends on these notions of fixity, reproducibility, and authorship, as many recent court cases, legislative acts, and international agreements attest. Bibliographic and textual scholarship, since the nineteenth century, has shown just how precarious and nuanced these concepts are. The destabilization of our ideas of fixed content began to accelerate, however, with the advent of audiovisual recording technologies. Daguerreotypes exist in only one version, because the image is exposed directly onto a metallic plate; wax cylinder recordings are also unique, each produced as a live recording.

Film-based images, however, do have a master—the photographic negative. For this reason, they can exist in multiple, nearly identical copies. Still, although the images are all made from one source (i.e., a negative), the negative inevitably wears with use, and the copies become less faithful. Through reproduction, the image on the negative can be effaced. This is not as true of print products. Engravings do deteriorate with each production, and books set with type can show wear from copy to copy; nevertheless, the loss of information for texts from copy to copy is generally not as striking as it is for visual and sound resources.

In non-print materials, the problem of "version control"—i.e., determining which version should be preserved as an original—is complicated by a further lack of stability over time and place. This factor characterizes broadcast media in particular. Take as an example a single television document that a news archives might wish to collect: the CNN news broadcast for January 15, 1998. What do the archives collect? The broadcast that originated in Atlanta, in London, or in Tokyo? This problem has existed among collectors of newspapers, of course, with libraries deciding often on the final edition as being the one of record and making efforts to collect several editions of a paper that tracks a particularly important event, such as an assassination or an election. But the scale of this problem for broadcast media on a 24-hour news cycle that constantly update news is of a different order.

The artifact that records an image or sound, moreover, can easily lose its originality or uniqueness. The adjective "unique" may haveonce been sufficient to identify a primary document in manuscript, and in some cases, such as legal documents or signed first editions, it may still have some meaning. But with newer formats, such as electronic and broadcast media that rely on refreshing and reformatting for longevity, the terms "original," "unique," "content fixity," and "material artifact" mean little.

The cardinal features of an artifact that have the highest research value—originality, faithfulness, fixity, and stability—retreating like a mirage as they worked their way from the 1800s into the twenty-first century. The three sections that follow look at how these four values work themselves out in print, analog audiovisual, and digital documents. These sections also explore how preservation strategies address these values and seek to preserve them. Preservation options, it will be seen, are shaped by such factors as the quantity and quality of resources, the instability of media, constraints of resource allocation, and the changing valuation of the artifact in research and teaching.

Relative Stability of Imprints

Books and other printed matter deteriorate over time as the result of their inherent chemical instability. For example, when paper made of wood pulp reacts with humidity and heat, it becomes brittle. Books also deteriorate as a result of mechanical strain. For example, the spine is stressed when an open book is placed on a photocopy machine. (Photocopying also exposes the paper to heat and light.) But there have been significant changes in how books, journals, and newspapers have been made since 1800, and these changes affect their significance as artifacts as well as their physical robustness.

In the 1970s, 1980s, and 1990s, much attention was focused on the legacy of brittle books created by the processes for making inexpensive paper. Now joined to this concern about the paper is concern about the structural support for that text block—the binding. The last few decades have seen an explosion of relatively inexpensive, soft-cover editions of books that were not designed to last.

Until the middle of the nineteenth century, paper was made from linen and cotton rags, which in principle make a strong and durable product. In the 1850s, wood pulp came into general usage for making paper more economically. The publishing industry rapidly converted to this process, following the lead of the newspapers, for which wood pulp was a source of inexpensive newsprint. The manufacturing process required that wood-pulp paper be treated with aluminum sulfate (alum) to keep the inks from running and to improve the hand. Alum, together with various bleaches and sizings usually added during the papermaking process, reacts with humidity to produce an acid that, over time, breaks down the molecular structure of the cellulose in the wood pulp.

In its worst form, damage leads to "brittle" paper that loses its flexibility and eventually crumbles when handled. While any given page may be readable, turning it may lead to several types of damage. In thin, hard-finish paper, the page becomes brittle and brown along the edges and can easily snap off along a fold line. Thick, pulpy paper tends to separate almost spontaneously under tensile stress in any direction, and whole blocks of text may come loose near the gutter and fall out of the volume.

Once paper becomes embrittled, nothing can arrest the decay. Such materials are candidates for preservation reformatting, that is, capturing the information content of the original and transferring it onto a stable medium such as preservation-quality microfilm. While acid paper of any sort is at risk, decay manifests itself unevenly. Manufacturing processes vary a great deal, and the conditions of storage and use can vary dramatically as well. Few places have proved to be as bad for wood-pulp paper as the humid, polluted eastern seaboard of the United States.

Many acid-paper items are not yet embrittled and can be stabilized to arrest the process of embrittlement. The two chief methods of stabilizing acid-based paper are deacidification and storage under optimal conditions. Deacidification is a chemical process whereby paper is treated with an alkaline buffering agent that neutralizes the acid content. It can be done on a single item or on many items at a time. There are facilities that can deacidify bound materials en masse, and some facilities can even treat unbound materials, such as sheet music, archival documents, and newspapers. Deacidification can stop further damage, but it neither reverses damage done nor strengthens already-brittle paper. Therefore, it is unsuitable for books that are damaged or weak.

Embrittlement can also be avoided or slowed by storing materials in stable environments with set parameters for temperature and humidity. These storage conditions cannot be obtained in open-access stacks. The conditions that slow the decay of library materials would be uninhabitable for most people. One of the reasons that libraries have been eager to build remote storage facilities is to lengthen the productive lives of their print collections.

Librarians have noted a disturbing trend during routine checking of new acquisitions for acidity. In many newly independent and emerging countries—countries from which U.S. libraries get a significant portion of their collections—printers continue to use unbuffered wood-pulp paper. A large portion of these acquisitions are at high risk for acidity. But more and more academic and trade presses in the developed countries are producing reprints—and an ever-increasing number of first press runs in paperback—on acid paper. Consequently, many new acquisitions, not only from Asia or South America but also from Europe and North America, may be at risk of embrittlement unless deacidification or other preventive measures are undertaken.

Artifact and Selection for Preservation

The recent interest in the production of knowledge has made materials that libraries acquired as secondary sources in the last two centuries into primary sources for this century. The lively field of printing history has made the book itself, rather than its content, the subject of investigation. This has promoted a large and not very physically robust category of resources to artifact status. It is not surprising that historians of print are interested in books that were created before the mechanization of printing and binding. Book production before the 1830s was craft work. Printers delivered unbound sheets to the booksellers, who then bound them into volumes that carried the printers' own imprints. One printing was distributed among a number of booksellers, each of which would bind the volumes differently. Consequently, the same printing could appear as a number of forms. Each set can be considered unique in its printing, binding, or dissemination and thus worthy of retention in a collection.

The introduction of mass production has not diminished the status of books from the latter two-thirds of the nineteenth century as items with artifactual interest. There were so many innovations in the business and art of printing during that period that there are now many candidates for special treatment as objects, irrespective of the content. While books printed before 1801 are usually managed as "rare" books, there is an increasing use of the category of "medium-rare" books of the nineteenth century that are served to patrons under somewhat stricter protocols than are general collection imprints. This could be because the books have illustrations that are of research value or are vulnerable to mutilation; have aesthetically significant bindings; or were produced by special printers or publishing houses. These books rarely receive the intensive, item-level treatment that a rare book would get; a global or collection-level treatment is sufficient to ensure that they survive in usable form. This is one example of preventive preservation that should be encouraged in libraries holding important collections of such materials.

One should not underestimate the amount of time it takes to select books for this kind of treatment. Some libraries pull these books during normal shelf inventorying or when they cross the circulation desk. Other libraries pull these books when they are selecting items for filming, scanning, deacidification, or secondary storage. To expect each library to develop a collection of artifacts relevant to the history of printing simply because it has books from eras relevant to that field, however, is neither feasible nor responsible.

Many paper-based collections other than books and periodical publications held in special collections libraries and departments are also at risk. Libraries, archives, historical societies, and museums house large collections of pamphlets, letters, brochures, broadsides, sheet music, printed maps, advertising art, playbills, restaurant menus, scrapbooks and memorabilia, almanacs, proof sheets, children's books, religious tracts, and other items printed between 1800 and 2000. Nevertheless, retention of these materials does not guarantee their survival. These collections are invaluable intellectual and cultural resources, and they must be considered in any national preservation strategy. While these materials fall outside the scope of consideration here, it is important to emphasize that these collections warrant separate investigation.

Creating Surrogates

Surrogates are created for one of two reasons: to create copies of works too fragile to use or to replace items in imminent danger of disintegration. In the former case, a rare book or collection of broadsides may be scanned and the originals retired from use, except under extraordinary circumstances. For materials that are on their last or next-to-last use, the content is reformatted onto a more stable medium, such as preservation microfilm, or is photocopied onto acid-free paper. For these types of books and other items that are in current demand, most libraries create paper copies, a far more convenient mode of access than is microfilm.

In most cases, the source is photocopied onto acid-free paper; however, at libraries with active digitization programs, the source materials are often scanned and the scans are used to recreate the original volume on acid-free paper on demand. Microfilming remains the gold standard for preservation reformatting of low-use materials. With proper storage and handling, preservation microfilm can remain faithful and legible for a century or more. Film is still considered to be the best medium for preservation of images. But microfilm is just that—images—and no more. Digital reformatting that includes optical character recognition (OCR) adds functionality, including the capability for full-text searching.

The preservation community has given much thought to making preservation microfilm whenever digital scans are made or to converting preservation microfilm into digital scans, but few libraries have embraced this more costly approach. Even though the money goes toward ensuring preservation after creating access, funders tend to be reluctant to put money into preservation when the same money can be put toward enhancing access to something else.

Digitization of low-use special-format collections, by contrast, is common. This predilection to scan special collections rather than monographs is based in part on the idea that special-collections materials—maps, photographs, manuscripts—have traditionally received little use because they exist in single copies in one collection. Once made easily accessible, these materials may become high-use items. One significant exception to the practice of not scanning low-use print materials is the Making of America (MOA) program at the University of Michigan and Cornell University. This digitization program focused on brittle American monographs and journals from the latter half of the nineteenth century, and the selection of materials was coordinated between the two libraries.

The visibility of digitized materials on the Web has facilitated their discovery, resulting in usage that greatly outstrips that of the paper copies that were slowly decaying on their shelves. A dedicated researcher may have consulted the print copies, but the secondary school student, the genealogist, the lexicographer, and the insurance company are unlikely to have engaged with the paper volumes as they are able to access these digitized publications on the Internet.

The scholars who were "hooked" reported that the searching techniques available were especially prized. The report noted that "the thoroughness with which searching is possible across any of the corpora covered by these databases means that once they have been recognized by a group of researchers in a particular field, their use is obligatory." The observation that use is "obligatory" means that these scholars are now able to avail themselves of otherwise-scarce texts.

All these instances testify that scholars are growing more comfortable with digital surrogates of texts. There is a need to develop and apply methodologies to track the growing use of large digitized collections and to evaluate how researchers use these aggregations. Their increasing use also raises the question of what value there will be for libraries to maintain their hard-copy collections of these texts, when the same collections, without gaps and items missing from the shelves, are accessible from a computer 24 hours a day from anywhere in the world.

Duplicative collections of materials that are not rare and are readily accessible on the desktop will have lost much of their original reason for being: to provide local access. Information technologies may allow libraries to develop a system of registration or other kind of tracking that can allow linking local preservation decisions and investments to the changing needs of a national and international research community. And with new models of distributed preservation responsibilities facilitated by digital technology, shared among libraries, must come financial and legal support for those actions taken on behalf of the group.

Responsible Retention Policies

Books are totemic objects that have developed a powerful status over centuries, both for their content and for their physical significance. At the same time, books, like other objects, have always been cultural variables. Codices were routinely expunged in the Middle Ages, their writing scraped off to make room for a new work, which, in turn, might be effaced by a later generation. The spiraling costs of basic library functions and the added demands of new and more expensive services and collections cannot be allowed to put libraries and their missions at risk. To ensure the continued accessibility of current library collections into the future, not to mention the extension of access to those collections through networked resources, economies of scale, some of which entail the forging of cooperative enterprises, must be achieved. The technical infrastructure, financial resources, and public support must also be secured to sustain those actions.

As a way of envisaging how responsible retention of reformatted materials might be reconciled with the economic realities of preservation, librarians can look to archivists for sound guidance. The benchmarks of sufficient quality film or digital capture include the following:

— The scan has captured all informational content—color, original formatting, full content, or whatever else is important in the source document.

— The document is fully accessible through a defined indexing-and-retrieval scheme.

— Access to the digital file will be maintained over time, and the data will be protected from loss, corruption, and technological obsolescence.

A consortium of leading American research libraries has proposed benchmarks for digital capture of text and image for libraries that posit technical specifications that would meet these requirements. If adopted and widely practiced, these would go a long way to building digital files on which researchers could rely for some minimal levels of capture and fidelity. Once a library has created scans of sufficient quality to serve as full surrogates, it should put in place a plan to maintain those resources over time. It should also consider the question of what to do with the original source material.

A plan for maintaining the files over time may one day become routine, but at present there are very few libraries or archives that can or would assert that their digital assets are secure for more than a few years hence. There is a need for what might be called digital service bureaus or utilities that would provide such services as scanning, managing files, delivering files to local users, and long-term archiving. This infrastructure needs to be in place before most libraries and archives could develop routine, cost-effective digital services.

Any scanned material that is rare and of artifactual value should be handled with care during scanning, and retained afterward, even if retired from active duty, and stored to prevent further damage. Items that are common, such as journals, and that have content value but little artifactual value may also be sent to storage. However, if hard copies exist at other sites, there is no compelling reason to retain them, unless the local patrons have a history of using hard copy even when digital files are available. What is important is that researchers who do need hard copy should be able to locate and retrieve it with relative convenience.

In many cases, this may mean developing shared repositories for originals, used and supported by several libraries that store their materials in one site and are able, thereby, to create richer and often more comprehensive shared collections. The custodians of artifacts need to design a plan that strives for the most comprehensive coverage of given journals or subject matter. This would almost certainly entail collaboration by the repositories of the original materials, support from their local constituencies, and concurrence that acting for the greater good might engender some local inconvenience.

The Five-College Library Depository is a model for this kind of shared storage. Such a repository might be able to afford collections services such as in-house preservation facilities, or even scan-on-demand services, that single institutions could not develop and sustain alone. Promoting better understanding of the importance of the artifact will require a clear, succinct framing of the issues and structured discussions. The objective should be to develop commonly understood and widely endorsed approaches to the problem of caring for an abundance of materials with limited resources. There will never be complete agreement: the matter of what to preserve and how to make that accessible will never be considered resolved for all time. Instead, interested parties should develop and declare a basis for making those decisions that must be made in the immediate future.

Audiovisual Materials

Audiovisual materials present many of the same preservation challenges as do resources on paper. They are recorded on media that decay and they are abundant, thereby forcing libraries and archives to make difficult choices in acquiring and preserving them. Researchers' demands for audiovisual products, like the demands for print resources, change over time. This reinforces libraries' sense that they need to collect masses of materials with no immediate demand in sight, in case they eventually prove to be of research value.

At the same time, in large part because of the extreme fragility of the recording media and the dependence on playback machinery that quickly becomes obsolete, audiovisual materials present new challenges to traditional notions of the intrinsic value of the artifact. For printed materials, the artifact is a single physical object that has some measure of fixity. That fixity is largely dependent on the fact that the object has been recorded on a relatively stable medium. The stability of the paper depends on its physical composition, the effects of handling and storage on the original imprint, and other variables; however, there is little confusion about what a book or a journal is and what constitutes the original.

Moreover, the role of the print artifact in research is fairly straightforward: it provides evidence, and does so through information that the physical object itself carries. This information offers a means of ensuring the authenticity of an object and of judging the veracity and accuracy of the information contained in it. It also brings researchers in some tangible way closer to the moment of creation of that object and, presumably, closer to the intentions of the creator.

A simple example can be used to illustrate the variety of ways in which audiovisual technologies assault the fundamental notion of artifact. While many humanists are familiar with print resources and the copyright regime that governs their distribution and permits timely preservation action, fewer scholars are familiar with the protocols that govern audiovisual resources. Their manufacture, preservation, and access protocols and, perhaps most significantly, the copyright laws that permit or restrict those protocols, are well-known only to specialists. Moreover, the history of collecting these materials differs dramatically from that of print resources.

The curatorial and preservation communities involved in audiovisual materials are widely dispersed—in media, government, and public and research libraries, as well as in museums, historical societies, and regional collecting institutions. There are as many conflicts as there are common interests between the creative community (such as film directors, photographers, and musical artists) and the rights holders (such as studios, news services, and major media companies), or between researchers (folklorists, ethnographers, and linguists) and their subjects.

These conflicts sometimes have serious commercial consequences, and the communities can come to blows over preservation issues such as colorization and letter-boxing, cropping and retouching, or enhancing recorded performances for re-release on CD by cleaning up the noise in an original long-playing (LP) record. Because these resources often have high entertainment and commercial value, the role of the marketplace must be considered in any strategy to preserve and make them accessible for research. In other instances, for unpublished and noncommercial recordings, serious ethical issues have arisen between some researchers and the communities that have been documented. This has led to new access restrictions on old bodies of evidence that beg the question of whether or not repositories should invest in preserving materials to which they may never be allowed to grant access. Some of the intricacies of rights management, commerce, and ethics are discussed in detail in two case studies about film preservation and folklore collections.

Still-image Collections

Many special-collections repositories also have significant still-image collections, often filed with printed, cartographic, or design materials in collections organized not by medium but by provenance or subject matter. No one knows exactly how much of this type of material exists in the United States or where it is stored. Nonetheless, it seems clear that the majority of historical documents that are image-based are not in academic research libraries but are scattered in historical societies, natural history collections, special-collections libraries, commercial archives, and local, municipal, state, and federal records offices. The charts that document land ownership and management; architectural drawings and engineering records of the built environment; photographs taken in the course of collecting news or creating journalistic essays; and archives of architectural firms, industrial design companies, and advertising enterprise—all these collections constitute invaluable historical records.

While many companies take excellent care of their business archives and offer some level of preventive preservation for the still images scattered throughout their records, most enterprises do not have preservation strategies for their archives, lack resources to develop and implement such strategies, and may not even be aware that they hold materials that are of great potential value to historians and others. Within research institutions, still-image collections have been slowly coming into their own as primary source materials. In public libraries such as the New York Public and the Library of Congress, both of which have premier visual resource collections, most users are professional picture researchers who are looking for images to reproduce in publications.

While professional picture researchers will always constitute a significant portion of users in public institutions, there is evidence that the current and future generations of humanities scholars will turn increasingly to visual documents for primary evidence. There are several reasons for this trend in research methodology. The first is chronology, pure and simple. The primary recording media of the past 100 years have been visual, and anyone studying that period can—or in many cases must—rely on still or moving images for information. A second reason is that the proliferation of photography and easy reproduction of images in magazines and books have exposed the current generation to more imagery. Some believe that this has led to a rise in "visual literacy"; others argue that exposure to many images does not create the ability to "read," or understand, an image critically—the true sign of literacy. The third reason is that the topics and methodologies of literary, historical, and sociological research have broadened to include many phenomena that are not well documented in texts but are so in visual resources.

In pictorial collections, the items that receive priority for selection and preservation include any work that is of artistic value or of a certain age, or that has been created by a well-known artist photographer, graphic artist, or cartoonist; has a significant provenance; constitutes an institutional priority; and so forth. Original works—vintage photographs and their negatives or original drawings—receive the best care. Color film and photographs are generally more fragile than are black-and-white film and photographs; however, any photograph printed on resin-coated or acid paper is at risk.

Film-based materials are often served in a high-quality surrogate, such as a digital image, slide, or copy print, unless the researcher is primarily interested in the object rather than the image content. One of the dilemmas of preservation is that the best conditions for storing an object often compromise the object's effectiveness for research. Still images, whether film or paper based, are often an integral part of a mixed-media collection. Such images might include photos in a personal archive, illustrations in a book, or architectural records in a business archive. Preservation would demand that they be physically separated from the original collection and stored elsewhere in cold vaults. Each medium has its own storage requirements; for example, requirements for black-and-white film differ from those for color.

There are large collections of documentary photography that gain research value as they are supplemented by a range of secondary materials—notebooks, work files, and contact sheets—that enlarge the evidential base of the documents under review. In many cases, it is sufficient to create surrogates that can be kept with the original collection. Copy photos or digital reproductions usually provide all the information needed, but creating high-quality surrogates can be costly.

While both public and private nonprofit archives have long been working to document and preserve film, it was the emergence of ancillary markets for resale of film inventories that moved the industry itself to invest resources in preservation. As videotape playback equipment became cheap enough for the consumer market, studios predicted that recycling old films for reissue would be worth the investment. That led to the introduction of colorization, theoretically to enhance the appeal of old movies to consumers. Colorization and cropping to fit a television screen, in turn, galvanized the creative community around issues of original intent and moral rights, which sparked a confrontation with commercial forces and a widening circle of discourse about the state of the global film heritage.

Many people disagree about whether digital preservation of film is necessary for analog films, because commercial entities still shoot with old-fashioned film stock. Editing is now done primarily on digital equipment, and some major filmmakers—George Lucas most famously—are shooting with digital cameras. As long as film stock continues to be manufactured, the debate will go on.

Recorded sound is a different matter. In this case, members of the preservation community will soon find themselves without the tape and equipment they need for analog reformatting. Acquiring the equipment needed to transfer analog to digital is a huge capital expenditure—one that many institutions that hold valuable recordings are not prepared to make. Consequently, many collecting institutions will have to outsource their preservation reformatting. Such a process is fraught with risk because few laboratories specialize in the art of old media.

Broadcast media

Broadcast media—radio and television—are the stepchildren of the audiovisual media. While everyone acknowledges their reach across the country and their power to shape public perceptions, interests, and thinking, few institutions take them seriously as sources of historical information, at least as evidenced by how few collect them. In US, the Library of

Congress has an unparalleled collection of black-and-white-era television holdings and some significant radio holdings, such as the Armed Forces Radio and Television Service Collection. But in general, at both the national and the local levels, what gets broadcast is woefully under-documented.

There is little local collecting, yet because broadcast media are the equivalent of newspapers in another era, the most significant materials are generated locally and should be collected and preserved at the local, not national, level. Those who decry the loss of newspapers from the past are well positioned to raise awareness about the present need to save broadcasting, because what they most value about old newspapers is present in the newer forms of news and entertainment—exquisite sources for popular opinion, advertising, and cultural phenomena of all types.

The Library of Congress has been authorized to create an archival record of national radio and television through the American Television and Radio Archives program. However, the state of local television news collections across the country is, in the words of an expert report, "extremely desperate". The state of collections of non-news television and of radio of all sorts is equally deplorable, if not more so. The Library of Congress report on the state of television and video preservation lays out the scope of the problem and proposes a national plan of shared responsibilities to ensure that at least some of the television and videotape in the country will survive. Should these broadcast documents not survive, it would be an irreparable loss for present and future generations.

Scholars can play a crucial role in making the academic communities of which they are members, as well as the public, aware of the value of this documentation, the extent of the challenges to future access, and the efforts under way to preserve these materials. It would be ironic and sad indeed if this generation of scholars, using ephemera and other artifacts of the nineteenth century to reconstruct the history and consciousness of that time, were to do nothing to articulate the need to safeguard the comparable artifacts of this era.

Digital Information Objects

It is in part the phenomenal growth of digital information in libraries that prompts this examination of the nature and importance of physical artifacts for research and teaching. Digital technology is changing the ways in which researchers and teachers are getting access to information and in some cases obviating the need to consult an original. The demand for electronic resources and the infrastructure needed to support their access and maintenance is affecting the budgetary climate in which artifactual preservation must fight for its share. Finally, the flooding of the information landscape by "nonartifactual" intellectual property influences our understanding of the notion of the artifact in ways that beg scrutiny. It is for reasons such as these that digital formats warrant special attention.

With respect to original artifacts, the salient questions to pose about digitized representations are as follows:

— When can a digital surrogate stand in for its source?

— When can a digital surrogate replace its source?

— When might a digital surrogate be superior to its source?

— What is the cost of producing and maintaining digital surrogates?

— What risks do digital surrogates pose?

In print, there is a great deal of secondary literature that is amenable to digitization. There is also a great deal of primary source material—dime novels, vintage photographs, and various ephemera—that, because of its scarcity, could be more widely accessible were it in digital form. Other items—for example, oversize materials such as posters, or books in fragile states—are easier and safer to use in the form of digital surrogates. The research tools available for digital materials, such as full-text searching, may make the surrogates more accessible to specific types of research questions than the originals are. Postscanning processes may make the use of damaged items easier because one can lighten dark patches or sharpen the resolution of faded inks.

For visual resources and recorded sound, reformatting for access purposes is nearly always recommended or required for the sake of preserving the integrity of the source material. There is a growing consensus that digital, rather than analog, reformatting will best meet the demand for accessibility, fidelity, ease of reproduction, and cost-effectiveness, although significant issues still must be addressed in standards for access, preservation, and rights management before this technology can fulfill its promise. For audiovisual resources, the funding of the preservation work that is required remains a hurdle.

In sum, there are many ways in which this new technology can create adequate and at times superior access to information in physical artifacts. There are also instances in which no surrogate, no matter how splendid, will serve the scholar's needs. Finally, the infrastructure needed to support and sustain such reformatting programs is still in its infancy. Before one can recommend digital reformatting for the preservation of or access to artifacts with intrinsic value as physical objects, it will be necessary to identify the hazards of digital representation of artifacts and to determine the true nature of an artifact in a digital environment. Physical artifacts bear all sorts of evidence about how they were created or manufactured, who had possession of them at what time, how they were used, how they have changed, whether the information they contain has been altered, and whether the alteration was intentional or inadvertent.

Artifactual Value in the Digital Realm

Libraries and archives have two distinct categories of digital objects—materials that exist only in digital form ("born-digital" information) and materials that are digitized versions of analog source materials ("reborn-digital" information). The two categories can exist side by side on a server, and the information technologists responsible for the maintenance of those files do not draw distinctions between them in terms of treatments. From the researcher's point of view, however, the distinctions are great, and they will be maintained here.

Digital technology can represent all genres and types of library and archival materials—textual, numeric, visual, and sound information. Because the technology of creating and disseminating information through digital means is relatively new, society has appropriated many terms specific to analog information and used them, almost by analogy, to describe digital objects. This goes beyond such examples as referring to individual instances of files uploaded to computer screens as "pages." It has also resulted in such awkward back-formations as "nondigital" information to mean everything that already exists in analog form.

The very value of the physical manifestation, together with the dependence on the physical medium, has created problems for preserving information printed on paper. That problem deepens with audiovisual information objects, because the mechanical processes that produce and record audiovisual information produce physical artifacts far more fragile than paper is. The concept of artifactual value is contingent not only on changes in cultural valuations but also on information technologies and their businesses—be they printing presses and paper mills or film stock manufacturers and playback equipment companies. All these complexities abound, and are perhaps even more problematic, in digital formats as well.

Digital Surrogates

Therefore, as a means of determining the value and appropriate use of digital surrogates for library holdings, it may be useful to divide original materials into those that are rare and those that are not, and to divide them further into those that are frequently used and those that are infrequently used.

Materials that are not rare and that are frequently used. In this case, we can assume that preservation of the original is not a particularly high priority (since the original is not rare); nevertheless, digital surrogates for such an object might be worth producing and providing, for several reasons:

— to reduce the cost associated with reshelving the object

— to make the object simultaneously available to multiple users (for example, through an electronic reserve desk)

— to replace the object, thereby doing away with the cost of housing it

The first two are obvious and uncontroversial benefits. The third is potentially problematic, even if the object in question is not rare, because it is not obvious that digital surrogates provide all the functionality, all the information, or all the aesthetic value of originals. Therefore, while it may be sensible to recommend that digital surrogates be used to reduce the cost and increase the availability of library holdings that circulate frequently, the decision to deaccession a physical object in library collections and replace it with a digital surrogate should be based on a careful assessment of the way in which library patrons use the original object or objects of its kind. It is not necessary that the digital surrogate possess all the qualities and perform all the functions of the original, but it is necessary that the digital surrogate answer to the identifiable needs and expectations of those who frequently used the original.

Materials that are not rare and that are infrequently used. Many libraries now store infrequently used books and other materials in long-term storage facilities. Those materials are retrievable and available to library patrons, but only after a wait of two or three days. With such materials, digital surrogates might help users to determine whether recalling an object from long-term storage was worth the wait—and worth the library's effort increase frequency of use (by providing searchable metadata, for example) reduce costs by replacing the object with a digital surrogate. The first two are obvious and uncontroversial benefits, and the third comes with the caveat that the digital surrogate should answer to the identifiable needs and expectations of those who (in)frequently used the original. At some point, especially with infrequently used materials that are not rare, libraries might be expected to evolve a calculus that balances functionality with actual use in order to help decide when digital surrogates that provide most of the functionality of originals are acceptable.

Libraries, as an institutional and cultural community, need to consider whether these infrequently used and commonly held materials are, in fact, being preserved in a concerted and deliberate way in their original form by any one (or more than one) library. If they are not, the sources for digital surrogates that are common today could easily become rare, or nonexistent, tomorrow. Another missing feature of the current digital library infrastructure is a central location from which to discover which analog collections have been digitized and how one can get access to them. One reason is that organizations that digitize use a great variety of standards, not only for capture but also for description. Some items are described at the item level, others at the collection level. Items that have been digitized more than once would not all appear in a search of the records as they currently exist.

Libraries are often short-staffed, and they cannot report regularly on what they are doing or planning to do. The absence of such reports would jeopardize the timeliness and reliability of such a registry. No single body has agreed to act as an organizing agency to create and maintain the information, and it is not clear from where the funding for such a body would come. The work of such a body would include securing the information and ensuring that changes in URLs were kept up-to-date.

Born-Digital Materials

Whereas digital surrogates always originate from physical source materials, a born-digital item has no previous manifestation in physical form. It is entirely dependent on hardware and software for accessibility, storage, and long-term access. Anyone who has tried to trace a citation to a digital source, only to find that the site no longer exists, understands that dedicated maintenance and resources are required to keep digital sources alive, let alone up-to-date. Beyond the problem of stability, it can be difficult to judge the authority or authenticity of Web-based information.

Digital information is by its nature perfectly replicable. To distinguish between the first and the forty-first instantiations of a digital file is a fool's errand. But born-digital information is of very great import for scholars interested in the artifact, for it challenges notions of originality and uniqueness, and even of authenticity, fixity, and stability. That it does so matters greatly, because of the sheer quantity of information that is being created in digital-only form.

In many digital objects, the chief value is in the informational content of the file, and that content is as good in one copy as in another. It is similar to the case of feature films, where the researcher will normally prize ease of access over fidelity to the original manifestation, within limits. But are there equivalents in the digital realm to the intrinsic values we have defined for the physical artifact, namely, originality, faithfulness, fixity, and stability? This is a subject of intense discussion among librarians, archivists, computer scientists, and security experts.

Originality in its simplest sense—that is, of "oneness"—is not a meaningful notion in the digital realm. Archivists have many ways of defining "digital original," all of which may suffice to meet core requirements for evidence. In a library context, however, the notion is more or less bankrupt. Faithfulness, by contrast, is not necessarily an empty notion. It is true that the bit streams that make up a file can be changed without evidence of the change, regardless of whether it was intentional or accidental. For example, someone who receives a forwarded plain-text file that has had three paragraphs deleted from it would not be able to see evidence of the deletion on a computer monitor.

Internal evidence, however, might lead an attentive reader to believe that "something is missing," and if the file comes with a digital signature—a public key or other mechanism for objectively verifying that the file has not been changed since the key was generated—then one does have some hope of determining faithfulness. Of course, few researchers perform forensic examinations on the physical artifacts they view. Users trust that a source found in a library, for example, is more reliable than one found posted to a billboard. So, too, many researchers place more trust in resources found on a library Web site than in information anonymously posted on the Web.

The issues of stability and fixity, however, are quite troublesome for digital texts. For analog sources, stability and concrete form are absolute requirements for proving the authenticity and provenance of unique documents. The malleability of digital information, the ease of creating several different and subtly tailored versions of digital documents for different audiences, and the difficulties of maintaining digital sources intact and accessible over time are similar to the problems associated with archiving the international television broadcasts. Efforts are under way to bring together libraries and publishing houses to address the many questions that surround the archiving of scholarly journals.

As to the intrinsic value of the digital artifact, as opposed to the value of the content that might easily be reformatted onto another medium, what are those features that drop out when content is reformatted? It could be the text formatting, as anyone who has imported a file created in one word-processing program into another program well knows. But in most cases, it is some sort of functionality that is lost.

Relational databases can export their data in a form that permits another database engine to import that content, but the relationships laid down among items in the original database will be lost, because there is no standard way of encoding those relationships.

Preservation of Digital Information

Like analog moving-image and recorded sound information, digital information is both technology- and medium-dependent. Digital technology appears to be evolving even more rapidly than analog recording media have evolved. Hardware and software have changed so quickly that information that has been recorded on one software program often is at risk of obsolescence in only three or four years. The media on which digital information is recorded, whether it is magnetic tape or a hard disk, are vulnerable to a startling array of new risk factors, including magnetic fluctuations, separation of information from the substrate caused by mild environmental disturbances, accidental overwrites, and "bit rot."

Precisely because the technologies used to encode, display, and enact digital information are changing so rapidly, the digital artifact that goes untouched for 10 or 20 years may well be unrecoverable. Its storage medium might require hardware that no longer exists, the software used to create it might no longer be available, or the operating system under which that software ran might be obsolete. Digital files must be "refreshed" and magnetic tape "exercised" to ensure that the bits keep their integrity and the recording medium does not suffer undue degradation. This constitutes minimal-level preservation for digital files. There is no such thing as putting the text on eight-inch floppies, putting the floppies in storage, and being able to retrieve the text 50 years later. Digital preservation programs will have to be much more active, and even aggressive, than book preservation programs are.

In the past, with information stored in more or less durable physical objects, the task of preservation has been to stabilize and, if possible, enhance the integrity of items (books, films, sound recordings) that had been around for generations because they had been acquired by a library. Some judgment has been made about the intellectual or cultural value of the item, and the question for preservation is not whether, but how, to preserve the item. With digital information, whose life span can be as short as one software upgrade, the decision to preserve must be made almost simultaneously with its creation. This turns the traditional preservation paradigm on its head.

The two most commonly advocated methods of preservation, both of which involve concerted efforts by custodians, are migration and emulation. Migration is essentially a moving of digital files from old hardware and software platforms onto new ones. Migration is a translation, and some measure of loss is inherent in the process. What happens when one reformats word-processing files from an old version of a program to a new one, or from a Mac platform to a PC? The content of the documents is usually preserved, but the formatting is corrupted to one degree or another. Migration has occurred, and loss has been incurred. Yet most people who look back at the costs and benefits of the process would probably decide that the benefits of not having to rekey whole documents outweigh the tinkering necessary to restore the original formatting.

At the same time, there are categories of digital documents, most of them nontextual, that might suffer unacceptable losses during migration. These include executable files, such as time-lapse simulations and interactive programs. For these, the goal is to preserve not only the content but all aspects of the behavior of the original content and of the software used to present it. This is what emulation is designed to do—create software that can simulate the hardware and software environment in which a document was created. The technology of emulation is still in its early stages.

When considering artifacts that are born digital, the first and possibly the most difficult question is "What is the artifact?" What information or value inheres in the carrier medium? Is the equipment originally used for display part of the digital artifact? Does the software that presents and actualizes the data qualify as a constituent element of the artifact? Thinking again of the criteria for determining intrinsic value in an artifact—as a way of understanding what the features of an artifact might be—it is evident that there are a number of practical ways in which these questions might surface.

The physical form of a document or program might be the subject for study if the records provide meaningful documentation or significant examples of the form. For example, the layout of a form used for collecting data on the Web might reveal a good deal about otherwise-inexplicable aberrations, omissions, or misconstructions in the data collected.

There are also aesthetic or artistic qualities that may require preserving, most notably digital art and literature (Lyman and Kahle 1998). Achieving that level of fidelity to the original, or original instantiation, would require running a program on originally specified system hardware and software. Early computer games are a popular species of programming wizardry that inspire heroic efforts at emulation, or recreation of original hardware and software platforms, for replay. One such emulation program can be found in Java, which runs Kaypro (Z-80/CPM-based) software on contemporary Intel/Windows-based systems. The challenges posed by preserving digital art are manifold, because the art is often designed, like a game, to provide real-time experience for the viewer—an experience that may or may not be intended to be replicable. The Guggenheim Museum of Art has developed a program, Variable Media Initiative, that "encourages digital artists to help establish preservation guidelines long before their equipment, code, and lives become history," as Wired recently reported (Jana 2001). Through this program, artists can record not only the technical specifications of a given work of art but also the artist's intentions or considerations for longevity.

A third form of digital preservation is the preservation of the original hardware and software for use at some time in the indefinite future. Similar to the saving of wax cylinders and the original play back equipment for listening, this is a strategy of last resort, one that is not scalable for the routine needs of moving massive amounts of information forward and making it readily accessible to users in the future.

These examples suffice to show that the relevant features of a digital artifact could include more than the fungible information contained in an electronic file. Although the Kaypro example may seem facetious, the many issues attendant to digital art and literature are not. The questions that the preservation of these digital objects bring forth are similar to those that collection development staff members ask about preserving all sorts of digital information that is dependent on specific software programs for its intrinsic value.

In many cases, the answer for libraries will be that they are, in fact, primarily concerned with collecting, preserving, and providing access to the fungible informational content of digital objects. In that case, the "preservation through handling" scheme is a likely winner; digital information that is frequently used by patrons stands a better chance of being migrated and refreshed, and therefore is more likely to continue to be available in future generations, than is little-used digital information. Indeed, migration may turn out to be a much more frequently recurring problem than is refreshing, because "today's optical media most likely will far outlast the capability of systems to retrieve and interpret the data stored on them".

Regrettably, it is easier and cheaper to refresh than to migrate. If libraries have reason to be hopeful in this regard, it lies in open, nonproprietary standards such as JPEG for images, MPEG for video, and SGML, XML, and XSL for textual data. There are still important data types for which no such standards exist (GIS data, for example). However, the trend over the last 20 years—accelerated significantly in the last decade by the advent of the World Wide Web—has been in the direction of support for nonproprietary standards, even in proprietary software.

Another promising strategy under development is called LOCKSS (Lots of Copies Keep Stuff Safe). The basic principle of LOCKSS is preservation through proliferation. Curiously, this strategy flies in the face of the new logic of preservation and access in the digital world: that libraries should not build redundant collections in a networked environment, but should develop cooperative collection development and preservation strategies. Duplication of effort is seen as not cost-effective.

In the digital realm, cold storage does not work. Born-digital artifacts will not benefit from living undisturbed in dead storage for years. On the contrary, digital artifacts seem to require preservation through handling. Such active intervention would seem to obviate redundancy. Nevertheless, there is plenty of room for experiments in this new environment, and if the future proves to be anything like the past, then many of our initial approaches to ensuring longevity will be stood on their heads.

With print originals, the "preservation through proliferation" strategy of duplicative collections assumes that one copy is as good as another, that is, that the value of the artifact is fungible and that it is the information, not the artifact, one wants to preserve. One copy cannot serve the access needs of a large research community, and the only way for two people to have access to a book is for each to have his or her own copy.

Barriers to Preservation

Libraries and archives are allowed to use copying technologies for preservation purposes under an exemption of the copyright code. When the Digital Millennium Copyright Act first appeared, there was no exemption for digital materials. The copyright community feared that it would be impossible to control the distribution of copied files, and that even those created for educational and preservation purposes would be a threat to the intellectual property rights of their creators or publishers.

These concerns have been addressed in further legislation that allows preservation copying, and technologies to encode data are adding desired layers of protection from infringement for rights owners. The real threat to preservation in the digital realm is that copyright law is being finessed by licensing agreements. Libraries do not purchase electronic databases and do not have ownership of materials as they do of analog materials. Libraries do not preserve materials that they do not own. At the same time, however, publishers are not in the preservation business.

6

Digitised Collections

Libraries have been digitizing collections for a decade or more. Their collective experience has produced a depth of technical expertise and a set of tested practices. That information is widely shared among digital library staffs and has been well reported at meetings and in publications. Every library, regardless of size or mission, will need to determine for itself how and when digitization will move from being an experiment to becoming a collection-development strategy that is well integrated into its daily practice.

While the great majority of research libraries have undertaken digitization projects of one type or another, only a few are developing full-scale digitization programs rather than focusing on discrete uses of digitization for specific purposes. How do the libraries that have undertaken full-scale efforts conceptualize the role of digitized collections in providing collections and services to their core constituencies? What are they doing, or what have they determined must be done, to move from project-based conversion to programs that, whether large or small, have a well-defined role in the long-term goals of the library?

A sustainable digitization program, in other words, would be fully integrated into a library's traditional collection-development strategies. A digitization program need not be large and production oriented to be sustainable. The role of conversion can be significant and well thought out, even when the conversion program serves limited purposes and has limited resources. Any assessment of what libraries have achieved so far must take into account two key factors common to sustainable collection development, be it of analog, digitized, or born-digital materials. These factors are

— a strategic view of the role of collections in the service of research and teaching or other core institutional missions, and

— life cycle planning for the collections, beginning with their identification and including acquisition, cataloging and preservation, and providing reference.

A strategic view can be revealed in many cases not only by looking at how closely the results serve the mission but also at the decision-making process itself—that is, who decides what to convert to serve which ends. When are the decisions made primarily by subject specialists based on existing collection strengths, and when is the selection process shaped by curricular development and other faculty needs? If the latter, then by what process are the faculty involved and how are teaching and research tools developed to meet their needs?

Ensuring long-term access to digital collections depends on careful life-cycle management. How does the library budget for not only the creation of the digital scans but also for the metadata, storage capacity, preservation tools (e.g., refreshing, migration), and user support—the sorts of things that are routinely budgeted for book acquisitions? How much of the program is supported by grant funding and how much by base funding? If the program is currently grant supported, what plans exist to make it self-sustaining? A sustainable digitization strategy may well include the creation of digital surrogates that serve short-term needs and do not demand long-term support. The crucial thing is to anticipate what support, if any, will be needed.

Selecting materials for digitization is more complex than is selecting materials for the purchase or licensing of born-digital materials, because it involves expending resources for items that are already in the library's collection rather than acquiring new ones. In theory, a library would choose to digitize existing collection items only if it could identify the value that is added by digitization and determine that the benefits outweigh the costs. But in practice, the research library community has, over the past decade, gone boldly forth with digitization projects not knowing how to measure their costs or benefits.

Digitization technology and its costs are constantly changing; as a result, budgeting models that make comparisons between libraries can be meaningless or downright misleading. Unlike selecting officials who decide the purchase or license of electronic resources, those responsible for digital conversion do not have a set of fixed prices for services and collections on offer. The only way for many libraries to get at the issue of cost is to undertake projects for their own sake, in the expectation that documentation of expenditures will yield some meaningful data. Libraries that have been able to secure funding for projects, document their activities and expenditures, and share that information with their colleagues have emerged as the leaders of the community, if only because of their policies to share their knowledge.

Policies and Guidelines

Very few libraries have developed their own formal written policies for conversion criteria. Those that do have such documents tend to refer to them as "guidelines." These documents tend to focus on technical aspects of selection and, even more, on project planning. When asked why they do not have a policy, most institutions reply that it is too early to formulate policies, that they have not gotten around to formulating them, or that the institution does not have written collection-development policies for other materials so it is unlikely to write them for digitized collection development.

These documents almost always focus on the planning of digital projects or of various elements of a larger program, rather than on the rationale for digitization. In US, the University of Michigan, for example, has a written policy that clearly aims to fit digitization into the context of traditional collection development. It states that "core questions" underlying digitization should be familiar to any research library collection specialist. These questions are as follows:

— Is the content original and of substantial intellectual quality?
— Is it useful in the short and/or long term for research and instruction?
— Does it match campus programmatic priorities and library collecting interests?
— Is the cost in line with the anticipated value?
— Does the format match the research styles of anticipated users?
— Does it advance the development of a meaningful organic collection?

These are fundamental collection-development criteria that assert the importance of the research value of source materials over technical considerations; however, they are quite general. The rest of Michigan's policy focuses not on how to select items for conversion but on how anticipated use of the digital surrogates should affect decisions about technical aspects of the conversion, markup, and presentation online.

Harvard's selection criteria offer far more detailed considerations than do those of Michigan. In common with the Michigan criteria, the Harvard criteria focus largely on questions that come after the larger, "why-bother-to-digitize-this-rather-than-that" issues have already been answered. Creation of digital surrogates for preservation purposes is cited as one legitimate reason for selection, as are a number of considerations aimed not at preservation but solely at increasing access.

The primary nontechnical criterion—research value—is a subjective one and relies on many contingencies for interpretation. What does it mean to say that something has intrinsic research value? Do research libraries collect any items that do not have such value? Should we give priority to items that have research value today or to those that may have it tomorrow? What relationship does current demand have to intrinsic value? Because the answers to these questions are subjective, the only things excluded under these selection criteria are items that are difficult to scan (for example, oversized maps) or things that are very boring or out of intellectual fashion.

Interestingly, foreign language materials are nearly always excluded from consideration, even if they are of high research value, because of the limitations of optical character recognition (OCR) software and because they often have a limited number of users. There are digital projects that have converted valuable historical sources, from Egyptian papyri to medieval manuscripts, into image files (such as the Advanced Papyrological Information System [APIS] and the Digital Scriptorium). In general, however, the conversion of non-English language sources into searchable text continues to be rare.

This high-level criterion of research value is also an intrinsic part of traditional collection-development policies. The difference is that in most libraries, the acquisition of monographs, to take an example, fits into a longstanding activity that has been well defined by prior practice. This practice governs the acquisition of new materials, that is, those that the library does not already hold. (The issue of how many copies is secondary to the decision to acquire the title.)

Selection of an item for digitization is reselection, and the criteria for its digitization, or repurposing, will be different from those for its acquisition. The meaning of research value will also differ, because the methods of research used for digital materials differ from those used for analog, and the types of materials that are mined—and how—are also fundamentally different. Several large digitization programs today are grounded in the belief that it is the nature of research itself that is "repurposed" by this technology, and it is often surprising to see which source material yields the greatest return when digitized.

As one librarian said, the guidelines addressing selection that are used routinely, whether official or not, are by and large "project oriented." It would be a mistake to confuse what libraries are doing now with what libraries should and would do if "we understood what higher purpose digitization serves." While guidelines for technical matters such as image capture and legal rights management are extremely useful and should be codified, formal collection-development policies are still a long way off.

Reasons for Digitization

Libraries usually identify two reasons for digitization: to preserve analog collections, and to extend the reach of those collections. Most individual projects and full-scale programs serve a mix of both purposes. As librarians have learned from tackling the brittle book problem through deacidification and reformatting, it is difficult and often pointless to separate preservation and access. When a library is seeking outside funding for digital conversion (apparently still the primary source of funding for many libraries), it tends to cite as many possible benefits from conversion as possible. For this reason, preservation and access are usually mentioned in the same breath. Nonetheless, because it has been generally conceded that digital conversion is not as reliable for preservation purposes as is microfilm reformatting, it is worthwhile to consider what institutions are doing in terms of preservation per se.

Preservation

Surrogates: The use of scans made of rare, fragile, and unique materials—from prints and photographs to recorded sound and moving image—is universally acclaimed as an effective tool of preventive preservation. For materials that cannot withstand frequent handling or, because of their value or content, pose security risks, digitization has proved to be a boon.

Replacements: For paper-based items, librarians generally agree that digital scans are the preferred type of preservation surrogates. They are widely embraced by scholars and are preferred over microfilm. However, most librarians also assert that scanning in lieu of filming does not serve preservation purposes, because the expectation that we can migrate those scans into the future is simply not as great as is our conviction that we can manage preservation microfilm over decades. There is a general hope that the problem of digital longevity will soon be resolved. In anticipation of that day, most libraries are creating "preservation-quality" digital masters—scans that are rich enough to use for several different purposes and are created to obviate the need to rescan the original. These masters are sometimes created together with preservation master microfilm.

Only one institution, the University of Michigan, has a policy to scan brittle books and use the scans as replacements rather than as surrogates. The university has created a policy for the selection and treatment of these books, and it explicitly talks of digital replacements as a crucial strategy for collection management. This policy is based on the premise that books printed on acid paper have a limited life span and that, for those items with insignificant artifactual value, the library is not only rescuing the imperiled information but also making it more accessible by scanning in lieu of filming.

The focus of Michigan's digital program is the printed record, not special collections such as rare books and photographs, and digitization has been made a key collection-management tool for these holdings. Cornell also has incorporated digitization into collection management (that is, it is not for access alone), although its efforts are not as systematic as are those of Michigan. At Cornell there is a preference for digital replacements of brittle materials with backup to computer output microfilm (COM) or replacement hard copies made from digital scans. The Library of Congress has also begun implementing preservation strategies based on digitization in its project to digitize the nineteenth-century journal, Garden and Forest. Most libraries, though, elide the issue of digitally replacing brittle materials because they scan chiefly items from special collections.

For audiovisual materials, digital replacements appear to be inevitable, although standards for archival-quality re-recording have yet to be established. Because the recording media used for sound and moving image demand regular, frequent, and ultimately destructive reformatting, migrating onto digital media for preservation, as well as access, is acknowledged to be the only course to pursue for long-term maintenance. The University of California at Los Angeles (UCLA) and LC, both deeply engaged in audiovisual preservation, intend to digitize analog materials to provide long-term access. This does not mean that these institutions will dispose of the original analog source materials, only that the preservation strategy for these items will not be based on routine use of that analog source material.

Access: In nearly all research libraries, digitization is viewed as service of collections in another guise—one that provides enhanced functionality, convenience, some measure of preservation, aggregation of collections that are physically dispersed, and greatly expanded reach. Among all the strands of digitization activities at major research institutions, there are essentially three models of collection development based on access: one that serves as outreach to various communities; one that is designed to build collections; and one that is driven by a specific need, such as demand by a user or preservation surrogates, or that is part of a larger effort to develop core infrastructure. All libraries engage in the first kind of access to one degree or another. Significant strategic differences are evident, however, in their approaches to the choice between mounting large bodies of materials in the expectation of use versus collaborating with identified users to facilitate their data creation.

There will continue to be times when academic libraries create digital surrogates of their analog holdings for reasons that are important to the home institution yet not directly related to teaching and research. Libraries will continue to be parts of larger communities that look to them for purposes that transcend the educational mission of the library per se. As custodians of invaluable institutional intellectual and cultural assets, libraries will always play crucial roles in fund raising, cultivating alumni allegiance, and public relations.

Occasions for selective digitization projects include exhibitions, anniversaries (when archives or annual reports often get into the queue), a funding appeal (digitization as a condition of donation), and efforts to build institutional identity. Careful consideration needs to be given to what goes online for whatever purpose because, once a collection is online, it becomes part of the institutional identity. Image building is a critical and often undervalued part of ensuring the survival of the library and its host institution. As custodians of the intellectual and cultural treasures of a university, libraries have an obligation to share that public good to the advantage of the institution.

Collection-driven Selection

The most common approach to digitization hinges on a collection-driven selection process in which a library decides to scan a set of materials identified by staff as having great research potential online. The terms "collection driven" and "use driven" are familiar from the preservation microfilming projects of the 1980s and 1990s. At that time, brittle books were conceptualized as a "national collection" that was held by a group of libraries, not just one. Each library could help preserve the national collection by filming a set of its holdings that were particularly strong, thereby avoiding duplication of effort by registering its filming activities and enhancing access to the endangered materials through the loan or duplication of microfilm.

Librarians would select books not on the basis of their documented use (by checking circulation statistics or going with items that cross the circulation desk), but on the basis of whether they constituted a coherent set of monographs (and occasionally serials) arranged by subject matter or date of publication, or both. This method, so well-known to preservation experts and subject specialists from the many grant-supported microfilming projects of the past two decades, has been transferred to the digital realm with one interesting twist: It has been extended primarily not to the general collections—monographs and serials—that are the heart of microfilming projects, but to special collections—materials that are rare or archival in nature or that are in nonprint format.

Within each group, libraries may attempt to be as comprehensive as possible in putting items from the collection online to simulate the comprehensive or coherent nature of the source collection. Libraries that depend on outside funding—the great majority of libraries digitizing collections—often assert that it is easier to raise funds if they propose to digitize special collections because they are more interesting and have greater appeal to the funding agencies. While academic libraries have many reasons for deciding to digitize special collections, the rationales of the two public institutions merit special consideration, in large part because they are so different from those of academic libraries. (Because of these differences, however, taking them as a model should be done with eyes wide open).

None of the research libraries with comparable deep collections claims cultural enrichment of the public as an explicit goal. And yet, as de Stefano points out, there are academic libraries that are mounting special collections of broad public appeal that is not matched to curricular needs.

Libraries face several issues as a consequence of undertaking digital conversion. Some of these issues are constraints that may limit the potential of digitization to enhance research and teaching. They must be identified and explored to assess accurately the costs and benefits of digitization. Other issues may not be constraining as such, but may put new pressures on libraries to expend further resources. They, too, must be scrutinized and managed if digital programs are to be developed cost-effectively and with the greatest possible benefit to the collections and their users.

Treatment and Disposition

Selecting for scanning must include an assessment of the source's physical condition and readiness for the camera. For those items that are rare, unique, fragile, or otherwise of artifactual value, preparation for scanning usually demands the attention of conservators, if only to confirm that the item will not be harmed by the camera. Some type of prescanning treatment may also be required, from strengthening or mending paper to removing environmental soil. In the case of certain media, such as medieval manuscripts or daguerreotypes, the institution may need to call upon the services of a consultant or vendor with special expertise. This involves more time and resources (e.g., for writing contracts and checking items that return from a vendor) and may divert resources normally dedicated to other conservation work.

The disposition of scanned source materials that are not unique or rare is a challenging subject that most libraries are just beginning to confront. When digitization becomes an acceptable, if not preferred, alternative to microfilm for preservation reformatting and those items that can be networked are, what criteria will libraries use to decide what to keep on campus, what to send to remote storage, and what to discard?

The library community never reached a consensus about this issue for microfilming. The historical inattention to originals on the assumption that some institution would retain an original has led to avoidable material losses and to a serious public relations problem. Recent trends in scholarship have forced libraries to reexamine old assumptions about the value of original serials and monographs—items that are not traditionally prized for their artifactual value. It is important that research libraries find cost-effective means of preserving originals and making them readily accessible. This does not mean that all libraries should keep multiple copies of items that researchers prefer to use electronically.

But 20 years from now, when many scholars may well prefer accessing these materials electronically over retrieving them from library shelves, will the library community have developed a collective strategy for preserving a defined number of originals for access purposes and reducing the redundancy of print collections? How will researchers who wish to have access to originals be able to find out where they are and how they can be viewed? Current plans to register digitized items in a nationally coordinated database include consideration of noting the location of a hard copy available for access, and the fate of originals is beginning to get the attention that researchers demand.

For certain very fragile media, such as lacquer sound discs or nitrate film, the original or master should seldom or never be used for access purposes. Service of those collections should always be done on reformatted (access) media. However, that is an expensive proposition for any library, and there is great resistance to push the costs of preservation transfer onto the user. Regrettably, a great number of recorded sound and moving image resources continue to be played back using the original. Until digitization is an affordable option for access to these media, their preservation will remain at very high risk.

Scalability

Digitizing either general or special collections presents challenges regarding size: How many items from any given collection will be sufficient to create added value? "Critical mass" is one selection criterion that shows up in nearly all the written guidelines for selection and is commonly noted in conversation. The magic of critical mass, in theory, is that if you get enough related items up in a commonly searchable database, then you have created a collection that is richer in its digital instantiation than in its analog original. This is premised on the notion that the technology has a transformative power—that it can not only re-create a collection online but also give it new functionality, allow for new purposes, and ultimately create new audiences that make it available for novel queries. It does this by, for example, turning static pages of text or numbers into a database.

Monographs are no longer limited by the linear layout of the bound volume or microfilm reader. By making texts searchable, librarians can create new resources from old ones and transform items that have had little or no use into something that receives hundreds or thousands of hits. In the case of general collections, or imprints, one must select enough that they, taken together, create a coherent corpus. In one case, time periods may set the parameters; in another, it might be genre or subject.

Critical mass could more accurately be thought of as "contextual mass," that is, a variable quantity of materials that provides a context for evaluation and interpretation. In the analog realm, searching within a so-called critical mass has always been very labor-intensive. It has taken great human effort and patience to identify the relationships in and among items in a collection, and it has been possible only within collections that are physically located together. But once those items are online, in a form that is word-searchable, one has a mass that is accessible to machine searching, not the more arduous human researching. Theoretically, when many related collections exist together on the Web, they create a significantly more meaningful source than these same collections would if not linked electronically. In reality, achieving such a contextual mass across institutional boundaries will remain elusive as long as the collections are not interoperable.

For archival-type collections, which are not necessarily text based and are usually under looser bibliographical control than are published works, the amount of material needed to get a critical mass can defy the imagination, or at least challenge the budget. If a collection is too large to digitize—for example, a photo morgue or institutional records—staff may choose to digitize a portion that represents the strengths of the collection. But what portion? How much is enough? These are subjective decisions, and they are answered differently by different libraries. In the public libraries, with no faculty to provide advice, the decisions have been made by the curatorial staff.

The California Digital Library (CDL) has inaugurated a project, called California Cultures, designed to make accessible a "critical mass of source materials to support research and teaching." Much of this documentation will reflect the social life, culture, and commerce of ethnic groups in California". The collection will comprise about 18,000 images. The California Digital Library sees collaboration as a key element in scalability. Because of funding and governance issues, the CDL believes that it must foster a sense of ownership and responsibility for these collections among creators statewide, locality by locality.

The role of scholars in selecting a defined set of contextually meaningful sources often works well for published items in certain disciplines. Agriculture and mathematics are examples where scholars have been able to come up with a list of so-called core literature that is amenable to comprehensive digitization. By way of contrast, curators may do a better job in selecting from special collections of unpublished materials—musical manuscripts, photo archives, personal papers—than scholars do. These are materials with which only curatorial staff members are sufficiently familiar to make selection decisions. While there are exceptions to this rule, the sheer quantity of materials from which to select often makes the involvement of scholars in all decisions impractical and hence unscalable. Scholars tend to have a different concept of the critical mass than do librarians.

Intellectual Control and Data Management

The scarcity of cataloging or description that can be quickly and cheaply converted into metadata is often a decisive factor in excluding a collection from digitization. Given that creating metadata is more expensive than is the actual scanning, it is necessary to take advantage of existing metadata—that is, cataloging. Often, money to digitize comes with promises by library directors that they will put up several thousand—even million—images. This is a daunting pledge.

These libraries have put enormous resources into creating descriptions, exhibitions, finding aids, and published catalogs of prized institutional holdings. One can assume that a collection that has been exhibited or made the subject of a published illustrated catalog has demonstrated research and cultural value. Some collections that are supported by endowments can make the transition to digital access more easily than can others, because funds may be available for this within the terms of the gift.

There are a number of grant applications that not only build the cost of metadata creation into the digitization project but also appear to be driven in part by a long-standing desire on the part of a library finally to get certain special collections under bibliographical control. It can be quite difficult, however, to harmonize descriptive practices that were prevalent 40 years ago with what is required today. The expansive bibliographical essays that once were standard for describing special collections need quite a bit of editing to make them into useful metadata. It is not simply a question of standards, which have always been problematic in special collections.

The problem is that people research and read differently on the Web than they do when sitting with an illustrated catalog or finding aid at a reading desk. Descriptive practices need to be reconceptualized for presentation online. This reconceptualization process is several years off, since we have as yet no basis for understanding how people use special collections online. For monographs and serials, genres for which the MARC record was originally devised and which is a standard well understood, retooling catalog records need not be complicated or expensive.

For materials that are published but not primarily text based, such as photographs, posters, recorded speech, or musical interpretations, the MARC record has noted limitations and those tend to be accentuated in the online environment. Unpublished materials share this dichotomy of descriptive practice between textual and nontextual. For institutions that have chosen to put their special collections online, tough decisions must be made about how much information can be created in the most cost-effective way. In some cases, rekeying or OCR can be used to produce a searchable text in lieu of creating subject access. For handwritten documents, non-Roman scripts, and audio and visual resources, searching remains a problem.

The context for interpretation needs to be far more explicit in the online environment than in the analog realm. It is interesting to think about why that is so. Are librarians creating too much descriptive material for online presentation of those collections that have successfully been served in reading rooms with no such level of description, or is it too little? Are librarians assuming that the level of sophistication or patience of the online user is far lower than that of the onsite researcher? It is commonly assumed that an online patron will not use a source, no matter how valuable, if it is accompanied by minimal-level description. This assumption may be well founded in principle, and it is certainly true that the deeper and more structured the description, the likelier it is that the item will be found through the various searching protocols most in use.

But by removing research collections from the context in which they have traditionally been used—the reading room—one also removes the reference staff who can guide the patron through the maze of retrieval and advise about related sources. Materials that the public has had little experience using are now readily available online. If patrons lack certain research skills, the resources will remain inaccessible to them. The ease of finding digitized items on library Web sites varies. A few sites are constructed in a way that makes finding digitized collections almost impossible for people who do not already know they exist.

Much less has been written about how to plan for the access to and preservation of digitally reformatted collections over time than about how to select materials for digitization. This is partly because we know nothing certain about maintaining digital assets over the long haul. We have learned a great deal as a result of failed or deeply flawed efforts—those of the "We'll never do that again!" variety told of some projects to reformat information onto CDs, for example—but such lessons tend to be only informally communicated. Exceptions include the University of Michigan, where one library that has a clear view of what role digitization plays—that of collection management and preservation—has developed and published preservation policies that support those goals.

The CDL is also an exception, perhaps because, as a central repository, establishing standards and best practices to which its contributors must adhere is paramount to building confidence as well as collections. Harvard University has published information about its plans for a digital repository, and Cornell has adopted policies for "perpetual care" of digital assets. In reality, however, many libraries have created digital surrogates for access purposes and have no strategic interest in maintaining them as carefully as they would have if they had created those files to serve as replacements. Nonetheless, at this point libraries are uncomfortable admitting that they have a limited commitment to many of their surrogates, should push come to shove. Those who are creating surrogates for access purposes alone still declare an interest in maintaining those surrogates as long as they can because the original investment in the creation of digital files has created something of enormous value to their patrons.

Moreover, the cost of having to re-create those surrogates and the physical stress it might impose on the source materials argue for maintaining those files as long as possible. The mechanism for long-term management of digital surrogates is theoretically no different from that for management of born-digital assets. While refreshment and migration of digital collections have occurred in many libraries, the protocols and policies for preservation are clearly still under development.

Many libraries have been sensitized to the fact that loss can be simple and catastrophic, beginning with the wrong choice of (proprietary) hardware, software, or medium on which to encode information and ending with negligent management of metadata. The Y2K threat that libraries faced in 1999 has led to systemic improvements in many cases. Not only did institutions become aware of how deleterious it is to allow different software to proliferate but they also developed disaster-preparedness plans. Many received funds for infrastructure upgrades that might have been awarded much later, or not at all, were it not for the sense of urgency that the coming of Y2K provided.

Libraries are anticipating the day when they must develop strategies for handling digital objects that faculty are creating without the involvement of the library. These are the often-elaborate constructions done by individual scholars or groups of collaborators that the library hears about only after the critical choices of hardware, software, and metadata have been made, often by people wholly unaware of the problems of long-term access to digital media. An increasing number of library managers have expressed concern about the digitized materials created by faculty that are "more than a Web site" yet less, often far less, than what the library would choose to accession and preserve.

While libraries acknowledge that this is a growing problem, none has been forced to do much about it yet, and thoughts about how to deal with faculty projects are just now evolving. Predictably, those that are collection-driven in approach are working to build a system for selecting what the library wishes to accession to its permanent collections. Most libraries recognize that the collections they now offer online require a different type of user support than that which they have traditionally given visitors to their reading rooms. In many cases, user support has been developed for "digital collections" or "digital resources," terms that almost invariably denote born-digital (licensed) materials.

Libraries have been keeping careful track of gate counts, for example, but when these counts go up or go down, what conclusion can one draw about the effect of online resources on use of on-site resources? Most libraries report having classes and other instructional options available for students and faculty. Some librarians report that instruction is not really necessary for undergraduates, who are quite used to looking first online, but that general orientations to library collections are needed more than ever.

7

Copyright Libraries

Copyright libraries have a statutory obligation to maintain and provide access to certain classes of non-unique information objects whose deposit is legally prescribed and enforced upon the objects' producers. Copyright libraries may supplement these core holdings through voluntary deposit and through acquisition (either through subscription or purchase), both to support their national roles in preservation and to fulfill other functions such as the provision of information both on site and through inter-library loan. Their use of the framework is governed by mandated deposit, the need to influence how publishers create electronic information objects, their orientation toward long-term retention and preservation of information which are covered by legal deposit materials and toward permitting the (possibly limited) secondary use of those materials. It is important to note, however that legal requirements to deposit electronic publications with copyright libraries is relatively new and to date, only a small number of countries have appropriate legislation in place.

Data Creation and Collection Development

Data Creation

Copyright libraries are expected to retain publications which are deposited under the terms of legal deposit legislation for the dual purposes of preservation and access. As such, they must be prepared to accession electronic publications combining different forms of data such as images and text and which can be hyper-linked to other resources. They are deposited in a wide variety of different formats, on a similarly wide range of media, and which are provided with varying degrees of documentation. In this respect, copyright libraries share certain characteristics with the data banks. Unlike the data banks which preserve data at the bit-stream level and leave content considerations to the depositor, the copyright library must also confront issues pertaining to the preservation and re-use of a data resource's content, appearance, and functionality. That is, it is or will be required to ensure that the content, appearance, and functionality of deposited electronic publications can be meaningfully rep resented on and accessed from contemporary hardware and software platforms. In this respect, the copyright library shares characteristics in common with the institutional and academic data archives.

Unlike the archives which ensure that the content of its data holdings remain viable by exercising some direct influence over how those holdings are created or by restructuring or enriching those holdings at accession, the copyright library exerts no such influence and the format and type of data deposited may mitigate against restructuring at accession. Additional constraints may be imposed upon the copyright library by the terms and conditions of legal deposit. Where those conditions permits only single user access to deposited holdings, for example, certain strategies for data management and access which may be preferable owing to their efficiency and cost effectiveness (those relying on centralised storage of network accessible information) may be prohibited.

Of course, the difficulties confronted by the copyright library are less severe where electronic publications are acquired through voluntary deposit or through purchase or subscription. There the copyright library may develop and employ selection criteria to ensure that only those materials are accessioned which can be managed effectively. Accordingly, the copyright library is or will be compelled to implement the widest possible range of data preservation and access strategies appropriate to the diverse preservation and access requirements imposed by the diverse characteristics of its electronic publications.

Given their lack of any formal influence over electronic publishers whose products are or are likely to be covered by legal deposit legislation, copyright libraries will typically:

— demonstrate an interest in reserving the right to select from amongst deposited electronic publications those which they will retain for the purposes of preservation and/or access;

— demonstrate a significant interest in working together with publishers to identify and promote those standards and best practice which help to ensure that electronic publications can be migrated across platforms and between individuals at minimal cost and with minimal loss of information content;

— demonstrate a significant interest in working together with government to ensure that the preservation and access obligations that are or may be imposed upon the library by legislation requiring the deposit of electronic publications are (a) achievable and (b) adequately resourced.

Data Acquisition

The selection process is likely to involve both content and technical criteria. Content criteria may reflect those used in print materials and differ depending upon whether accessions are to be acquired by voluntary deposit, by purchase/ subscription, or by mandatory deposit (where selectivity of such materials is permitted). Additional technical criteria may also be applied to electronic publication as a means of assessing the extent to which they may be retained and made accessible to readers in light of any technical and financial constraints. Mechanisms used to identify and claim print publications (comprehensive lists based on standardised and unique publication identifiers, regularised information exchanges with appropriate copyright and other agencies, publishers awareness of the copyright library's mission with regard to deposit) were either non-existent or poorly developed for electronic ones. Where on-line publications were concerned, Internet search engines offered only moderate assistance in the identification of appropriate electronic materials.

"De-selection" is likely to reflect library retention policies as they apply to particular collection levels and classes of objects within its collection. The British Library's retention policy for example, recognises three categories of object: heritage and unique; long-term research; and current (including duplicates etc.). The on-line publications in the PANDORA archive are equivalent to the heritage and unique level at the British Library and reflect the NLA's underlying philosophy for all publications - to ensure comprehensive collections of Australian materials are preserved in perpetuity. With regard to digital on-line publications, the NLA looks towards a co-operative national model where the State and possibly other libraries (e.g. large university libraries) and organisations will share responsibility within a national framework for archiving and providing access to electronic publications. The SCOAP guidelines make a contribution toward the development of that framework (as, indeed, does the PANDORA project which acts in some respects as a test case) and provide selection criteria. Generally, content criteria prevail and there is no discrimination against on-line publications on the grounds of their technical formats (though see below) or of the costs involved in accessioning and preserving such materials.

Implementing the guide-lines proved to be more resource intensive than originally expected. Identifying on-line publications was an initial hurdle, and only moderate help was available from Internet search engines and logically structured gateways. The evaluation of publications once discovered was also resource intensive, requiring detailed evaluation of their content and technical characteristics. Given the inherent diversity of electronic publications, no single evaluative method could be employed - the information required to support it could be available (if at all) in different places and accessible via different means with different publications.

Data Management

In the copyright library, data storage and data structuring reflects preservation and access strategies. With PANDORA, data are structured as they are accessioned. In order that their look, feel, and content may be preserved. The fact that PANDORA is dealing with web-based publications whose construction and presentation are constrained by the web and by the formats and structures appropriate to it is a further deterrent. In most cases, data prepared for web-based delivery are prepared according to de jure or de facto standards which are presently widely recognised by appropriate software.

Data may be restructured under the following circumstances. Where published data are compressed, PANDORA will normally ask for utilities used by the publishers to uncompress them so they may be stored in the archive in an uncompressed format. Where published materials are "locked", PANDORA will normally ask that publishers provide that archive versions be "unlocked" versions for the archive. Where published data exist in idiosyncratic formats or are presented in ways which would make archived versions difficult to access or use, PANDORA may consider restructuring them. Note that cost considerations involved in accessioning and archiving a data resource would neither force nor inhibit data restructuring.

With CDs' the difficulties involved in determining their architecture makes emulation the most appropriate long-term preservation strategy. Migration is likely to be considered as a potentially less costly option for those publications whose architecture is known and relatively simple. In either case, CD publications would have to be restructured periodically to reflect changing technical regimes; comprehensively so where emulation is concerned. In addition, all CD publications will need to be copied from time to time onto newer CD platforms given their (often indeterminate) volatility.

Use considerations also apply, particularly where legal deposit legislation imposed the same single-user access constraints on electronic publications that are imposed upon printed ones. In such cases, readers may require physical access to the CD for use in a reader-accessible computer. Consequently, the physical location of a CD may become a storage issue as frequently used CDs would arguably need to be housed in proximity to an appropriately equipped reading room.

Data Documentation and Description

Cataloguing standards used by the copyright library for electronic publications are likely to reflect those used with printed ones, and thus to rely upon MARC and accompanying standards (e.g. in the English speaking world at any rate, on Anglo-American Cataloguing Rules, Library of Congress Subject Headings, and on the Dewey Decimal Classification system). The approach promises to integrate information about relatively new digital information objects with that already available for printed ones, an d thus to fulfill a national bibliographic function which is typically performed by the copyright library.

The adoption of MARC has also been validated by research, successful thus far, into the use of MARC extensions to document distinctive characteristic s of digital information objects. Cataloguing practices are also likely to continue little changed with digital objects, with records generated by in-house staff, though some may be requested from publishers by cataloguing staff, notably about an electronic publication's technical characteristics, and, where on-line publications are concerned about patterns of publication, terms and condition of use, etc.

PANDORA prepares a full MARC record for archived publications and enters it onto the National Bibliographic Database. A catalogue record is also entered into the NLA's web-accessible OPAC through which users have integrated access to the NLA's diverse and mixed media holdings. In addition, a title entry pages are manually created for archived publications providing information about the publication, including a copyright statement, terms and conditions of use, and, where serials are concerned, information about the number of issues and their pattern of publication. Critically, the title entry page also provides a link to the publishers' home page encouraging users to use the current rather than the archived version.

In its CD-ROM demonstrator project, the BL found that UKMARC, AACR2, Library of Congress Subject headings and Dewey Decimal classification were appropriate and that records could be generated for CD-ROM's in about twice the time required for printed publications, principally owing to the need to read the CDs (and thus to load and then de-install appropriate software).

Data Preservation

Preservation strategies appropriate for electronic publications are substantially different than those which are appropriate for books, not least of all because such strategies need to be worked out when (even before) an electronic publication is accessioned on the basis of the publication's technical characteristics which are not always transparent or even available. Inevitably, the copyright library will have to adopt a range of different strategies as appropriate to the diverse kinds of electronic publications in their collections, and to the terms and conditions imposed on the library with regard to their maintenance and use. Migration may be preferred as a least costly option with data resources for which it is appropriate. Emulation will also be required particularly with electronic publications produced in non-standard and undocumented proprietary formats and/or those implementing proprietary software or hardware. There are a number of outstanding concerns, however:

— about the prospects for preserving some electronic publications, for example those fitted with hardware or software keys which time out and render the electronic publication inaccessible after a given period of time;

— about the physical security of items such as CD-ROMs which need to be handled physically by readers (e.g. those whose content cannot be migrated onto a central computing server for network distribution), and which, as such might be removed from the library or damaged through use;

— about the absence of clear cost models for any of the preservation strategies (but particularly for emulation) that the copyright library is likely to be required to adopt given the extensively diverse electronic publications that will be deposited;

— about the relative shortage of information about financial resources likely to be available in the longer term as necessary to determining appropriate and achievable preservation strategies for electronic publications accessioned now.

With regard to preservation procedures, copyright libraries may currently lack the large-scale infrastructure needed for mass computer storage and access available at the data banks and the institutional archives reflecting their historic orientation t o paper-based materials and other artefacts. The development of that infrastructure or of partnerships with agencies which maintain it may become an issue for copyright libraries in future.

PANDORA has adopted both short-term and long-term preservation strategies which are worked out for electronic publications based upon the technical evaluation which takes place before accession. Short term strategies involve routine and cumulative back -up of the on-line filestore to DLT cartridges. Long term strategies involves data migration through changing technological regimes. There are also potential roles for technology preservation and for emulation where on-line publications are only accessible via proprietary (non-third-party) software developed for and used by the publisher. In these cases, PANDORA would seek to work with the publisher to ensure that the software is migrated across changing technological regimes or that the look, feel, and content of the publication can otherwise be emulated.

The preservation of CD-ROMs has already been addressed above. Migration may be appropriate for CDs with relatively simple data architectures. Most, however, are likely to require emulation. Given the volatile nature of many CD-ROMs as data storage media over the longer-term, all CD publications will need periodically to be copied onto new discs.

Remote Management

Remote management may become an issue for copyright libraries, particularly where electronic publications covered by legal deposit legislation are dynamic, that is, available from a third-party supplier in a form which is constantly being amended and updated. The serial publications archived by the PANDORA project are examples of dynamic publications. Others include on-line reference materials such as bibliographic databases, which are periodically updated with new entries. Another example is the national large-scale mapping of the UK held in the Ordnance Survey's National Topographic Database. The Ordnance Survey is the UK's national mapping agency and previously produced traditional printed editions of large-scale maps. With computerisation, maps are now produced on demand for customers and the database is constantly updated with new survey information.

There are at least two strategies for dealing with such data as are covered by legal deposit legislation. One, adopted by PANDORA with its serial publications, is to create an archive copy of new issues as they are added to the serial. If applied to dynamic databases, the same strategy would entail the periodic creation of snapshots of the data resource for archival storage. A second strategy is to manage the data remotely according to agreements struck between the copyright library and the third-party data supplier. In such cases, the academic data archive's approach to remote data management may be instructive.

Data Use

Data use in the copyright library is likely to reflect and to integrate with practices pertaining to printed publications. It will also be contingent upon terms and conditions of use imposed by depositors or, where publications are deposited under copyright legislation by the terms worked out between the libraries, government, and publishers. Supporting access to electronic publications also make a range of new demands on the copyright libraries. Reading rooms need to be equipped with appropriately enabled workstations and the workstations need to be supported technically. Users will require adequate documentation and support services and possibly even training given the broad public which the library generally serves.

The PANDORA project makes information about its archived holdings accessible from the OPAC which supplies a hypertext link from the OPAC record to archived holdings' title entry pages which themselves encourage users to link to the publishers' site where this is still available on line. The holdings are made available via the Internet and web browsers, either from the publishers' site (the preferred port of entry for users) or the archive mirror of them.

Users are supported with information on the title entry pages and with on-line information made available by PANDORA about the archive and its use. Information about the archive and its activities is currently supplied to potential depositors individually by email, though formal depositors' guidelines or information packs may be considered. With CD-ROMs, usage will be dependent upon what a library will be permitted to do by national legislation or rights holders in terms of providing networked or single access as with printed books. Single use can introduce administrative problems for monitoring users, usage, and ensuring non-disappearance of or damage to portable format e publications. There are also implications for reader services in terms of staff, equipment, training, technical support, user support, storage, and retrieval for users.

Rights Management

For the copyright library, rights management practices are likely to be prescribed by any copyright legislation and will reflect the extensive discussions which will take place between government, publishers, and the copyright libraries that inform that legislation. In general, rights management practices will need to mediate between publishers who may seek to restrict access to deposited materials, users who may seek to extend access to published materials, and the copyright library which may seek some influence over the construction and management of copyright materials in order to ensure that they can be preserved over the longer term and made accessible to end users under what ever terms and conditions ultimately apply.

8

Methods and Practices of Digital Library

As the needs and expectations of library users change in the digital environment, libraries are trying to find the best ways to define their user communities, understand what they value, and evolve digital library collections and services to meet their demands. In part, this effort requires a closer, more formal look at how library patrons use and respond to online collections and services.

Libraries are struggling to find the right measures on which to base their decisions. Working with data is essential, time-consuming, and costly—so costly that libraries are beginning to question, and in some cases even measure, the costs and benefits of gathering and analyzing different data. Respondents know that they need new measures and composite measures to capture the extent of their activities in both the digital and traditional realms. The libraries are considering, beginning, or completing needs assessments of the data they currently gather, or think they should gather, for internal and external purposes.

How can libraries measure what they do, how much they do, or how well they do, when the boundaries keep changing? Developing skills to gather, analyze, interpret, present, and use data. Even if libraries gather the right measures for their purposes, developing the requisite skills to analyze, interpret, present, and use the data are separate challenges. Sampling and research methods are available to recruit research subjects and assess use and usability of the digital library, which methods are best suited for which purposes, and how to analyze, interpret, present, and use the quantitative and qualitative data they gather to make effective decisions and strategic plans.

Planning Assessment

Planning assessment from conception through follow-up also presents challenges. Ideally, the research process should flow seamlessly—from deciding to gather data to developing and implementing plans to use the data. People assigned responsibility for certain steps in the process may lack the requisite skills. Staff turnover or competing priorities may intervene. Respondents also made it clear that the more people involved in the research process, the longer it takes. The longer the process takes, the more likely it is that the results will be out of date, momentum will be lost, or other phenomena will intrude before the results are implemented.

Organizing assessment as a core activity. At some institutions, user studies are centralized and performed by recently hired experts in the field. At others, user studies are decentralized and performed systemwide; they involve efforts to teach librarians and staff throughout the organization how to conduct research using different methods. Still other institutions, sparked by the interests of different personnel, take an ad hoc approach to user studies. A few libraries have established usability testing programmes and laboratories. If the goal is a culture of assessment, then making assessment a core activity and allocating human and financial resources to it is essential. The key is not how a study is organized, but that it is organized and supported by commitment from administrators and librarians.

Compiling and Managing

Libraries need a simple way to record and analyze quantitative and qualitative data and to generate statistical reports and trend lines. Development of management information system (MIS) to compile and manage statistical data. They are wrestling with questions about how long data should be kept, how data should be archived, and whether one system can or should manage data from different kinds of assessments. Existing systems typically have a limited scope. For example, one site has a homegrown desktop reporting tool that enables library staff to generate ad hoc reports from data extracted and to update them regularly from the integrated library system.

Users can query the data and run cross-tabulations. The tool is used for a variety of purposes, including analysis of collection development, materials expenditures, and the productivity of the cataloging department. Reports can be printed, saved, or imported into spreadsheets or other applications for further analysis or manipulation. New systems being developed appear to be more comprehensive; for example, they attempt to assemble statistical data from all library departments. The ability to conduct cross-tabulations of data from different departments and easily generate graphics and multiyear trend lines are important features of the new systems.

Acquiring sufficient information about the environment to understand trends in library use. Emerging new measures will assess how library use is changing in the networked environment, but these measures will not explain why library use is changing. Academic libraries need to know how students and faculty find information, what resources they use that the libraries do not provide, why they use these resources, and what they do with the information after they find it. This knowledge would provide a context for interpreting existing data on shifting patterns of library use and facilitate the development of collections, services, and tools that better meet user needs and expectations. Library user studies naturally focus on the use and usability of library collections, services, and Web sites. The larger environment remains unexplored.

User Studies

User studies reflecting the user-centered focus of their operations. One respondent referred to the results of user studies as "outcome" measures because, although they do not measure the impact of library use on student learning or faculty research, they do indicate the impact of library services, collections, facilities, and staff on user experiences and perceptions. Some take an ad hoc approach; others use a more systematic approach. Some sites have dedicated staff experts in research methodologies who conduct user studies; others train staff throughout the libraries to conduct user studies. Some libraries take both approaches. Some have consulted experts on their campuses or contracted with commercial firms to develop research instruments and analyze the results.

Libraries that conduct user studies use spreadsheet, database, or statistical analysis software to manage and analyze the data. In the absence of standard instruments, guidelines, or best practices, institutions either adapt published efforts to local circumstances or make their own. Learning how to prepare research instruments, analyze and interpret the data, and use the results is a slow process. Unfortunately, however, the ability to quickly apply research results is often essential, because the environment changes quickly and results go out of date.

Libraries are conducting many user studies employing a variety of research methods. The results of these studies run the gamut: they may reinforce librarian understanding of what users need, like, or expect; challenge librarian assumptions about what people want; or provide conflicting, ambiguous, misleading, or incomplete information that requires follow-up research to resolve or interpret. Multiple research methods may be required to understand fully and corroborate research results. This exacerbates an already complicated situation and can frustrate staff. Resources may not be available to conduct follow-up studies immediately.

In other cases, new priorities emerge that make the initial study results no longer applicable; in such a case, any attempt at follow-up is worthless. Moreover, even when research data have been swiftly analyzed, interpreting the results and deciding how to apply them may be slowed if many people are involved in the process or if the results challenge long-held assumptions and preferences of librarians. Finally, even when a plan to use the results is in hand, implementation may pose a stumbling block. The longer the entire research process takes, from conception to implementing the results, the more likely the loss of momentum and conflict with other priorities, and the greater the risk that the process will break down and the effort will be wasted. The issue appears to be related to the internal organization and support for the library's assessment effort.

Survey Questionnaire

Survey questionnaires are self-administered interviews in which the instructions and questions are sufficiently complete and intelligible for respondents to act as their own interviewers. The questions are simply stated and carefully articulated to accomplish the purpose for which the survey is being conducted. Survey questions typically force respondents to choose from among alternative answers provided or to rank or rate items provided. Such questions enable a simple quantitative analysis of the responses. Surveys can also ask open-ended questions to gather qualitative comments from the respondents.

Surveys are an effective way to gather information about respondents' previous or current behaviors, attitudes, beliefs, and feelings. They are the preferred method to gather information about sensitive topics because respondents are less likely to try to please the researcher or to feel pressured to provide socially acceptable responses than they would in a face-to-face interview. Surveys are an effective method to identify problem areas and, if repeated over time, to identify trends. Surveys cannot, however, establish cause-effect relationships, and the information they gather reveals little if anything about contextual factors affecting the respondents. Additional research is usually required to gather the information needed to determine how to solve the problems identified in a survey.

The primary advantage of survey questionnaires is economy. Surveys enable researchers to collect data from large numbers of respondents in relatively short periods of time at relatively low cost. Surveys also give respondents time to think about the questions before answering and often do not require respondents to complete the survey in one sitting. The primary disadvantage of survey questionnaires is that they must be simple, impersonal, and relatively brief. If the survey is too long or complex, respondents may get tired and hurriedly answer or skip questions.

Instructions and questions must be carefully worded in language meaningful to the respondents, because no interviewer is present to clarify the questions or probe respondents for additional information. Finally, it is possible that someone other than the selected respondent may complete the survey. This can skew the results from carefully selected samples. When necessary, survey instructions may explicitly ask that no one complete the survey other than the person for whom it is intended. Libraries have conducted surveys to assess the following:

— Patterns, frequency, ease, and success of use

— User needs, expectations, perspectives, priorities, and preferences for library collections, services, and systems

— User satisfaction with vendor products, library collections, services, staff, and Web sites

— Service quality

— Shifts in user attitude and opinion

— Relevance of collections or services to the curriculum

A few respondents reported conducting surveys as a way to market their collections and services; others commented that this was an inappropriate use of survey research. One respondent referred to this type of survey as "push polling" and stated that there were easier, more appropriate ways than this to market what the library offers.

The data gathered from surveys are used to inform decision making and strategic planning related to the allocation of financial and human resources and to the organization of library units. Survey data also serve political purposes. They are used in presentations to faculty senates, deans' councils, and library advisory boards as a means to bolster support for changes in library practice. They are also used in grant proposals and other requests for funding.

Libraries conduct some surveys routinely; these include annual surveys of general library use and user priorities and satisfaction. Other surveys are conducted sporadically; in this category might be, for example, a survey to determine user satisfaction with laptop-lending programmes. The library administrator's approval is generally required for larger, more formal, and routine surveys. Smaller, sporadic, less expensive surveys are conducted at the discretion of middle managers. Once the decision has been made to conduct a survey, libraries convene a small group of librarians or staff to prepare the survey instructions and questionnaire, determine the format of the survey (for example, print, e-mail, Web-based), choose the sampling method, identify the demographic groups appropriate for the research purpose, determine how many participants to recruit in each group and decide how to recruit them, and plan the budget and timetable for gathering, analyzing, interpreting, and applying the data.

Different procedures are followed for formal surveys than for small surveys. The former require more work. Because few libraries employ survey experts, a group preparing a formal survey might consult with survey experts on campus to ensure that the questions it has drafted will gather the information needed. The group might consult with a statistician on campus to ensure that it recruits enough participants to gather statistically significant results. When a survey is deemed to be extremely important and financial resources are available, an external consulting or research firm might be hired.

If the survey is to be conducted in-house, time and financial constraints and the skills of library staff influence the choice of survey format. Paper surveys are slow and expensive to conduct. Follow-up may be needed to ensure an adequate response rate. Respondents are not required to complete them in one sitting; for this reason, paper surveys may be longer than electronic surveys. E-mail surveys are less expensive than paper surveys; otherwise, their advantages are similar.

Web-based surveys might be the least expensive to conduct, particularly if scripts are available to analyze the results automatically. They also offer several other advantages. For example, they can be edited up to the last minute, and the capabilities of the Web enable sophisticated branching and multimedia surveys, which are difficult or even impossible, in other formats. Both Web and e-mail surveys are easier to ignore than are paper surveys, and they assume participants have computer access.

Web surveys have the further disadvantage that they must be completed in one sitting, which means they must be relatively short. They also require HTML skills to prepare and, if results are to be analyzed automatically, programming skills. Whether Web-based surveys increase response rate is not known. One DLF library reported conducting a survey in both e-mail and Web formats. An equal number of respondents chose to complete the survey in each format.

Considerable time and effort should be spent on preparing the content and presentation of surveys. Instructions and questions must be carefully and unambiguously worded and presented in a layout that is easy to read. If not, results will be inaccurate or difficult or impossible to interpret, worse yet, participants may not complete the survey. The choice of format affects the amount of control libraries have over the presentation or appearance of the survey. Print offers the most control; with e-mail and Web-based formats, there is no way for the library to know exactly what the survey will look like when it is viewed using different e-mail programmes or Web browsers. The group preparing e-mail or Web surveys might find it helpful to view the survey using e-mail programmes and Web browsers available on campus to ensure that the presentation is attractive and intelligible.

Libraries pilot test survey instructions and questions with a few users and revise them on the basis of test results to solve problems with vocabulary, wording, and the layout or sequence of the questions. Pilot tests also indicate the length of time required to complete a survey. Libraries appear to have ballpark estimates for how long it should take to complete their surveys. If the time it takes participants to complete the survey in the pilot tests exceeds this figure, questions might be omitted. The survey instructions include the estimated time required to complete the survey.

Using different approaches to distribute or provide access to surveys, based on the sampling method and survey format. For example, when recruiting volunteers to take Web-based surveys, the survey might automatically pop up when users display the library home page or click the exit button on the online public access catalog (OPAC). Alternatively, a button or link on the home page might provide access to the survey. Posters or flyers might advertise the URL of a Web-based survey or, if a more carefully selected sample is needed, an e-mail address to contact to indicate interest in participating. Paper surveys may be made available in trays or handed to library users. With more carefully selected sample populations, e-mail containing log-in information to do a Web-based survey, or the e-mail or paper survey itself, is sent to the targeted sample. Paper surveys can be distributed as e-mail enclosures or via campus or U.S. mail. DLF respondents indicated that all of these methods worked well.

Libraries use spreadsheet or statistical software to analyze the quantitative responses to surveys. Cross-tabulations are conducted to discover whether different user groups responded to the questions differently; for example, to discover whether the priorities of undergraduate students are different from those of graduate students or faculty. Some libraries compare the distribution of survey respondents with the demographics of the campus to determine whether the distribution of user groups in their sample is representative of the campus population. A few libraries have used content analysis software to analyze the responses to open-ended questions.

Libraries share survey results with the people empowered to decide how those results will be applied. The formality of the survey and the sample size also determine who will see the results and participate in interpreting them and determining how they will be used. High-profile, potentially contentious survey topics or research purposes tend to be treated more formally. They entail the use of larger samples and generate more interest. Survey results of user satisfaction with the library Web site might be presented to the library governing council, which will decide how the results will be used. Data from more informal surveys might be shared strictly within the department that conducted the survey.

For example, the results of a survey of user satisfaction with the laptop-lending programme might be presented to the department, whose members will then decide whether additional software applications should be provided on the laptops. Striking or significant results from a survey of any size seem to bubble up to the attention of library administrators, particularly if follow-up might have financial or operational implications or require interdepartmental cooperation. For example, results of a survey of reference service that suggest that users would be better served by longer reference desk hours or staffing with systems office personnel in addition to reference librarians should be brought to the addition of library administration.

Survey data might also be shared with university administrators, faculty senates, library advisory boards, and similar groups, to win or bolster support for changing directions in library strategic planning or to support requests for additional funding. Multiyear trends are often included in annual reports. The results are also presented at conferences and published. Although survey results often confirm expectations and validate what the library is doing, sometimes the results are surprising. In this case, they may precipitate changes in library services, user interfaces, or plans.

Costs and Benefits of Surveys

General surveys are not very helpful. Broad surveys of library collections and services do provide baseline data and, if the same questions are repeated in subsequent surveys, offer longitudinal data to track changing patterns of use. However, such surveys are time-consuming and expensive to prepare, conduct, and interpret. Getting people to complete them is difficult. The results are shallow and require follow-up research. Some libraries believe the costs of such surveys exceed the benefits and that important usage trends can be tracked more cost-effectively using transaction log analysis.

Point-of-use surveys that focus on a specific subject, tool, or product work as well as, or better than, general surveys. They are quicker to prepare and conduct, easier to interpret, and more cost-effective than broad surveys. However, they must be repeated periodically to assess trends, and they, too, frequently require follow-up research.

User satisfaction surveys can reveal problem areas, but they do not provide enough information to solve the problems.

Service quality surveys, based on the gap model (which measures the "gap" or difference between users' perceptions of excellent service and their perceptions of the service they received), are preferred because they provide enough information to plan service improvements. Unfortunately, service quality surveys are much more expensive to conduct than user satisfaction surveys.

Frequency of Surveys

Surveys are concern about their number and frequency. Over-surveying can decrease participation and make it more difficult to recruit participants. When the number of completed surveys is very small, the results are meaningless. Conducting surveys as a way to market library resources might exacerbate the problem.

Composing Survey Questions

The success of a survey depends on the quality and precision of the questions asked—their wording, presentation, and appropriateness to the research purpose. In the absence of in-house survey expertise, adequate training, or consultation with an expert, library surveys often contain ambiguous or inaccurate questions. In the worst cases, the survey results are meaningless and the survey must be entirely revised and conducted again the following year. More likely, the problem applies to particular questions rather than to the entire survey.

Composing well-worded survey questions requires a sense of what respondents know and how they are likely to respond. DLF respondents reported the following examples. A survey conducted to assess interface design based on heuristic principles did not work well, probably because the respondents lacked the knowledge and skills necessary to apply heuristic principles to interface design. Surveys that ask respondents to specify the priority of each service or collection in a list yield results where everything is simply ranked either "high" or "low," which is not particularly informative.

Similarly, surveys that ask respondents how often they use a service or collection yield results of either "always use" or "never use." Where it is desirable to compare or contrast collections or services, it is important to require users to rank the relative priority of services or collections and to rank the relative frequency of use. Otherwise, interpreting the results will be difficult. Asking open-ended questions and soliciting comments can also be problematic. Many respondents will not take the time to write answers or comments. If they do, the information they provide can offer significant insights into user perceptions, needs, and expectations.

A few libraries have attempted to automate the process using content analysis software, but none of them was pleased with the results. Perhaps the problem is trying to extract quantitative results from qualitative data. The preferred approach appears to be to limit the number of open-ended questions and analyze them manually by developing conceptual categories based on the content of the comments. Ideally, the categories would be mutually exclusive and exhaustive. After the comments are coded into the categories, the gist would be extracted and, if possible, associated with the quantitative results of the survey.

Lack of Analysis

Theoretically, the process is clear: prepare the survey, conduct the survey, analyze and interpret the results, decide how to apply them, and implement the plan. In reality, the process frequently breaks down after the survey is conducted, regardless of how carefully it was prepared or how many hundreds of respondents completed it. Survey results were analyzed and recommendations made, but nothing happened after that. No one knew, or felt comfortable enough to mention, who dropped the ball. No one claimed that changes in personnel were instrumental in the failure to analyze or apply the survey results. Instead, they focused on the impact this has on the morale of library staff and users. Conducting research creates expectations; people expect results. Faculty members in particular are not likely to participate in library research studies if they never see results. Library staff members are unlikely to want to serve on committees or task forces formed to conduct studies if the results are never applied.

The problem could be loss of momentum and commitment, but it could also be lack of skill. Just as preparing survey questions requires specific skills, so too do analysis, interpretation, and application of survey results. Libraries appear to be slow in acquiring the skills needed to use survey data. The problem is exacerbated when survey results conflict with other data.

Lack of Resources

Paper surveys distributed to a statistically significant sample of a large university community can cost more than $10,000 to prepare, conduct, and analyze. Many libraries cannot afford or choose not to make such an investment. Alternative formats and smaller samples seem to be the preferred approach; however, even these take a considerable amount of time. Furthermore, surveys often fail to provide enough information to enable planners to solve the problems that have been identified.

Libraries might not have the human and financial resources to allocate to follow-up research, or they could simply have run out of momentum. The problem could also be a matter of planning. If the research process is not viewed from conception through application of the results and follow-up testing, the process could likely halt at the point where existing plans end.

Focus Groups

A focus group is an exploratory, guided interview or interactive conversation among seven to ten participants with common interests or characteristics. The purpose of a focus group is to test hypotheses; reveal what beliefs the group holds about a particular product, service, or opportunity and why; or to uncover detailed information about complex issues or behaviors from the group's perspective. Focus group studies entail several such group conversations to identify trends and patterns in perception across groups. Careful analysis of the discussions reveals insights into how each group perceives the topic of discussion.

A focus group interview is typically one to two hours long. A trained moderator guides the conversation using five to ten predetermined questions or key issues prepared as an "interview guide." The questions are open-ended and noncommittal. They are simply stated and carefully articulated. The questions are asked in a specific sequence, but there are no predetermined response categories. The moderator clarifies anything that participants do not understand. The moderator may also ask probing follow-up questions to identify concepts important to the participants, pursue interesting leads, and develop and test hypotheses. In addition to the moderator, one or two observers take detailed notes.

Focus group discussions are audio- or videotaped. Audiotape is less obtrusive and therefore less likely to intimidate the participants. Participants who feel comfortable are likely to talk more than those who are not; for this reason, audiotape and well-trained observers are often preferred to videotape. The observers' notes should be so complete that they can substitute if the tape recorder does not work.

Focus groups are an effective and relatively easy way to gather insight into complex behavior and experience from the participants' perspective. Because they can reveal how groups of people think and feel about a particular topic and why they hold certain opinions, they are good for detecting changes in behavior. Participant responses can not only indicate what is new but also distinguish trends from fads. Interactive discussion among the participants creates synergy and facilitates recall and insight.

A few focus groups can be conducted at relatively low cost. Focus group research can inform the planning and design of new programmes or services, be it a means for evaluating existing programmes or services, and facilitate the development of strategies for improvement and outreach. Focus groups are also helpful as prelude to survey or protocol research; they may be used to identify appropriate language, questions, or tasks, and as follow-up to survey or protocol research to get clarification or explanation of factors influencing survey responses or user behaviors.

The quality of the responses to focus group questions depends on how clearly the questions are asked, the moderator's skills, and the participants' understanding of the goals of the study and what is expected of them. A skilled moderator is critical to the success of a focus group. Moderators must quickly develop rapport with the participant, remain impartial, and keep the discussion moving and focused on the research objectives. They should have background knowledge of the discussion topic and must be able to repress domineering individuals and bring everyone into the conversation. Before the focus group begins, the moderator should observe the participants and, if necessary, strategically seat extremely shy or domineering individuals.

For example, outspoken, opinionated participants should be placed to the immediate left or right of the moderator and quiet-spoken persons must be placed at some distance from them. This enables the moderator to shut out the domineering person simply by turning his or her torso away from the individual. Moderators and observers must avoid making gestures (for example, head nodding) or comments that could bias the results of the study.

Moderators must be carefully selected, because attitude, gender, age, ethnicity, race, religion, and even clothing can trigger stereotypical perceptions in focus group participants and bias the results of the study. If participants do not trust the moderator, are uncomfortable with the other participants, or are not convinced that the study or their role is important, they can give incomplete, inaccurate, or biased information. To facilitate discussion, reduce the risk of discomfort and intimidation, and increase the likelihood that participants will give detailed, accurate responses to the focus group questions, focus groups should be organized so that participants and, in some cases, the moderator are demographically similar.

The selection of demographic participant groupings and focus group moderator should be based on the research purpose, the sensitivity of the topic, and an understanding of the target population. For example, topics related to sexual behavior or preferences suggest conducting separate focus groups for males and females in similar age groups with a moderator of the same age and gender. When the topic is not sensitive and the population is diverse, the research purpose is sufficient to determine the demographic groupings for selecting participants. For example, three focus groups—for undergraduate students, graduate students, and faculty—could be used to test hypotheses about needs or expectations for library resources among these groups.

Mixing students and faculty could intimidate undergraduates. Although homogeneity is important, focus group participants should be sufficiently diverse to allow for contrasting opinions. Ideally, the participants do not know one another. This is because if they do, they tend to form small groups within the focus group and make it harder for the moderator to manage. The primary disadvantage of focus groups is that participants may give false information to please the moderator, stray from the topic, be influenced by peer pressure, or seek a consensus rather than explore ideas.

A dominating or opinionated participant can make more reserved participants hesitant to talk, which could bias the results. In addition, data gathered in focus groups can be difficult to evaluate because such information can be chaotic, qualitative, or emotional rather than objective. The findings should be interpreted at the group level. The small number of participants and frequent use of convenience sampling severely limit the ability to generalize the results of focus groups, and the results cannot be generalized to groups with different demographic characteristics. However, the results are more intelligible and accessible to lay audiences and decision makers than are complex statistical analyses of survey data.

A final disadvantage of focus groups is that they rely heavily on the observational skills of the moderator and observer(s), who will not see or hear everything that happens, and will see or hear even less when they are tired or bored. How the moderators or observers interpret what they see and hear depends on their point of reference, cultural bias, experience, and expectations. Furthermore, observers adjust to conditions. They may eventually fail to recognize language or behaviors that become commonplace in a series of focus groups.

In addition, human beings cannot observe something without changing it. The Heisenberg principle states that any attempt to get information out of a system changes it. In the context of human subjects research, this is called the Hawthorne or "guinea pig" effect. Being a research subject changes the subject's behavior. Having multiple observers can compensate for many of these limitations and increase the accuracy of observational studies, but it can also further influence the behaviors observed. The best strategy is to articulate the specific behaviors or aspects of behavior to be observed before conducting the study. Deciding, on the basis of the research objectives, what to observe and how to record the observations, coupled with training the observers, facilitates systematic data gathering, analysis of the research findings, and the successful completion of observational studies.

Libraries have conducted focus groups to assess what users do or want to do and to obtain information on the use, effectiveness, and usefulness of particular library collections, services, and tools. They have also conducted focus groups to verify or clarify the results from survey or user protocol research, to discover potential solutions to problems identified in previous research, and to help decide what questions to ask in a survey. One participant reported conducting focus groups to determine how to address practical and immediate concerns in implementing a grant-funded project.

Data gathered from focus groups are used to inform decision making, strategic planning, and resource allocation. Focus groups have the added benefit of providing good quotations that are effec tive in public relations publications and presentations or proposals to librarians, faculty, university administrators, and funders.

Questions asked in focus groups, unlike those included in surveys, are not repeated; they are not expected to serve as a basis for assessing trends over time. The decision to convene a focus group appears to be influenced by the organization of the library and the significance or financial implications of the decision to be informed by the focus group data. For example, in a library with an established usability programme or embedded culture of assessment (including a budget and in-house expertise), a unit head can initiate focus group research. If the library must decide whether to purchase an expensive product or undertake a major project that will require the efforts of personnel throughout the organization, a larger group of people might be involved in sanctioning and planning the research and in approving the expenditure to conduct it.

Once the decision has been made to conduct focus groups, one or more librarians or staff prepare the interview questions, identify the demographic groups appropriate for the research purpose, determine how many focus groups to conduct, decide how to recruit participants, and plan the budget and timetable for gathering, analyzing, interpreting and applying the data. Focus group questions should be pilot tested with a group of users and revised on the basis of the test results to solve problems with vocabulary, wording, or the sequence of questions, and to ensure that the questions can be discussed in the allotted time.

Libraries have used e-mail, posters, and flyers to recruit participants for focus group studies. The invitations to prospective participants briefly describe the goals and significance of the study, the participants' role in the study, what is expected of them, how long the groups will last, and any token of appreciation that will be given to the participants. Typically, focus groups are scheduled for 60 to 90 minutes. If food is provided during the focus group, a 90-minute session is preferred. When efforts fail to recruit at least six participants for a group, some libraries have conducted individual interviews with the people they did recruit. In addition to preparing interview questions and recruiting and scheduling participants, focus group preparation entails the following:

— Recruiting, scheduling, and training a moderator and observer(s) for each focus group

— Scheduling six to twelve (preferably seven to ten) participants in designated demographic groups, and sending them a reminder a week or a few days before the focus group

— Scheduling an appropriate room for each focus group.

The focus group moderator or an observer typically arrives at the room early, adjusts the light and temperature in the room, arranges the chairs, and retests and positions the recording equipment. If audiotape is used, a towel or tablet is placed under the recording device to absorb any table vibrations. When the participants arrive, the moderator thanks them for participating, introduces and explains the roles of moderator and observer, reiterates the purpose and significance of the research, confirms that their anonymity will be preserved in any discussion or publication of the study, and briefly describes the ground rules and how the focus group will be conducted.

The introductory remarks emphasize that the goal of the study is not for the participants to reach consensus, but to express their opinions and share their experiences and concerns. Disagreement and discussion are invited. Sometimes the first question is asked round-robin, so that each participant responds and gets comfortable talking. Subsequent questions are answered less formally, more conversationally. The moderator asks the prepared questions and may ask undocumented, probing questions or invite further comments to better understand what the participants are saying and test relevant hypotheses that surface during the discussion.

When the focus group is over, the moderator thanks the participants and might give them a token of appreciation for their participation. The moderator may also answer any questions the participants have about the study, the service or product that was the focus of the study, or the library in general. Observer notes and tapes are labeled immediately with the date and number of the session. Libraries might or might not transcribe the focus group tapes. Some libraries believe the cost of transcribing exceeds the benefits of having a full transcription.

The clerical help is typically unfamiliar with the vocabulary or acronyms used by focus group participants and therefore cannot accurately transcribe the tapes. This means that a professional must also listen to the tapes and correct the transcriptions, which significantly increases the cost of the study. When the tapes are transcribed, a few libraries have used content analysis software to analyze the transcriptions, but they have not been pleased with the results, perhaps because the software attempts to conduct a quantitative analysis of qualitative data. Even when the tapes are not transcribed, at least one person listens to them carefully and annotates the notes taken by observers. Analysis of focus group data is driven by the research purpose. Ideally, at least two people analyze the data—the moderator and observer—and there is high interrater reliability.

Decisions as to who applies the results of focus group research and how it is applied depend on the purpose of the research, the significance of the findings, and the organization of the library. Focus groups provide excellent quotations in support of cases being presented to university administrators, faculty senates, and deans' councils to gain support for changing library directions or receiving additional funding.

Issues in focus groups

Unskilled Moderators and Observers

If the moderator of a focus group is not well trained or has a vested interest in the research results, the discussion can easily go astray. Without proper facilitation, some individuals can dominate the conversation, while others may not get the opportunity to share their views. Faculty in particular can be problematic subjects. They frequently have their own agendas and will not directly answer the focus group questions. A skilled, objective moderator equipped with the rhetorical strategies and ability to keep the discussion on track, curtail domineering or rambling individuals, and bring in reticent participants is a basic requirement for a successful focus group.

Similarly, poor observer notes can hinder the success of a focus group. If observers do not know what comments or behaviors to observe and record, the data will be difficult, if not impossible, to analyze and interpret. The situation worsens if several observers attend different focus group sessions and record different kinds of things. Decisions should be made before conducting the focus groups to ensure that similar behaviors are observed and recorded during each focus group session. Following are the characteristics of the focus group participants:

- Descriptive phrases or words used by participants in response to the key questions
- Themes in the responses to the key questions

— Subthemes held by participants with common characteristics

— Indications of participant enthusiasm or lack of enthusiasm

— Consistency or inconsistency between participant comments and observed behaviors

Interpreting and Using the Data

A shared system of categories for recording observations will simplify the analysis and interpretation of focus group data. No DLF respondent mentioned establishing such a system before conducting a focus group study. Imposing a system after the data have been gathered significantly complicates interpreting the findings. The difficulty of interpreting qualitative data from a focus group study can lead to disagreement about the interpretation and delay preparation of the results. The limited number of participants in a typical focus group study, and the degree to which they are perceived to be representative of the target population, exacerbate the difficulty of interpreting and applying the results. The greater the time lapse between gathering the data and developing plans to use the data, the greater the risk of loss of momentum and abandonment of the study.

User Protocols

A user protocol is a structured, exploratory observation of clearly defined aspects of the behavior of an individual performing one or more designated tasks. The purpose of the protocol is to gather in-depth insight into the behavior and experience of a person using a particular tool or product. User protocol studies include multiple research subjects to identify trends or patterns of behavior and experience. Data gathered from protocols provide insight into what different individuals do or want to do to perform specific tasks.

Protocol studies usually take 60 to 90 minutes per participant. The protocol is guided by a list of five to ten tasks (the "task script") that individuals are expected to perform. Each participant is asked to think aloud while performing the designated tasks. The task script is worded in a way that tells the user what tasks to accomplish, but not told how to accomplish the tasks using the particular tool or product involved in the study. Discovering whether or how participants accomplish the task is a typical goal of protocol research. A facilitator encourages the participants to think aloud if they fall silent. The facilitator may clarify what task is to be performed, but not how to perform it.

The participant's think-aloud protocol is audio- or videotaped, and one or two observers take notes of his or her behavior. Some researchers prefer audiotape because it is less obtrusive. Experts in human-computer interaction (HCI) prefer videotape. In HCI studies, software can be used to capture participant keystrokes. Protocols are very strict about the observational data to be collected. Before the study, the protocol author designates the specific user comments, actions, and other behaviors that observers are to record. The observers' notes should be so complete that they can substitute for the audiotape, should the system fail.

In HCI studies, observer notes should capture the participant's body language, selections from software menus or Web pages, what the user apparently does or does not see or understand in the user interface, and, depending on the research goals, the speed and success (or failure) of task completion. Employing observers who understand heuristic principles of good design facilitates understanding the problems us ers encounter, and therefore the recording of what is observed and interpretation of the data.

User protocols are an effective method to identify usability problems in the design of a particular product or tool, and often the data provide sufficient information to enable the problems identified to be solved. These protocols are less useful to identify what works especially well in a design. Protocols can reveal the participant's mental model of a task or the tool that he or she is using to perform the task. Protocols enable the behavior to be recorded as it occurs and do not rely on the participants' memories of their behaviors, which can be faulty.

Protocols provide accurate descriptions of situations and, unlike surveys, can be used to test causal hypotheses. Protocols also provide insights that can be tested with other research methods and supplementary data to qualify or help interpret data from other studies. For protocols to be effective, participants must understand the goals of the study, appreciate their role in the study, and know what is expected of them. The selection of participants should be based on the research purpose and an understanding of the target population. Facilitators and observers must be impartial and refrain from providing assistance to struggling or frustrated participants. However, a limit can be set on how much time participants may spend trying to complete a task, and facilitators can encourage participants to move to the next task if the time limit is exceeded. Without a time limit, participants can become so frustrated trying to complete a task that they abandon the study.

In HCI studies, it is essential that the participants understand it is the software that is being tested, not their skill in using it. The primary disadvantage of user protocols is that they are expensive. Protocols require at least an hour per participant, and the results apply only to the particular product or tool being tested. In addition, protocol data can be difficult to evaluate, depending on whether the research focuses on gathering qualitative information (for example, the level of participant frustration) or quantitative metrics (for example, success rate and speed of completion). The small number of participants and frequent use of convenience sampling limit the ability to generalize the results of protocol studies to groups with different demographic characteristics or to other products or tools. Furthermore, protocols suffer from the built-in limitations of human sensory perception and language, which affect what the facilitator and observer(s) see and hear and how they interpret and record it.

With rare exception, libraries appear to view think-aloud protocols as the premier research method for assessing the usability of OPACs, Web pages, local digital collections, and vendor products. Protocol studies are often precipitated or informed by the results of previous research. For example, focus groups, surveys, and heuristic evaluations can identify frequently performed or suspected problematic tasks to be included in protocol research.

When protocols are conducted to identify problems in a user interface, often they are repeated later, to see whether the problems were solved in the meantime. In the absence of an established usability-testing programme and budget, the decision to conduct protocols can involve a large group of people because of the time and expense of conducting such research. After the decision has been made to conduct user protocols, one or more librarians or staff members prepare the task script, choose the sampling method, identify the demographic groups appropriate for the research purpose, determine how many participants to recruit in each group, decide how to recruit them, recruit and schedule the participants, and plan the budget and timetable for gathering, analyzing, interpreting and applying the data.

Jakob Nielsen's research has shown that four to six subjects per demographic group is sufficient to capture most of the information that could be discovered by involving more subjects. Beyond this number, the cost exceeds the benefits of conducting more protocols. Sometimes protocols are conducted with only two or three subjects per user group because of the difficulty of recruiting research subjects.

Some libraries prepare a recording sheet that observers use to structure their observations and simplify data analysis. Some also prepare a written facilitator guide that outlines the entire session. Pilot testing can help solve problems with the vocabulary, wording, or sequencing of protocol tasks or survey questions; it also can target ways to refine the recording sheet to facilitate rapid recording of observations. Pilot testing also enables the researcher to ensure that the protocol and follow-up research can be completed in the time allotted.

Libraries have used e-mail, posters, and flyers to recruit participants for user protocol studies. The recruitment information briefly describes the goals and significance of the research, the participants' role, and what is expected of them, including the time it will take to participate and any token of appreciation that will be given to the participants. Other than preparing the instruments and recruiting participants, preparation for a user protocol study closely resembles preparation for a focus group. It involves the following steps:

— Recruiting, scheduling, and training a facilitator and one or more observers; in some cases, the facilitator is the sole observer

— Scheduling the participants and sending them a reminder a week or a few days before the protocol

— Scheduling a quiet room; protocol studies have been conducted in offices, laboratories, or library settings.

— If necessary, ordering computer or videotape equipment to be delivered a half hour before the protocol is to begin

— Photocopying the research instruments

— Testing the audio-or videotape equipment and purchasing tapes

The facilitator or an observer arrives at the room early, adjusts the light and temperature in the room, arranges the chairs so that the facilitator and observers can see the user's face and the computer screen, and tests and positions the recording equipment. If audiotape is used, a towel or tablet is placed under the recording device to absorb any table vibrations. The audiotape recorder is positioned close enough to the user to pick up his or her comments, but far enough away from the keyboard to avoid capturing each key click. If computer or videotape equipment must be delivered to the room, someone must arrive at the room extra early to confirm delivery, be prepared to call if it is not delivered, test the computer equipment, and allow time for replacement or software reinstallation if something is not working.

Though HCI experts recommend videotape, all but some libraries reported using audiotape to record user protocols. The library that used videotape observed that the camera made users uncomfortable and the computer screen did not record well, so the group used audiotape instead for the follow-up protocols. Few other libraries have the resources or facilities to videotape their research, and the added expense of acquiring these might also be a deterrent to using videotape. When participants arrive, the facilitator thanks then for participating, explains the roles of facilitator and observer(s), reiterates the purpose and significance of the research, confirms that anonymity will be preserved in any discussion or publication of the study, and describes the ground rules and how the protocol will be conducted.

Libraries immediately followed protocol sessions with brief interviews or a short survey to capture additional information and give participants the opportunity to clarify what they did in the protocol, describe their experience, and articulate expectations they had about the task or the user interface that were not met. Protocol research is sometimes followed up with focus groups or surveys to confirm the findings with a larger sample of the target population. When the protocol is over, the facilitator thanks the participant and usually gives him or her a token of appreciation. The facilitator also answers any questions the participant has. Observer notes and tapes are labeled immediately. Libraries might or might not transcribe protocol tapes for the same reasons they do or do not transcribe focus group tapes. If the tapes are not transcribed, at least one person listens to them and annotates the observer notes.

Libraries have used significant findings from protocol analysis to inform processes that resulted in the following:

- Customizing the OPAC interface, or redesigning the library Web site or user interfaces to local digital collections. Examples of steps taken based on protocol results include:
  - rearranging a hierarchy
  - changing the order and presentation of search results
  - changing the vocabulary, placement of links, or page layout
  - providing more online help, on-screen instructions, or suggestions when searches fail
  - changing the labeling of images
  - changing how to select a database or start a new search
  - improving navigation
  - enhancing functionality
- Revising the metadata classification scheme for image or text collections
- Developing or revising instruction for how to find resources on the library Web site and how to use full-text e-resources and archival finding aids

The results of protocol studies have also been used to suggest revisions or enhancements to vendor products, to verify improvements in interface design and functionality, and to counter anecdotal evidence or suggestions that an interface should be changed.

Issues, Problems, and Challenges in User Protocols

Librarians can also be a problem when it comes to interpreting and applying the results of user protocols. Those trained in social science research methods often do not understand or appreciate the difference between HCI user protocols and more rigorous statistical research. They may dismiss results that challenge their own way of thinking because they believe the research method is not scientific enough or the pool of participants is too small.

Lack of Resources

User protocols require skilled facilitators, observers, and analysts and the commitment of human and financial resources. Requisite skills might be lacking to analyze, interpret, and persuasively present the findings. Even if the skills are available, there could be a breakdown in the processes of collecting, analyzing, and interpreting the data, planning how to use the findings, and implementing the plans, which could include conducting follow-up research to gather more information. Often the process is followed to the last stage, implementation, where Web masters, programmers, systems specialists, or other personnel are needed. These people can have other priorities.

Human and financial resources or momentum can be depleted before all the serious problems identified have been solved. Limited resources frequently restrict implementation to only the problems that are cheap and easy to fix, which are typically those that appear on the surface of the user interface. Problems that must be addressed in the underlying architecture often are not addressed.

Interpreting and Using the Data

Effective, efficient analysis of data gathered in user protocols depends on making key decisions ahead of time about what behaviors to observe and how to record them. For example, if quantitative usability metrics are to be used, they must be carefully defined. If the success rate is to be calculated, what constitutes success? Is it more than simply completing a task within a set time limit? What constitutes partial success, and how is it to be calculated? Similar questions should be posed and answers devised for qualitative data gathering during the protocols.

Otherwise, observer notes are chaotic and data analysis may be as difficult as is analyzing the responses to open-ended questions in a survey. The situation worsens if different observers attend different protocols and record different kinds of things. Such key decisions should be made prior to conducting the study. If made afterward, they can result in significant lag time between data gathering and the presentation of plans to apply the results of the data analysis. The greater the lag time, the greater the risk of loss of momentum, which can jeopardize the entire effort.

Recruiting Participants

At least one librarian is considering conducting screening tests to ensure that protocol participants can think aloud. Enhancing the skills of the facilitator (through training or experience) and including a pretest task or two for the participants to get comfortable thinking aloud would be preferable to risking biasing the results of the study by recruiting only participants who are naturally comfortable thinking aloud.

Effective Research Methods

Discount usability research can be conducted to supplement more expensive usability studies. This informal research can be done at any point in the development cycle, but is most beneficial in the early stages of designing a user interface or Web site. When done at this time, the results of discount usability research can solve many problems and increase the efficiency of more formal testing by targeting specific issues and reducing the volume of data gathered. Discount usability research methods are not replacements for formal testing with users, but they are fruitful, inexpensive ways to improve interface design.

Heuristic Evaluations

Heuristic evaluation is a critical inspection of a user interface conducted by applying a set of design principles as part of an iterative design process. The principles are not a checklist, but conceptual categories or rules that describe common properties of a usable interface and guide close scrutiny of an interface to identify where it does not comply with the rules. Following are the Nielsen's heuristic principles of good design, mentioning the following:

— Visibility of system status
— Match between system and real world
— User control and freedom
— Consistency and standards
— Recognition rather than recall
— Flexibility and efficiency of use
— Aesthetics and minimalist design
— Error prevention
— Assistance with recognizing, diagnosing, and recovering from errors
— Help and documentation

Heuristic evaluations can be conducted before or after formal usability studies involving users. They can be conducted with functioning interfaces or with paper prototypes. Applying heuristic principles to a user interface requires skilled evaluators. Nielsen recommends using three to five evaluators, including someone with design expertise and someone with expertise in the domain of the system being evaluated. According to his research, a single evaluator can identify 35 percent of the design problems in the user interface. Five evaluators can find 75 percent of the problems. Using more than five evaluators can find more problems, but at this point the cost exceeds the benefits.

Heuristic evaluations take one to two hours per evaluator. The evaluators should work independently but share their results. An evaluator can record his or her own observations, or an observer may record the observations made by the evaluator. Evaluators follow a list of tasks that, unlike the task script in a user protocol, may indicate how to perform the tasks. The outcome from a heuristic evaluation is a compiled list of each evaluator's observations of instances where the user interface does not comply with good design principles. To guide formulating solutions to the problems, each problem identified is accompanied by a list of the design principles that are violated in this area of the user interface.

Heuristic evaluations have several advantages over other methods for studying user interfaces. No participants need to be recruited. The method is inexpensive, and applying even a few principles can yield significant results. The results can be used to expand or clarify the list of principles. Furthermore, heuristic evaluations are more comprehensive than think-aloud protocols are, because they can examine the entire interface and because even the most talkative participant will not comment on every facet of the interface. The disadvantages of heuristic evaluations are that they require familiarity with good design principles and interpretation by an evaluator, do not provide solutions to the problems they identify, and do not identify mismatches between the user interface and user expectations. Interface developers sometimes reject the results of heuristic evaluations because no users were involved.

Few digital libraries have conducted their own heuristic evaluations or have made arrangements with commercial firms or graduate students to do them. The evaluations were conducted to assess the user-friendliness of commercially licensed products, the library Web site, and a library OPAC. In the process, libraries have analyzed such details as the number of keystrokes and mouse movements required to accomplish tasks and the size of buttons and links that users must click. The results of these evaluations were referred to as a "wake-up call" to improve customer service. It is unclear from the survey whether multiple evaluators were used in these studies or the study was conducted in-house, and whether the libraries have the interface design expertise to apply heuristic principles or conduct a heuristic evaluation effectively.

Paper Prototypes and Scenarios

Paper prototype and scenario research resembles think-aloud protocols, but instead of having users perform tasks with a functioning system, this method employs sketches, screen prints, or plain text and asks users how they would use a prototype interface to perform different tasks or how they would interpret the vocabulary. Paper prototype and scenario research is portable, inexpensive, and easy to assemble, provided that the interface is not too complicated. Paper prototypes do not intimidate users. If it is used early in the development cycle, the problems identified can be rectified easily because the system has not been fully implemented.

Paper prototypes are more effective than surveys to identify usability, navigation, functionality, and vocabulary problems. The disadvantage is that participants interact with paper interfaces differently than they do with on-screen interfaces; that is, paper gets closer scrutiny. One library used scenarios of horizontal paper prototypes, which provide a conceptual map of the entire surface layer of a user interface, and scenarios of vertical paper prototypes, which cover the full scope of a feature, such as searching or browsing.

Card-Sorting Tests

Vocabulary problems can arise in any user study, and they are often rampant in library Web sites. A few respondents reported conducting research specifically designed to target or solve vocabulary problems, including card-sorting studies to determine link labels and appropriate groupings of links on their Web sites. Card-sorting studies entail asking individual users to

— Organize note cards containing service or collection descriptions into stacks of related information
— Label the stacks of related information
— Label the service and collection descriptions in each stack

Reverse card-sorting exercises have been used to test the labels. These exercises ask users what category (label) they would use to find which service or collection. Alternatively, the researcher can simply ask users what they would expect to find in each category, then show them what is in each category and ask them what they would call the category. The primary problem encountered in conducting card-sorting tests is describing the collections and services to be labeled and grouped. Describing "full-text" e-resources appears to be particularly difficult in card-sorting exercises, and the results of surveys, focus groups, and user protocols indicate that users often do not understand what "full-text" means. Unfortunately, this is the term found on many library Web sites.

Transaction Log Analysis

Transaction log analysis (TLA) was developed about 25 years ago to evaluate system performance. Over the course of a decade, it evolved as a method to study unobtrusively interactions between online information systems and the people who use them. Today, it is also used to study use of Web sites. Researchers who conduct TLA rely on transaction monitoring software, whereby the system or Web server automatically records designated interactions for later analysis. Transaction monitoring records the type, if not the content, of selected user actions and system responses.

For example, a user submits a query in the OPAC. Both the fact that a query was submitted and the content of that query could be recorded. In response, the system conducts a search and returns a list of results. Both the fact that results were returned and the number of results could be recorded. Transaction monitoring software often captures the date and time of these transactions, and the Internet Protocol (IP) address of the user. The information recorded is stored in an electronic file called a "transaction log." The contents of transaction logs are usually formatted in fields to facilitate quantitative analysis. Researchers analyze transaction logs to understand how people use online information systems or Web sites with the intention of improving their design and functionality to meet user needs and expectations.

TLA is an effective method to study such activities as the frequency and sequence of feature use; system response times; hit rates; error rates; user actions to recover from errors; the number of simultaneous users; and session lengths. In the library world, if queries are logged, it can reveal why searches fail to retrieve results and suggest areas for collection development. If the IP addresses of users are logged, it can reveal whether the user is inside or outside of the library. The information extracted from transaction logs can be used to assess patterns of use and trends over time, predict and prepare for times of peak demand, project future system needs and capacities, and develop services or interfaces that support user actions. For TLA to be effective, transaction monitoring software must record meaningful transactions, and data mining must be driven by carefully articulated definitions and purposes.

TLA is an unobtrusive way to study user behavior, an efficient way to gather longitudinal usage data, and an effective way to detect discrepancies between what users say they do (for example in a focus group study) and what they actually do when they use an online system or Web site. Transaction log analysis is also a good way to test hypotheses; for example, to determine whether the placement or configuration of public computers (for example, at stand-up or sit-down stations) in the library affects user behavior.

The primary disadvantages of TLA are that extracting data can be time-consuming and the data can be difficult to interpret. Though systems and servers have been logging transactions for decades, they still do not incorporate software to analyze the logs. If analysis is to be conducted routinely over time, programmers must develop software or scripts to mine the data in transaction logs. If additional information is to be mined, someone must do it manually or the programmer must add this capability to the routine. Often, extracting the data requires discussion and definitions.

Even after the data have been mined, interpreting the patterns or trends discovered in the logs can be problematic. For example, are a large number of queries necessarily better than a small number of queries? What if users are getting better at searching and able to retrieve in a single query what it might have taken them several queries to find a few years ago? Are all searches that retrieve zero results failed searches? What if it was a known-item search and the user just wanted to know whether the library has the book? What constitutes a failed search? Zero results? Too many results? How many is too many? Meaning is contextual, but with TLA, there is no way to connect data in transaction logs with the users' needs, thoughts, goals, or emotions at the time of the transaction. Interpreting the data requires not only careful definitions of what is being measured but additional research to provide contextual information about the users.

A further disadvantage is that transaction logs can quickly grow to an enormous size. The data must be routinely moved from the server where they are captured to the server where they are analyzed. Keeping log files over time, in case a decision is made to mine additional data from the files, results in massive storage requirements or offline storage that can impede data mining.

TLA or using TLA data provided by vendors to study use of the library Web site, the OPAC and integrated library system (ILS), licensed electronic resources, and, in some cases, local digital collections and the proxy server. They have used TLA data from local servers to:

— Identify user communities
— Identify patterns of use
— Project future needs for services and collections
— Assess user satisfaction
— Inform digital collection development decisions
— Inform the redesign and development of the library Web site
— Assess whether redesign of the library Web site or digital collection has had any impact on use
— Assess whether providing additional content on the library Web site or digital collection has any impact on use
— Target marketing or instruction efforts
— Assess whether marketing or instruction has any impact on use
— Drive examinations of Web page maintenance requirements
— Inform capacity planning and decisions about platform
— Plan system maintenance
— Allocate human and financial resources
— Vendor-supplied TLA data from licensed electronic resources have been used to
— Help secure funding for additional e-resources from university administrators
— Inform decisions about what subscriptions or licenses to renew or cancel
— Inform decisions about which interface(s) to keep
— Determine how many ports or simultaneous users to license

— Assess whether instruction has any impact on use of an e-resource

— Determine cost per-use of licensed e-resources

Web Sites and Local Digital Collections

Practices vary significantly across institutionsfrom no analysis to extensive analysis. Digital libraries track use of their Web sites and Web-accessible digital collections using a variety of homegrown, shareware, or commercial software. The server software determines what information is logged and therefore what data are available for mining. The logging occurs automatically, but decisions concerning what data are extracted appear to be guided by library managers, administrators, or committees.

For example, as libraries adopt new measures for digital library use, Web server logs are being mined for data on virtual visits to the library. In some libraries a great deal of discussion is involved in defining such things as a "virtual visit." In other libraries, programmers are instructed to make their best guesstimate, explain what it is and why they chose it, and use it consistently in mining the logs. As with user studies, the more people involved in making these decisions, the longer it can take. The longer it takes, the longer the library operates without answers to its questions.

Many libraries do not use Web usage data because they do not know how to apply them or do not have the resources to apply them. Some libraries, however, are making creative use of transaction logs from the library Web site and local digital collections to identify user communities, determine patterns of use, inform decisions, assess user satisfaction, and measure the impact of marketing, instruction, interface redesign, and collection development. They do this by mining, interpreting, and applying the following data over time:

— Number of page hits

— Number and type of files downloaded

— Referral URLs (that is, how users get to a Web page)

— Web browser used

— Query logs from "Search this site" features

— Query logs from digital collection (image) databases

— Date and time of the transactions

— IP address or Internet domain of the user

— User IDs (in cases where authentication is required)

In addition, several libraries have begun to count "click throughs" from the library Web site to remote e-resources using a "count use mechanism." This mechanism captures and records user clicks on links to remote online resources by retrieving and logging retrieval of an intermediate Web page. The intermediate page is retrieved and replaced with the remote resource page so quickly that users do not notice the intermediate page.

Writing a script to capture click throughs from the library Web site to remote resources is apparently simple, but the mechanism requires that the links (URLs) to all remote resources on the library Web site be changed to the URL of the intermediate page, which contains the actual URL of the remote resource. Libraries considering implementing a count use mechanism must weigh the cost of these massive revisions against the benefits.

The count use mechanism provides a consistent, comparable count of access to remote e-resources from the library Web site, and it is the only way to track use of licensed resources for which the vendor provides no usage statistics. The data, however, provide an incomplete and inaccurate picture of use of remote resources because users can bookmark resources rather than click through the library Web site to get to them, and because the mechanism counts all attempts to get to remote resources, some of which fail because the server is down or the user does not have access privileges to the resource.

OPAC and Integrated Library Systems

Both OPAC and ILS log transactions, but different systems log different information; therefore, each enables analysis of different user activities. For example, some systems simply count different types of transactions. Others log additional information, such as the text of queries, the date and time of the transaction, the IP address and interface of the client machine, and a session ID, which can be used to reconstruct entire user sessions. Systems can provide an on-off feature to allow periodic monitoring and reduce the size of log files, which can grow at a staggering rate if many transactions and details are captured.

Integrated library systems provide a straightforward way for libraries to generate summary reports of such things as the number of catalog searches, the number of items circulated, the number of items used in-house, and the number of new catalog records added within a given period. Use of different interfaces, request features (for example, renewals, holds, recalls, or requests for purchases) and the ability to view borrowing records might also be tracked. This information is extracted from system transaction logs using routine reporting mechanisms provided by the vendor, or special custom report scripts developed either in-house or prepared as work for hire by the vendor for a fee.

Customized reports are produced for funding agencies or in response to requests for data relevant to specific problems or pages (for example, subject pages or pathfinders). Often Web and ILS usage data are exported to other tools for further analysis, manipulation, or use; for example, circulation data and the number of queries are exported to spreadsheet software to generate trend lines. In rare cases, Web forms and functionality are provided for staff to generate ad hoc reports.

Staff members generate monthly usage reports and distribute or make them available to all staff or to the custodians of the Web pages or digital collection. Overall Web site usage (page hits) or the 10 most heavily used pages might be included in a library's annual report. However, though usage reports are routinely generated, often the data languish without being used. At institutions where the data are used, many different people use the data for many different purposes. Interface designers, system managers, collection developers, subject specialists, library administrators, and department heads all reap meaning and devise next steps from examining and interpreting the data.

Page hits and referral URLs are used to construct usage patterns over time, understand user needs, and inform interface redesign. For example, frequently used Web pages are placed one to two clicks from the home page; infrequently used links on the home page are moved one to two clicks down in the Web site. Data on heavily used Web pages prompt consideration of whether to expand the information on these pages. Similarly, data on heavily used digital collections prompt consideration of expanding the collection. Subject specialists use the data to understand how people use their subject pages and pathfinders and revise their pages based on this understanding.

Page hit counts also drive examination of page maintenance requirements with the understanding that low-use pages and collections should be low maintenance; high-use pages should be well maintained, complete, and up to date. Such assessments facilitate appropriate allocation of resources. Data on low-use or no-use pages can be used to target publicity campaigns. Cross-correlations of marketing efforts and usage statistics are performed to determine whether marketing had any measurable effects on use. Similarly, correlating interface redesign or expansion of content with usage statistics can determine whether redesign or additional content had any effect on use.

Data on use of "new" items on the Web site are used to determine whether designating a resource as "new" had any measurable effects on use. Tracking usage patterns over time enables high-level assessments of user satisfaction. For example, are targeted user communities increasingly using the library Web site or digital collection? Do referral URLs indicate that more Web sites are linking to the library Web site or collection?

Query logs are also mined, interpreted, and applied. Frequent queries in "Search this site" logs identify resources to be moved higher in the Web site. Unsuccessful queries target needed changes in Web site vocabulary or content. Query logs from image databases are used to adjust the metadata and vocabulary of digital collections to match the vocabulary and level of specificity of users and to help decide whether the content and organization of digital collections are appropriate to user needs.

TLA also informs system maintenance and strategic planning. Time and date stamps enable the monitoring of usage patterns in the context of the academic year. Libraries have analyzed low-use times of day and day of week to determine good times to take Web servers down for maintenance. Page hits and data on the number and type of files downloaded month-to-month are used to plan load and capacity, to characterize consumption of system resources, to prepare for peak periods of demand, and to make decisions about platform and the appropriate allocation of resources.

Although the use of dynamic IP addresses makes identification of user communities impossible, libraries use static IP addresses and Internet domain information (for example, .edu, .com, .org, .net) in transaction logs to identify broad user communities. Libraries are defining and observing the behavior of different communities. Some libraries track communities of users inside or outside the library. Some track on-campus, off-campus, or international user communities;

others track communities in campus dormitories, libraries, offices, computer clusters, or outside the university.

In rare cases, static IP addresses and locations are used to affiliate users with a particular school, department, or research center—recognizing that certain IP address locations, such as libraries, dormitories, and public computing clusters, reveal no academic affiliation of the users. Where users are required to authenticate (for example, at the proxy server), the authentication data are mapped to the library patron database to identify communities by school and user status (such as humanities undergraduate). If school and user status are known, some libraries conduct factor analysis to identify clusters of use by user communities.

Having identified user communities in the transaction logs, libraries then track patterns of use by different communities and the distribution of use across communities. For example, IP addresses and time and date stamps of click-through transactions are used to identify user communities and their patterns of using the library Web site to access remote e-resources. IP addresses and time and date stamps of Web site usage are used to track patterns of use inside and outside the libraries. The patterns are then used to project future needs for services and collections.

9

Role of Research Libraries

The past two decades have been a time of tremendous social, economic, and institutional change for all sectors of higher education, including the r development of technology, colleges and universities have also addressed issues of social relevance, accountability, diversity, and globalization. Although academic institutions are notoriously slow to change, they have experienced considerable ferment, prompting shifts in priorities and constituencies and within disciplines.

Because research libraries support all sectors of academic life, they reflect a context where these issues converge. This presents them with a challenge of unusual scale and complexity. In response, libraries have embraced new technologies and adjusted to the programme priorities of their parent institutions. As the so-called information revolution has taken shape, libraries have also demonstrated broader leadership in bringing their intellectual and service missions to bear on the issues raised.

However, libraries face significant challenges in responding to change while sustaining their traditional functions. With the explosion of information technology have come powerful competitive forces that raise fundamental questions about the role of libraries and librarians. Libraries are taking on far more diffuse roles within the campus community and beyond. That is, libraries are becoming more deeply engaged in the creation and dissemination of knowledge and are becoming essential collaborators with the other stakeholders in these activities.

The roles emerging through this evolution are based in part on extrapolations of existing functions, yet they also represent fundamentally new roles for academic libraries. These changes reflected in the library's shift from:

— emphasizing the value of collections to emphasizing the value of expertise

— supporting information description and access to taking responsibility for greater information analysis

— serving as a support agency to serving as a collaborator

— a facility-based enterprise to a campus-wide enterprise

This analysis of library roles covers the 10 to 15 years in which distributed computing, the Internet, and the World Wide Web took hold. The environment that nurtured and catalyzed library activities was influenced by myriad forces, both technical and nontechnical; however several overriding themes merit attention. These themes reflect a developmental path for the evolving roles of libraries in the digital age. This path can be described in three phases: the growth of distributed technologies, the development of open paradigms and models, and the emergence of the library as a diffuse agent.

Distributed Computing Technology

In the 1990s, distributed computing and the Web democratized technology by bringing it to the desktop. As a result, many individuals and institutions now have the basic capabilities for publishing and creating "libraries." This has prompted an explosion of information goods and services for both the general and scholarly markets. For libraries, it has created both potential competitors and potential partners.

Two areas of technology development have contributed significantly to shaping the opportunities for libraries: the emergence of content standards and the maturation of more intelligent systems. These developments have progressed as the distributed environment has taken shape and continue to enable new capabilities for libraries.

Emergence of standards

The evolution of standards for creating, structuring, and disseminating digital content has allowed libraries and other content-rich organizations to move away from the proprietary methods of information access and management that characterized the early days of electronic information. As libraries gained experience with new modes of delivering content and the new genre of digital collections, these standards were embraced and integrated into library operations.

Distributed computing introduced a panoply of players in the information arena; consequently, the emergence of these standards was a critical step toward achieving a more unified information environment and interoperability among distributed collections and content providers. These standards have offered libraries new opportunities for handling content (e.g., to add functionality, deliver content differently for different audiences, or to sustain digital collections over time) and for enhancing the library's classic roles in information access and preservation.

Maturation of tools and systems

Intelligent tools and systems allow invisible mediation between content and user. They facilitate forms of information inquiry and analysis that were heretofore impossible. These developments could lead to the perception that libraries have become irrelevant, since system capabilities can assume mediation functions previously provided by libraries, often with human involvement. However, libraries can harness these capabilities to build far more robust and useful information environments. The challenge is to make resources seamless without making the library's role invisible.

Libraries coming to terms with distributed tools and systems and beginning to incorporate these distributed resources into existing functions. Efforts to lay the groundwork needed to develop relationships among the new stakeholders are evident, as are subtle shifts in the traditional stewardship functions of libraries.

Open Paradigms Models

At the start of the twenty-first century, we see evidence of several movements based on "open" paradigms. For example, the Open Source movement—the concept of software development wherein the source code is shared and development is collaborative—reflects a fundamental shift away from proprietary software and systems. These open models are appearing in an interesting array of new applications and venues, such as the Open Knowledge Initiative to share learning technologies and the OpenLaw programme as a collaborative approach to crafting legal arguments. This trend toward open models may presage more generalized acceptance of collaborative development and sharing of intellectual goods and services.

Cyberlaw expert Lawrence Lessig suggests that the creation of a "commons," wherein the free exchange of ideas and collaboration prevail, is fundamental to an open society. This belief stands in stark contrast to that of commercial and other interests, whose goal is to control the Internet and its content. One could argue that the notion of the commons also reflects a departure from models that embrace central control mechanisms—a model that has characterized library operations in the past.

Themes of openness and collaborative exchange have also emerged in the context of publishing, particularly with respect to the relationship between authors and commercial publishers. For example, the Open Archives Initiative (OAI) seeks to address concerns within the scholarly community about certain aspects of traditional journal publishing, especially the notion of a "gift economy," wherein intellectual property is ceded to the for-profit sector and then repurchased for community use. These concerns have given birth to new conventions, such as e-print archives, for distributing content.

As information becomes more distributed and open models of exchange become more common, the library's relationship with content creators, publishers, and consumers will change. There is in these open trends evidence of a shift from publication as product to publication as process. When content can be enhanced or supplemented over time by others, it becomes more dynamic and the "versions" become more cumulative. Some have forecast this shift as the ultimate challenge to current copyright law, which is based on objects fixed in time and space. Such a shift has significant impact on organizations whose current role is to manage publications in both traditional and new forms and to sustain the scholarly record for the future. As this shift continues, there are likely to be further changes in the library's information management functions and in its role as an agent in scholarly communication.

In this phase in the evolution of library roles, the library starts to engage in collaboration as a strategy to address its core mission of building collections, maintaining access, and providing service. Building on distributed structures, the library begins to involve other stakeholders in fulfilling its functions, and sustaining relationships among stakeholders becomes an essential activity. As responsibilities for content and services become more distributed, models of central control give way to new mechanisms for coordination and collaboration. Ultimately, the processes of scholarly communication become as critical as traditional publication products.

Library as a Diffuse Agent

As the evolution proceeds, libraries increasingly adopt distributed models for information access and management, and more often use open and collaborative models for developing library content and services. With the incorporation of distributed technologies and more open models, the library has the potential to become more involved at all stages, and in all contexts, of knowledge creation, dissemination, and use. Rather than being defined by its collections or the services that support them, the library can become a diffuse agent within the scholarly community.

In physics, "diffusion" refers to the spreading out of elements, an intermingling (though not a combining) of molecules. Applying this analogy to libraries, we see the library becoming more deeply engaged in the fundamental mission of the academic institution—i.e., the creation and dissemination of knowledge—in ways that represent the library's contributions more broadly and that intertwine the library with the other stakeholders in these activities. The library becomes a collaborator within the academy, yet retains its distinct identity.

As is often the case in times of change, organizational structures and the language for describing an organization's activities do not adequately reflect the transformations under way. Consequently, while the descriptions that follow derive from traditional functions of libraries (collection development, cataloging and access, user services, and place) these descriptions fall short in the contemporary context.

Functions of Collection Development

Libraries have been in the collection business for centuries and are defined largely by the functions of collection development and management, that is, by a continuum of processes to select content appropriate for a particular community, make it accessible, manage it, and preserve it. These discrete functions have been viewed as necessary components of good collection stewardship, and they have obvious definition in a physical context. Libraries bought books (which they then owned), organized them, made them available through library facilities, and took steps to ensure the longevity of the volumes for future use.

To some extent, this full stewardship model is being followed in the digital arena. Libraries acquire and secure ownership of digital content (typically through license), store the content on local servers, and make it accessible to a target community. Libraries attempt, as protocols permit, to ensure long-term access to the digital collection through license conditions and through practices to create backup and redundancy, and to migrate the content over time.

In a variation of the model, some libraries host commercial content or centrally manage content of other campus units. In both of these cases, the classic collection stewardship model is sustained largely intact. A defining characteristic of this traditional model is the library's ability to exercise primary responsibility for and control over the content and future access to that content.

Federated Systems

Increasingly, the capabilities of the distributed environment prompt an unbundling of the discrete component functions of traditional collection development and management responsibilities. Models in which the library retains central control over content, its access, and its longevity may no longer be appropriate or sustainable. Consequently, we see instances of libraries providing access to electronic content that they neither own nor manage. The library may also preserve and archive content that is not accessible to users.

An interesting illustration of this unbundling of collection functions can be found in a model of collection federation. These efforts typically create structures with both decentralized and centralized responsibilities. Federated systems allow distributed content to be brought together and used as an integrated collection. Individual content managers retain ownership and governance over each discrete collection, but the content is made accessible under the principles of the larger federating system. The University of Michigan Library's Image Services provides a good example. This programme offers mechanisms to integrate image content (e.g., photographs, art, or architecture) from independent providers and to represent it in a larger access system. The collection providers retain control, managing the individual image collections in a variety of different local database systems. Differing types of descriptive metadata are used for each collection, but each is converted to a standard encoding (using SGML or XML), and fields are mapped to minimal Dublin Core metadata in the federating system.

Image Services is optimized to provide access, without the overhead of a management system for the image collections themselves. Users can access each collection individually and exploit the full access protocols for each collection or search across all collections or a subset using the mapped, core metadata elements. User tools are also incorporated, allowing image analysis (e.g., pan and zoom) and comparison, subset creation, and presentation options within the federated system. Thus, the functional benefits of federation can be achieved without diminishing the features and specialized functionality of each independent collection.

Federation may seem to be a simple approach to bringing content together; however, the underlying design principles and intellectual effort involved suggest a far more complex role for the library. The difference from the full stewardship model is also significant. Whereas traditional models bring content control to the library and create a central access strategy, the federating model balances distributed content and collection-specific functionality with cross-collection functionality and tools.

Distribution and Responsibilities

First, content providers have to be identified for inclusion and evaluated by the federating agent. Negotiation and education are often required to secure the participation of content providers. Contractual agreements may be necessary that specify the responsibilities of each party and the conditions for the use of the content. Each collection database structure must be analyzed and understood to map metadata schema. At the federating system level, user assessment and task analysis are needed to inform the design of the search system, and analytic tools must be incorporated. A system architecture needs to be developed to implement the search, display, and tool functions that draw on distributed content. Finally, federation requires ongoing assessment of system functionality and maintenance of the relationships with the content providers.

Organizationally, the service reflects a melding of expertise related to the subject domain, content characteristics, access, service, and technology. One could add to the list skills related to human-computer interaction, interface design, and usability assessment. Technology infrastructure is imperative, as are the "organizational infrastructure," (i.e., the server and software apparatus) and the "relationship apparatus" reflected in sustaining the federation partnership. Threaded throughout programmes of this sort are often issues of intellectual property, licensing, and rights management. The organizational implications are significant. There are obvious investments required to build the technology components. Perhaps more critical than any financial investment, however, is organizational support for the coalescing of expertise within and outside of the library.

An additional implication of the federating model relates to the responsibility for documenting and preserving scholarly resources over time. In the federated model, the library controls neither the content nor the permanence of these resources. To the extent that component collection databases are dynamic and subject to decisions of the distributed collection managers, the library must forgo its traditional archiving role. However, this prompts a new responsibility for the library in influencing and educating individual content providers, the institution, and the community about the requirements for preservation and archiving of resources.

Library's Role in Publishing Process

As a second example of new paradigms for the library's role in collection development, we see libraries becoming more engaged in the publishing process, including content presentation, management, and distribution policies and practices. This moves the library closer to the point of creation and distribution in the publishing process and broadens its functions beyond archiving and mediation for published works.

There are several variations on the theme of library-as-publisher. In some instances, the focus has been on providing robust distribution services for established society and university presses. Other enterprises, such as the California Digital Library's e-Scholarship programme, serve more as incubators, providing tools and services to facilitate innovation in publishing, particularly e-print or similar repositories. The content creators and producers are within the University of California system, where they may serve institutional interests as well. Finally, there are examples such as the Electronic Publishing Initiative at Columbia (EPIC), where the partner organizations exercise direct control over content, pricing, and distribution in a classic publishing model.

Although these three publisher/distributor examples differ in the degree of control over content (e.g., content evaluation and editorial control), they share some features. Each model engages the library directly in the processes of publishing. Consequently, there is an opportunity for libraries to advocate for responsible practices (e.g., on pricing, licensing, or archiving) as well as to develop new relationships with publishers. The ideologies that inform these new roles in publishing are potentially in keeping with the values of libraries and the emerging interests of institutions and authors relative to intellectual property ownership and conditions of use. In some cases, there are opportunities to respond to institutional interests regarding the retention of copyright and cost-effective processes and products that can be sustained for the future. Less clear is the extent to which these new roles tap the core expertise of libraries and librarians.

Libraries usually bring expertise in information dissemination and use, rather than contribute to the editorial or evaluative aspects of publishing. Consequently, it seems more likely that publishing ventures for libraries will be carried out in partnership with other organizations that have these necessary skills. Library involvement in publishing and content distribution plays off of the fundamental experiences libraries have with information acquisition, access, use, and preservation.

Access to Information

Organizing and providing access to information is another classic role of libraries. The twin functions of cataloging and classification have allowed published works to be fixed in a framework of knowledge and to be given multiple access points for retrieval—a combination that has supported general inquiry over time. These functions have brought predictability and a cumulative order to vast amounts of material. As protocols for structuring and sharing bibliographic data were developed for automated systems and networks, libraries have been able to share these data and build more flexible access systems. In many respects, bibliographic utilities such as OCLC and RLIN and the model of shared cataloging represent early, primitive models of distributed and open approaches to library functions. As distributed forces prevail, models are emerging that no longer rely on central data and capabilities, but rather harness resources through new, distributed mechanisms.

Traditional access activities have been largely undifferentiating and unintrusive; that is, all materials added to libraries have generally had the same descriptive treatment and the functionality or structure of the works themselves have not been materially altered by these processes. As new types of digital content emerge that are structured, include multimedia, and encompass associative links to other resources, it is unlikely that these classic techniques for access can suffice.

Doug Greenberg has offered a stark characterization of the contrast between traditional library and Internet techniques of access:

— If the key to the library's power is its rigid, counterintuitive arrangement of static information in a comprehensible and hierarchical structure, the key to the Internet's power is its flexible arrangement of dynamic information that permits the human mind literally to jump from one thing to another and back again with no more than stream of consciousness as a guide. It is anybody's guess which of these systems is better adapted to human creativity and curiosity.

— The challenge for libraries is to sustain the significant capabilities developed through standards-based bibliographic processes while taking advantage of new access strategies that have been created as a result of new media standards and communication protocols.

— Libraries have responded to the challenges of content description for new digital media, extrapolating from existing cataloging practices to develop various metadata schema. These schema have recognized the new types of attributes necessary to represent digital objects and services fully, that is, to describe more than just their content and topic. Administrative and structural metadata, for example, add significant value and capture information about provenance, property rights, and methods of creation or capture, as well as information about the object's structure that can be used by retrieval systems.

Communities and Collaboratories

Metadata developments generally reflect an extension of cataloging practices to new dimensions of content and access. Libraries are seeking to understand how these new access strategies might better serve target user communities. In particular, libraries now analyze how content should be represented to achieve the desired functionality within access systems. Assessing functionality increasingly requires an understanding of how content is used, and by whom. For example, metadata for a collection of plant or animal specimens might incorporate scientific as well as popular names to serve both research investigators and K12 users. Or a research user may need to map specimen data for geographic analysis, thus requiring the specification and inclusion of spatial references.

As the information environment has become more distributed and more collaborative, how have these forces affected the library's role in facilitating access? Two interesting examples can be found in the OAI and in the functions of metadata harvesting. Although OAI initially focused on e-print archives and new models of scholarly communication, it now is involved in the development and promotion of "interoperability standards that aim to facilitate the efficient dissemination of content . . . independent of both the type of content offered and the economic mechanisms surrounding that content".

Metadata harvesting techniques address the inability of the popular network search engines to tap the riches of digital libraries and other content that lives within databases and repositories (the so-called deep Web). Metadata harvesting projects involve both "exposing" metadata associated with digital library collections (using specified protocols) and developing harvesting services that can gather these exposed metadata and create access services appropriate for specific uses or user communities. In the early phase of development, both general and specialized services have been proposed; the latter require attention to domain-specific vocabulary or other characteristics associated with specific formats, uses, or users.

As an example of a specialized service, the University of Virginia's proposed American Studies Information Community will draw on harvesting protocols to bring together disparate types of information (text, data, media, images) for a community, defined as a group of scholars, students, researchers, librarians, information specialists, and citizens with a common interest in a particular thematic area. The project is being undertaken collaboratively with other institutions and content providers (e.g., Thomas Jefferson Foundation, Virginia Tech University, and the Smithsonian National Museum of American Art). The University of Virginia describes these information communities as "learning and teaching environments in which subject-driven websites are developed around print and digital versions of our collections and the teaching interests of our faculty members . . . Information communities will foster interdisciplinary and collaborative research and publication amongst scholars with common interests."

This access model is interesting because it reflects several trends that are also evident in the broader landscape. The new service will take advantage of a distributed collection model and a range of partners. The descriptive techniques will reflect enhanced attributes appropriate to the subject area and the diverse formats in the distribut ed collections. Analytic tools will be incorporated to add value to the content and to stimulate collaboration. Perhaps most significant, the access system is explicitly designed to serve a social role as a catalyst for an interdisciplinary community—a far more intrusive role than is provision of access alone.

A similar model for creating a collaborative environment that mixes content and tools can be found in the construct of a collaboratory, having its genesis in the research community. In many respects, collaboratories are a new incarnation of the "invisible college" of the past, in that they focus on creating a communication environment. Collaboratories have been defined as "tool-oriented computing and communication systems to support scientific collaboration" (National Research Council 1993). An often-cited example of a collaboratory, the Space Physics and Aeronomy Research Collaboratory (SPARC), provides an online knowledge environment for atmospheric scientists worldwide. SPARC incorporates the ability to control remote telescopes and instrumentation, to review and collaboratively analyze observational data of atmospheric events, to create and archive vast amounts of research data, and to use tools to manipulate the data.

To the extent that libraries begin to develop access techniques in response to a community and to support the potential development of collaboratories for these communities, we see them assuming a far more integral role within the scholarly arena. In contrast to the approaches to access created in the past, which were focused on published content and largely independent of the less formal aspects of scholarly communication (as in the invisible colleges), this emergent model has the potential to bridge formal and informal communication structures and to develop these structures working closely with the target community of content creators and users. The role of the library moves from manager of scholarly products to that of participant in the scholarly communication process.

Semantic Web

A second example of new dimensions of access—an exploration of the emerging Semantic Web—is still in a formative stage. The creator of the World Wide Web, Tim Berners-Lee, is the intellectual force behind the Semantic Web as well. Berners-Lee notes, "the Semantic Web is not a separate Web but an extension of the current one, in which information is given well-defined meaning, better enabling computers and people to work in cooperation". The Semantic Web brings together metadata, a language to structure the data, and a road map (or ontology, as known in the artificial intelligence community) that explains relationships between terms. These ingredients for knowledge representation—structured content, rich metadata, and a framework or ontology of relationships—allow software agents in computer systems to make inferences and therefore retrieve more intelligently from the vast body of distributed information on the Internet.

Designing the Semantic Web will require a mix of skills, and librarians have the potential to contribute significantly to this effort. One area in which they may become involved is metadata creation, where librarians' expertise in descriptive techniques has obvious relevance. The more complex arena of ontologies—defining relationships between entities such as classes and subclasses or properties and subproperties—is one in which librarians have latent experience in areas such as thesaurus development. Primarily the domain of computer scientists, ontologies and their specification could involve the library community in more multidimensional description, defining and specifying the logic of relationships between metadata elements and objects, e.g., "This document is a digital manifestation of a print object."

In addition to benefiting from rules for representing content and defining relationships, the Semantic Web will benefit from establishing a means of certifying the authenticity and provenance of the content. Otherwise, the diversity of providers and the scarcity of benchmarks to discern quality will seriously limit the Internet as an information retrieval system. How do we know the origin of what we retrieve, whether the descriptive information matches the object, and whether we can believe and trust the metadata? To move the Web from an unstructured and undifferentiated mass of information to a more useful and scaleable information environment, systems of trust and provenance will be essential.

Trust in the Semantic Web can be established through context (e.g., content or metadata from a known group or an authoritative source) or through digital signatures to verify authorship. While the Semantic Web is still in an early stage, one can imagine a scenario in which content selected by or associated with a library access service could establish a context in which the integrity of the information could be validated, in the same way that library acquisition of content in physical collections reflects a selection decision. This possibility, coupled with the proposed methods to validate the source (for example, with digital signatures that certify the content in a similar fashion to publisher imprints), could significantly enhance the library's role in refining retrieval.

Greater intelligence in information systems (for example, through software agents) can make connections between resources, respond to user preferences, and retrieve content on the basis of an array of attributes. A critical aspect of the library's future may lie in the notion of trust. In the past, a user would make general inferences about a resource on the basis of the fact that it was "associated with a library and its collection" and through use of descriptive information provided by the library. By continuing its descriptive role and using new virtual mechanisms to convey context for users, the library can continue to be a signifier that the resource or collection has been examined and formally described, and that a decision has been made about inclusion. This context could be created through well-defined collections of content and services, use of metadata to represent content attributes fully, and development of structures that can validate content and its source.

Library's role—in this case, providing access to information—is being reshaped by distributed forces and open models. Here, too, we see the potential for the library's more active engagement and collaboration. Moving beyond simple, descriptive access, libraries will be challenged to understand and fulfill community requirements for robust retrieval and for providing assurance of the integrity and authenticity of content.

User Services

Library user services have traditionally focused on collections support (i.e., helping users identify, retrieve, and use resources) or educational activities to help patrons use their libraries more effectively. These activities have largely been distinct; for example, reference services respond to individuals with specific questions, and instructional programmes target classes with general educational needs. The analysis that follows provides examples of more distributed approaches to user services that reflect the development of complex and integrating systems of support.

Evidence of changing user behavior has been documented but is not fully understood. Academic libraries have reported declining in-library attendance and declining use of in-library services such as reference and circulation, although some are experiencing increases in instructional activity. Other data indicate a rise in the use of and preference for electronic content. Institutional instructional management systems are offering alternative venues for course reserve materials, and the use of traditional course reserve methods has declined.

While the profession has yet to analyze fully the relationship among these trends, they suggest increased location-independent use of library and non-library content and heightened interest in acquiring the skills needed to make better use of the myriad systems and services now available on the network. Course-management systems also reflect the increasing desire for services that integrate resources (e.g., syllabi, readings, lecture notes, chat capabilities). These shifts in user behavior and interests prompt the library both to extend traditional services in the networked environment and to consider the broader set of user needs to be addressed in systems of user support.

Virtual Reference Systems

The past decade has seen a rise in reference services to support more virtual inquiry. Whereas, initially, the library mainly served remote users who were affiliated with the institution, it eventually came to serve a more global market. Virtual reference methods began with simple communication exchanges, such as reference via e-mail. They now incorporate tools that allow reference librarians to more fully understand the nuance of the reference interview context (e.g., using video technology to capture nonverbal behaviors) or to provide real-time assistance with electronic resources (e.g., through "chat" functions and through technologies to "capture" the user's workstation and guide or "co-browse" networked resources).

Many non-library reference services have blossomed on the Internet. These "expert" or "Ask-a" services may match users and experts, offer specific topic strengths, or incorporate natural language technologies to parse the inquiry and provide a more rapid, automated response. A recent survey of such services suggests that these sites are most effective in response to fact-based inquiries, and that the niche for digital reference services in academic libraries may lie in supporting more in-depth and source-dependent questions.

Consequently, users may seek answers to simpler questions on the "greater network" and use library services for more complex inquiries. Given the unlikely coordination between commercial and library services, an interesting set of "design" issues arises. Should libraries develop specialized services, assuming that the Internet will fulfill general needs? Will non-library services of the Internet be of sufficient quality and reliability to satisfy users?

If users are already beginning to differentiate their sources of support, libraries will have no choice but to determine how best to develop services in the context of what is commonly available on the Internet. Directing users to available fact-based reference sites may be one option, particularly during times of the day when libraries cannot provide human-mediated assistance. The bottom line is that when designing services, libraries must take into account the broader service landscape and user behaviors.

The evolution of electronic reference from single to multi-institutional services creates a more complex framework for virtual assistance. In these models, reference services are collaboratively staffed and mechanisms are developed to profile staff and institutional specializations in systematic and structured ways. In addition, the services often incorporate capabilities for real-time discussion and knowledge databases to store the results of reference transactions for future use. The Collaborative Digital Reference Service developing an international infrastructure that is designed to manage inquiries submitted by users worldwide and is staffed by librarians worldwide. While the model highlights seamless access to global resources, it also harnesses the human capital of library professionals. Expertise is as important as the network of library collections.

As more functional and intelligent systems are being developed for collection access, the development of reference systems has also involved the specification of standards to enable interoperability among sites and to allow more complex functionality. Evolving protocols and metadata will specify the representation, communication, and archiving of user transactions. The emergence of these standards, along with the move from institutional to collaborative models, is creating a more finely articulated system that supports transactions, communication, and management needs for distributed services.

There are three developmental stages described earlier, virtual reference services are early in the second stage, beginning to test collaborative approaches. Mechanisms for coordination are still relatively primitive, and the descriptive metadata infrastructure needed to support collaboration is nascent. There are reasons for this rate of development. Developing techniques to describe individual or institutional expertise or to capture complex questions will entail significant effort.

The organizational and governance issues are equally challenging. Earlier cooperation among institutions for reference services was done largely through hierarchical systems of referral within state or regional cooperatives (where size of collection and staff determined placement in the hierarchical tiers). The "point-to-point" systems now emerging in virtual, cooperative reference represent a far different model of collaboration—one in which the rules of engagement must be newly specified.

Characteristics of more diffuse activity will become more tangible as virtual reference systems are more widely adopted and integrated seamlessly into the library organization and the instructional and research systems of the academic community. Within library organizations, the next phase of development is likely to show evidence of greater integration between on-site and virtual services, integration of reference and technology expertise, and more finely specified tiers of service and referral.

Reference systems may be included as visible and discrete services in online instructional and research environments, or they may be seamlessly interwoven to allow automatic support. For example, a library reference system could be incorporated into a research collaboratory environment as a separately identifiable resource to be selected when help is needed. Alternatively, mechanisms may be developed within access systems to prompt users to seek reference assistance when they are having problems (e.g., after several unsuccessful searches or inquiries). These prompts could be mediated by librarians or addressed by automated "Help" files tied to the specific problem.

Research on user failure in libraries has documented areas where users frequently experience problems; for example, the library may not own the desired item, users may ineffectively use the catalog or other access services, or a desired item may not be found on the shelf. Often, the user does not interpret these problems as "failures," and they do not necessarily result in a request for assistance. In the electronic environment, there is an opportunity to build in mechanisms to capture problematic interactions between content and user. This opportunity to provide point-of-problem guidance, along with the ability to collect detailed data on use, may allow the library to be a presence in an area where it previously was unable to provide support. A key challenge will be striking the right balance between proactive and reactive assistance.

While the traditional notion of library services focuses on user-initiated requests within a library facility, the more diffuse constructs bring reference and technical expertise to a wide range of contexts, within both physical libraries and online environments. Query-based services are expanded and enhanced with more context-sensitive or resource-specific support. Ultimately, the library's presence becomes more pervasive and its services more fully integrated into the processes of learning and research.

Information Literacy

Instruction—helping people use library resources more effectively through directed and structured educational activities—is another core service that libraries have traditionally offered users. (Such support has been geared typically, although not exclusively, to undergraduate students.) In the digital age, putting bounds around "library resources" has become a daunting task. Moreover, the instructional needs of users have changed dramatically as new methods for teaching and learning have emerged.

In the 1990s, higher education was influenced by two forces that, though unrelated in principle, ultimately became intertwined in reshaping the educational experience. First, technologies emerged that enabled distance-independent, asynchronous venues for instruction. These technologies were adopted not only for use in distance education programmes but also for more generalized applications on campus. The second phenomenon was the growing pressure to rethink the academy's approaches to teaching and learning, particularly with respect to the undergraduate community. These two forces have created a volatile environment, but one that offers tremendous opportunities for libraries.

A number of perspectives have been brought to bear in understanding these new dimensions of learning and associated skills. These perspectives generally articulate two dimensions of literacy. One dimension reflects the need for skills to exploit technology to use information effectively. The second dimension is the need for a conceptual understanding of information and knowledge processes. In reality, a marriage of these fluencies is needed. The traditional functions of identifying, finding, and evaluating information are joined with more conceptual notions of inquiry, information analysis, and use. These information skills are now interwoven with technology skills.

Building an understanding of the characteristics of information is also important to literacy; issues of intellectual property, authenticity, and provenance are critical in a networked environment where the traditional signifiers of quality are absent. Libraries are then challenged to articulate a conceptual framework for instruction that integrates these concepts and skills in support of student learning. Two different models of information literacy programmes illustrate how these practical and conceptual dimensions are integrated.

The library has a continued role as place. In the past, this function has been characterized as a location for individuals and information to interact—a place for users to tap collections or for library staff to bring users and information together. The physicality of libraries and their collections is an often-cited value. The ability to browse and experience the gestalt of an array of resources has been a time-honored technique for inquiry, and the physical experience of books, maps, or manuscripts is important for many. Library facilities also serve a social function, providing a common ground for users to interact or a neutral site for individuals from different disciplines to come together.

The changes in library roles discussed thus far have obvious consequences for library facilities. Once the physical centerpiece of a campus with large, central collections, library resources are now more distributed and library users more nomadic. The challenge is twofold: reconceiving library buildings to reflect changing user behavior and needs, and developing the library's network presence as a virtual place of comparable value.

Libraries face a paradox with respect to facilities and their use. The University of Washington's ongoing survey of users reflects these trends, with the most recent responses indicating decreased facility use by faculty and graduate students, and a modest increase in use reported by undergraduates. Washington has a 24-hour undergraduate library facility and well-established computer facilities within libraries, which the survey data indicate are heavily used.

While most libraries have incorporated computing capabilities, the characteristics of new computer facilities are noteworthy. These new uses of facilities are consistent with the changes in the curriculum and research methods noted earlier. While still serving as a place for collections, library facilities increasingly serve as environments for learning and collaboration.

As geography loses its primacy as a basis for organizing libraries and as the phenomenal growth of digital content continues, libraries are challenged to identify ways to make their virtual roles visible and tangible to their campus communities. Too often, users do not know where responsibility lies for networked content and services; information and services are simply there, and presumably free.

While the nature of library facilities will change, the notion of library as place remains important in both physical and virtual contexts. Increasingly, this sense of place serves strategically to further the development of new roles.

Transformation of Libraries

The transformation of libraries to fulfill more diffuse roles within the academy reflects a shift in perspective both for the library and for the other stakeholders in this arena. There are significant challenges to be overcome, not the least of which is the pace of technology development. The volatility of technology contrasts with the glacial speed of change within higher education regarding core values and structure.

Libraries have thus far evolved fairly predictably in developing a digital presence and digital capabilities, particularly with respect to technology infrastructure and expertise. There is an initial phase wherein an individual library's activity is largely project-based. Involvement of others outside the organization is minimal and resource commitments are typically nonrecurring. In this stage, libraries experiment with and exploit distributed technology capabilities. In the next stage, the "adolescent" library has far more interest in its peers.

Collaborative activity within the library community emerges, and outreach to others within the campus environment becomes more prevalent. Often in this phase, groundwork is laid for more stable production capabilities for content, access, and services. Libraries add staff and develop new work processes. Resources are reallocated, but often the activities are still viewed as separate from the mainstream.

Nearing a more mature phase of digital capacity, the library organization is better positioned with secure infrastructure and leadership to collaborate with other libraries and other stakeholders. Workflow becomes more integrated, and investment is consistent with mission; i.e., permanent sources of support and organizational structures are put in place. Relationships with other stakeholders are often more "open,""that is, characterized by leveraging each other's expertise and strengths to the benefit of a programmatic goal.

While it is possible that a large infusion of funds might hasten this developmental cycle (particularly as it relates to building technology infrastructure), the organizational development necessary to integrate complementary expertise and adjust goals is likely to come only with experience and time. Consequently, these evolutionary stages—moving from distributed, to open, to diffuse roles—may be a requirement, a rite of passage.

Residential campuses are unlikely to disappear, and instructional and research programs are unlikely to abandon their interests in traditional libraries for the foreseeable future. Yet the evidence of changes in institutional priorities (e.g., with respect to outreach, new markets, and intellectual property) and in individual user behavior (with respect to expectations and needs) suggests that caution will be shortsighted.

The transformations under way in teaching, learning, and research will require a far different conception of the library. At a minimum, structures for the acquisition and description of digital content need to be in place and services developed to respond to a more nomadic and virtual clientele. These minimal requirements, however, merely extrapolate existing roles for collections, access, and user support. Seizing opportunities for more diffuse roles will require investment in both tangible components and in intangible elements such as leadership and organizational development.

Tangible Investments

Certain investments must be made if the library is to emerge as a player in the changing environment. Participation in new learning communities, in new ventures for knowledge management or dissemination, or in service to new markets requires investment in technology infrastructure and expertise in the handling of digital resources and tools. In developing digital library infrastructure, there is a tendency to assume that each institution must develop a full complement of capabilities. This assumption is attractive because hands-on experience does provide invaluable developmental opportunities for staff.

However, it is also becoming clear that institutions may have difficulty in sustaining the ongoing development of the local infrastructure. Further, an isolationist approach may not allow libraries to leverage institutional strengths or the benefits of a high volume of activity. Consequently, collaborative development of tools, services, and capabilities will be far more common in the future.

Competition has become intense for qualified professionals who can manage and develop new library roles. While many library or information-science graduate programs have revamped their curricula, it is impractical to assume that the needed leadership can come exclusively from newly minted professionals. Investment in professional development and participation in collaborative opportunities that can help advance organizational development are essential. Insights are often born of exposure to new ideas and of the freedom to explore.

Consequently, professional development models that include support for experimentation, experiential methods of stimulating creative thinking, and focused interaction with colleagues from other institutions are particularly useful. Technological expertise is in demand, but it is equally important that the profession attract individuals with agility in applying or exploiting new technologies in the service of new roles. It is essential that these individuals have a deep understanding of the communication structures and processes within disciplines. Such capabilities, while informed by technology, reflect development beyond task-specific skills such as cataloging to a contextual knowledge of scholarly processes and user needs. The challenge is to assemble the constellation of technology, subject, and application expertise and to facilitate the necessary collaboration between functional divisions of the library.

Intangible Investments

Infrastructure, expertise, and tools, while enabling, cannot forge a new agenda for the library. Leadership must be present to leverage the library's full range of assets. The examples cited throughout this analysis show how the library adds value through its expertise and its resources. Nonetheless, the prevailing forces also create an environment in which the library's efforts to support virtual collections and services can make the library less visible. An important aspect of leadership in the digital age will be the ability to articulate these new roles in a way that makes the library's contributions substantive and visible.

Seizing opportunities and articulating the library's potential, in turn, require organizational agility, i.e., the flexibility of budget and human capital that allows responsiveness and, when needed, redirection of activity. In the new environment, a culture of collaboration will be essential if the library is to fulfill its potential for providing services and collections. Collaboration will mean not only embarking on successful joint projects, but also managing campus and external relationships to ensure that the library is present at the table for relevant institutional dialogue and decision making.

The development of diffuse libraries will entail an understanding and appreciation of the shifts under way in all sectors of the academy, investment in infrastructure, and an organizational culture that nurtures and catalyzes relationships. Distributed, open, diffuse—these characteristics describe the stages that mark the library's evolution. Ultimately, the transformed, diffuse library will embody an intimacy of purpose and a full engagement both with institutional goals and with the practical conduct of learning, teaching, and research.

10
Usage of Electronic Resources

Over the last decade, libraries of all kinds have been spending larger and larger shares of their budgets to acquire or gain access to electronic resources from publishers and vendors. Electronic resources have enabled libraries to improve services in a variety of ways. First, most electronic resources come equipped with powerful search-and-retrieval tools that allow users to perform literature searches more efficiently and effectively than was previously possible. In addition, because most relevant electronic resources are now available through the Web, users can have desktop access to them 24 hours a day. In many cases, users also can now navigate directly from indexing databases to the full text of an article and can even follow further links from there.

Most users have welcomed these developments. Nevertheless, libraries face a number of technical, financial, and organizational challenges as they seek to continue offering the high level of services that users have come to expect. In an attempt to be as inclusive as possible, the term "commercially available resources" is defined as virtually any electronic product or service for which libraries spend funds. Librarians today tend to characterize pricing models, or the information marketplace in general, as sustainable or not, and this is the sense in which the word has been used recently in some influential documents. For example, a document issued in 1998 by the International Coalition of Library Consortia (ICOLC) states that "current pricing models for e-information, which are developing during a period of experimentation, are not sustainable".

Another document, "Principles for Emerging Systems of Scholarly Publishing," employs the word somewhat similarly, but it also declares that the current system of scholarly publishing and communication "has become too costly for the academic community to sustain". Vendors and providers of electronic resources also need to be concerned about the economic sustainability or viability of their products, and their views of what may be required for sustainability may conflict with what libraries view as the realities of their funding situations.

Libraries and vendors alike have important roles to play in fostering an environment in which resources and services are sustainable for both communities. These broad definitions of commercially available resources and of sustainability affected the scope of this study. Most important, they limited the number of libraries whose internal policies and practices could be surveyed and the way in which the survey could be done.

There are 10 issues and practices related to selection and presentation. The first issue is the economic context of electronic resource selection. There are two most visible means libraries have developed for dealing with the pricing of electronic resources: consortial purchasing and alternative scholarly communication initiatives. Digital libraries have gradually increased the amount of money spent for electronic resources over the last decade or so, and they are spending an increasing proportion of their budgets on such resources.

There is good reason to predict that e-resource expenditures will accelerate rapidly over the next few years. For example, more and more journals from established publishers are becoming available on the Web, and tens of thousands of electronic books are now available through a single new company: netLibrary. Questia, another new company, has begun to offer an extensive collection of electronic resources directly to users. Although it is too early to tell whether such new services will take hold, there is substantial concern in some libraries that they must respond to this competition if they are to remain important sources of information on their campuses. For these libraries, one response to this new "competitive space" will be to invest more heavily in electronic resources.

As libraries spend more money acquiring electronic resources or access to them, there are growing concerns over the interrelated problems of vendor pricing and institutional finances. In particular, there is a common perception that libraries are at a disadvantage when acting alone in this environment and that collaborative effort is necessary. This is perceived to be especially true when libraries negotiate with large corporate entities. Two important and fairly distinct types of collaboration have begun to shape the electronic resource market. The first of these is cooperative purchasing through library consortia, and the second is the development of alternative outlets for scholarly communication. The ultimate impact of each of these developments on prices and the marketplace remain to be seen.

Importance of Consortial Purchasing and Pricing

The importance of consortia and consortial buying has become obvious to librarians around the world who are involved in acquiring electronic resources. Consortia have been formed for a variety of reasons and exhibit a number of similarities and differences. Some of them, such as OhioLINK, VIVA, and the California Digital Library (CDL), are state-based and limited to academic libraries. Other academic library consortia, such as the Committee on Institutional Cooperation, include members in multiple states within a region. The NorthEast Research Library (NERL) consortium also includes members from several states, but its members are primarily private universities.

There are also many state-based multitype consortia, such as NC Live in North Carolina and INCOLSA in Indiana, as well as national consortia based in the United Kingdom, Canada, Australia, and elsewhere. Some of these consortia originated with broad mandates to foster resource sharing through online catalogs; they are relevant to this report to the extent that they attempt to negotiate better prices and other terms for libraries that are purchasing electronic resources.

Consortial arrangements for databases can benefit libraries financially in various ways. Usually, as the buying group expands, prices are lowered. One common practice is to put in place a price per full-time equivalent (FTE) student that is based on a sliding scale; as more FTE students are added to the consortial contract, the price is lowered. Another approach, taken by journal publishers, is to determine the scope and content of a consortial e-journal collection on the basis of library holdings within the consortium. Examples of this include the arrangements that OhioLINK and NERL have with Elsevier under which members have access to all ScienceDirect titles.

Since no individual library is likely to be able to subscribe to all of this publisher's titles on its own, even the best funded of them stand to gain access to considerable content under such arrangements. Smaller libraries may be able to dramatically improve access to resources for relatively small amounts of money. Consortial purchasing also must be profitable for publishers and vendors, and many of them see these arrangements as opportunities to reduce marketing and invoicing costs. It has been argued that consortial contracts for e-journal packages enable publishers to gain revenue from smaller institutions that could not otherwise afford to subscribe to any of these journals.

Although consortial arrangements can provide libraries with much better pricing or other advantages, those benefits must be weighed against the costs of doing business consortially, which can include substantial staff time and some losses of local control and flexibility. An added complication is that libraries can be formal or informal members of a number of different, and sometimes competing or overlapping, consortia and buying groups. Deciding which arrangements make the most sense in a given situation may be difficult.

Appropriate consortia Web sites were then checked to determine whether there seemed to be a consortial role, and further contact was made with a few key individuals to double-check the information.

Scholarly Communication Reform Initiatives

Although the consortial movement appears to have had a significant effect on prices, the recent development of Web-based alternative outlets for scholarly communication may also influence the market for scholarly information. One of the earliest and most successful of these alternatives is the physics preprint server at the Los Alamos National Laboratories, now known as arXiv, which is provided free of charge and serves researchers in a wide variety of physical science disciplines. Within a relatively short time, it has become an important part of the research culture in several of these disciplines.

The American Research Library (ARL) has organized several initiatives aimed at addressing the problem of high journal prices. Most recently, these efforts have focused on three complementary programs. The first of these is the Scholarly Publishing and Resources Coalition (SPARC), which has helped fund the development of a number of electronically based scientific journals and resources. One of SPARC's main goals is to foster competition in the STM journal market; consequently, some SPARC journals have been developed to compete directly with specific journals deemed to have especially high prices. SPARC's related Create Change and

Declaring Independence initiatives are aimed at raising journal editors' awareness of pricing issues and at encouraging them to take remedial actions to restrain prices. Suggested strategies include negotiating with publishers about pricing policies or, if pricing negotiations are unsuccessful, starting competing journals.

Although libraries seem to have good reason to support both the consortial and scholarly communication reform movements, a number of recent articles have pointed to a tension between the two approaches. For example, Landesman and Van Reenen have posited that there is a natural affinity or congruence between consortia and large publishers or vendors. Both are looking for the economies of scale that are represented by large packages, and although these packages typically do provide subscribers with more content for their money than individual print subscriptions used to, the large dollar commitments required can quickly claim larger and larger shares of scarce resources. These commitments will appear more justified as usage climbs because of visibility and easy availability. When that happens, there will be less money to pay for the individual titles and smaller packages that consortia are poorly equipped or unprepared to handle; these will tend to be the more modestly priced offerings from the scholarly associations and university presses.

In response, supporters of such package deals have emphasized the added content that may be made available and the importance of user choice. They have also stated that libraries do not surrender their ability to negotiate terms when they enter such agreements. There seems to be much value in both the consortial and "reform" approaches to influencing the market, and thoughtful people might reasonably lean in one or the other direction. However, as Landesman and Van Reenen suggest, consortia could help ensure the success of SPARC-like initiatives if those initiatives could be made more "consortia friendly." Bundling significant amounts of content, as the SPARC BioOne initiative is doing, seems to be one way to address the need for economies of scale.

Some for-profit publishers have also found that consortial contracts can provide them with new income from smaller institutions if the contracts provide those institutions with substantial content for little money. In addition to supporting these institutions financially, consortia could facilitate faculty education efforts and help create alternatives to established publishing outlets.

Policies and Plans

Faced with high user expectations, rapid change, and competitive pressures, it is not surprising that many librarians characterize local selection decisions as ad hoc or opportunity driven. Such decisions are also sometimes described as having strong political elements; this may be especially apt when the purchase of one expensive service for a particular group rules out the acquisition of another service that a different constituency may feel it needs.

Many libraries have tried to overcome such tendencies and perceptions and to give shape to their licensed digital collections by writing and adopting formalized local policies and plans. It seems clear that such documents should reflect and support the differing missions of these libraries and their parent institutions, and several do, although sometimes in only in a general way. For instance, Massachusetts Institute of Technology's (MIT's) document, entitled "Toward a Networked Resources Policy," begins by noting that the library "seeks to acquire access to the primary digital information resources which support the educational and research missions of the Institute".

A general sense of institutional mission may or may not prove helpful in making real-life decisions. Libraries that are funded to serve broader state, regional, or national constituencies face special dilemmas in the digital environment. For example, the US Library of Congress has traditionally served an archival function for printed materials, and that will be more difficult when these materials are both digital and licensed. Similarly, the libraries of large, state-funded universities are often expected to share their resources with other libraries or individuals in their states. When subscriptions to scholarly e-journals come with significant license-based restrictions or prohibitions on use for interlibrary loan, the institution can find itself caught in a new way between the priorities of local users and other groups.

Several selection-policy documents also refer to the need to support programs or to define the constituency to be served by a given resource. The documents mention other interesting considerations, including the need to maintain a balance among disciplines or subject areas, or with traditional formats, when choosing electronic resources. Some policies stipulate that there need to be identifiable and strong reasons for selecting electronic access over print or other formats.

The decision to acquire a given resource must consider these "non-content" costs and ramifications; as has been seen, questions of policy, strategy, and mission may also be involved. It is not surprising that libraries have recently been experimenting with different organizational approaches to these questions. Some have tried to address the apparent tension between centralized and decentralized decision-making models. Several institutions have made large amounts of money available to centralized budget lines. This seems particularly appropriate when resources are heavily interdisciplinary or multidisciplinary, when large amounts of resource funds are involved, or when there is a contractual requirement to maintain a certain level of expenditure with a given publisher.

On the other hand, many institutions believe it important that subject selectors or specialists have the leeway to spend noncentral or subject funds for electronic resources without having to go through multiple levels of review and approval. These considerations have prompted some institutions to write guidelines on such questions as how different categories of funds should be used, who should be involved in decision making, and how to develop new committee structures.

Many large libraries have invested substantial time and effort in trying to understand, document, streamline or rationalize, and communicate their local procedures for acquiring e-resources. The resulting documentation may be of significant value to other libraries grappling with the same issues. Many different pieces of information must be gathered and organized as a particular acquisition makes its way through most local processes. As with the acquisition of traditional materials, much of this information, such as basic descriptive information, vendor, selector or selectors, and fund or funds involved, is fairly standard.

For resources accessed through the Web, the appropriate URL or URLs, relevant user names and passwords, Internet protocol ranges from which they are available, and system requirements are needed. The ability to determine the status of a resource within the overall selection process is also important, and that can be a complex question. For example, libraries typically establish trials of resources that they are considering buying, and it is important to know when and to whom the resources are available for review, how and by whom input about them is to be received, and so on. Establishing funding for large expenditures can also take time, as can resolving license details and issues.

Licensing Issues and Practices

One of the biggest and most often-discussed changes facing libraries as they increase their reliance on electronic resources is that the use of these resources is typically governed by contract rather than solely by copyright. The full significance of this development and its impact on libraries have yet to be realized, but there are reasons for concern. For example, while existing copyright law provides for the time-honored practice of interlibrary loan, licenses may forbid or so constrain this practice that it becomes too costly or otherwise impractical.

Such license provisions can undermine a library's ability to continue serving as a regional or state resource.

Licenses may also interfere with a library's archival roles and responsibilities if ongoing access rights are excluded or if there are severe restrictions on photocopying. There may also be prohibitions against user copying that the library is unable to enforce. Noncompliance by library staff or end users may permit the vendor to discontinue the service without a refund for time remaining on the contract. In addition, the parent institution may be put at financial risk if its libraries are required to accept responsibility for user actions or agree to indemnify the provider against third-party damage claims. Finally, if, as frequently happens, a distant state's or country's laws and courts are named as the contractual authority, the institution could incur substantial travel and other costs in the event of litigation.

Many of these issues are now widely recognized within the library community, partly because of initiatives that have been organized over the last few years to help educate librarians. For example, for several years ARL has offered excellent training materials and classes for librarians wishing to upgrade their skills and to institute organized local processes for dealing with licensing issues. The popular Liblicense Web site and Liblicense-l listserv have also had considerable impact, because they facilitate discussions among librarians and publishers about licensing issues.

Efforts to develop more favorable license terms and standardized language have also been important. For example, the International Coalition of Library Consortia's "Statement of Current Perspective and Preferred Practices for the Selection and Purchase of Electronic Information" articulates a library-oriented viewpoint on several licensing issues, including fair use and perpetual access rights and liability for user actions. The concentrated purchasing power within that group has undoubtedly prompted some vendors to be more responsive to the concerns of potential buyers about licensing terms.

Some consortia and individual libraries have clarified and strengthened their bargaining positions by defining their own sets of standardized license terms or requirements. Despite these noteworthy efforts, libraries may still agree to terms that they regard as less than ideal. For example, if libraries are not required to accept responsibility for user behavior, they may still agree to make "reasonable efforts" to inform users of license terms.

It should be relatively simple for libraries to adopt and use such a general disclaimer, but because license details vary from one product or service to another, a general statement may be insufficient to make users aware of relevant terms. Some licenses require that subscribing libraries route their users through a "click-through" page containing standardized language about use restrictions and may also require users to certify that they are eligible to use the product. It seems impractical for libraries to consider investing the staff time required to write and maintain such pages for a large number of products.

If vendors do not provide rules of use or brief versions of license terms through their Web sites and services, libraries must devise and implement their own ways of tracking license terms and making them available to users and staff. Several libraries have done so. As interesting and promising as their efforts appear to be, there are still significant barriers to developing truly efficient systems for addressing this problem. One alternative that has recently been proposed is for libraries to share the effort of analyzing and reporting license details, much as cataloging effort is shared through bibliographic utilities.

Libraries could then incorporate a license profile for a given product into appropriate gateway or catalog descriptions of the resource. This idea seems to have merit, but since licenses for a product can vary among institutions, it could be difficult to establish the canonical version. The development of standard definitions of key provisions could facilitate the growth of such a system.

Strategies of Web Presentation

There are three general strategies for providing access to commercially available electronic resources: local loading by an individual library, loading by a consortium, and relying on vendor sites. Individual libraries have generally been moving away from the local load strategy because of its cost. Consortia have done likewise, although there are notable exceptions. Whether reliance on publisher and vendor services is truly the most cost-effective strategy is an interesting question, since an argument can be made that it entails a range of hidden costs. Local loading provides some important advantages, including control over the number and functioning of user interfaces and normalization of usage measurement.

Presenting electronic resources effectively to users poses challenges for collections of locally digitized, commercially available, and "free" Web resources, and each type of resource has its own distinctive issues and complications. The role online catalogs should play in providing access to these resources is controversial because users accustomed to the Web expect to be able to locate resources through just a few mouse clicks. This is especially true of students who, without a quick means of retrieval, will tend to rely even more extensively on Web search engines than they currently do. A number of institutions have observed that the use of specific resources jumps or declines quickly on the basis of their gateway placement and visibility, and this phenomenon has recently been documented.

Large libraries appear to follow a strategy in which resources are presented both through catalogs and e-resource gateways. These gateways typically provide alphabetical or subject lists of databases or electronic journals, along with an effective gateway search tool. Providing such multiple paths to resources in a cost-effective manner requires establishing synergy between cataloging and the methods used to generate lists, which can be accomplished by systematically deriving metadata from an online catalog system and using it to create a separate database from which resource lists are generated.

Several writers have pointed to the extent and importance of the trend toward customized services, and there have recently been efforts aimed at providing closer fits between user needs and the organization of resources than may be provided through established subject schema. For example, a system at the University of Pennsylvania organizes resources according to flexibly defined communities of interest. In this system, bibliographers identify the resources they believe to be the most critical to a particular user community, and new resources are brought to the attention of users through highlighting.

Both established and newer presentation strategies tend to treat e-resources as distinct entities that are located and then searched and used one at a time. However satisfactory the presentation of distinct databases may be, users may find the effective integration of disparate resources to be just as important. One step in that direction was the development of broadcast search functions, which were introduced first for traditional indexing and abstracting databases. Useful as those functions are, it is also important to integrate full-text content with the indexing and abstracting services.

Until recently, few libraries had been able to systematically make users aware of what periodicals were included in which aggregator databases; however, techniques for doing so are now being developed. An important step toward making the content of these collections more visible and usable is the development of the jake initiative and the related jake2marc program. Both of these services are available to interested libraries free of charge. jake incorporates periodical holdings or coverage information for nearly 200 databases and enables users to determine which database or databases include a given title. Institutions can customize jake to reflect their own holdings. The jake2marc service uses the jake database to enable libraries to generate catalog records for local use.

Libraries clearly have reasons to want more universal, standardized solutions to the problem of providing such links to full text. One new approach is Crossref; an industry-based initiative aimed at enabling article linkages across participating publishers. Although the initiative includes a significant number of for-profit and nonprofit publishers, it has some drawbacks, the most important of which may be libraries' inability to control which links are enabled. This can be an important issue, since publishers can provide Crossref links only for their "premiere" e-journal services, and links to less-costly alternatives from a given publisher may not work.

Some librarians believe that what is needed is a single utility that can be used to establish and maintain full-text links for indexing databases from various publishers and that gives them control over which links are enabled. More visionary is the idea of establishing a broader "scholars' portal" or commons that could be searched more or less like such established Web search engines as Yahoo, Alta Vista, and Google. The advantage of such an approach is that it combines convenient access with appropriately "vetted" academic content. Practical means toward achieving such a vision may be available through metadata harvesting, a method being investigated and developed through the Open Archives Initiative. The viability of the scholars' portal idea may depend on the availability of consistent and comparable metadata, and this may be difficult to achieve.

User Support

As libraries have increased their investments in electronic resources, providing ongoing support has become more complex. For example, as libraries rely more heavily on access through multiple remote vendors, interfaces and potential points of failure have proliferated. As indexing services and e-journal collections become more closely linked, such "pieced-together" or eclectic systems present additional possible points of failure. Any number of problems may arise for users accessing licensed resources remotely. For example, a particular service may suddenly become slow to respond or unavailable because of technical problems, Web browser configuration or unrelated connectivity issues, or invoicing and payment problems.

Users coming to a library's gateway through a commercial Internet service provider may also find services to be unavailable to them and not realize that this is because they have not authenticated themselves through a proxy service. Most users of Web-based services expect these services to be understandable and usable with a minimum of help or intervention from others. When users do need support, their expectations are high.

For example, users may wish to use a consortium's or library's gateway at any time of day and may expect live support at those times. Just what support may be needed and how it is to be provided are continuing questions, and libraries' responses to them are based on local perceptions, resources, and priorities. Of course, users need to know what services are available, who is eligible to use them, and how to connect to them. These basic needs have typically been addressed through the design of gateway Web pages and e-resource lists mentioned in the previous sections. These approaches can be helpfully supplemented by basic "how to use" instructions.

Connectivity and other technical problems are more difficult and seem likely to require ongoing efforts of various kinds. Provision of basic information about how to make a library-specific connection may be necessary. Lists of known problems and solutions can be posted for users, as can browser configuration pages that inform users if they need to adjust settings and that provide information on how to contact staff for help. Some libraries have begun to experiment with online "chat" functions for reference and other services, and it seems reasonable to suppose that such an approach would work for asking questions and receiving advice on access problems.

Several libraries and consortia have determined that they can respond more effectively to support problems if the work can be distributed among a number of units or individuals, such as those identified as resource coordinators or liaisons. This strategy necessitates some coordination and orchestration; some libraries have done this by establishing and communicating triage paths for different situations. Doing so may be easier if vendor contact information is assembled and maintained centrally.

Evaluation of Usage Information

Libraries have long had a strong interest in knowing how, how much, and by whom their collections are being used. A prevailing motivation has been to focus spending on those parts of the collection that appear to be used most heavily, although it has long been recognized that some specialized materials are likely never to receive much use. Measuring the use of print collections has been approached in various ways; early efforts to develop and apply unobtrusive techniques have given way to reliance on online systems for tracking external circulation and systematically recording in-library use.

It has been possible to track the use of electronic resources for many years, and many libraries have considerable experience gathering, analyzing, and presenting such data for internal and external consumption. In addition, libraries have come to expect vendors to provide usable and useful data. Although it may be possible to state such an expectation fairly simply, defining it has proved to be difficult. Just what should be measured, how the information should be presented, what data might mean, and how they might be used confidently in decision making are all questions without obvious answers.

There are some obvious impediments to obtaining data useful for these purposes. First, most libraries currently depend on vendors for usage information, and many supply no data at all. Libraries and consortia such as OhioLINK, which rely on their own equipment and staff for access to electronic resources, are well positioned to develop and initiate measurement and presentation methods that could become standards in the future. The usage measurement and presentation methods developed at the University of Pennsylvania demonstrate that it is possible to be innovative without an extensive local investment in infrastructure. Some libraries are also attempting to show how electronic resources affect student learning or facilitate research productivity. If successful, these efforts could also be widely emulated.

Classification-based Interfaces

Organizing books and documents in a digital library interface by an a priori classification system may seem to be a weak alternative to the variety of ad hoc organizations possible in response to searches. However, a consistent structure, reflecting a commonly agreed upon organization of knowledge, may help orient the user.

Indeed, an interface which reflects the structure of the classification system essentially provides suggestions to a user about further options to pursue following a search. That is, after a search a user can select from the node labels of the classification system near the search hits to identify the subdivisions that may help further refine the search. The classification system can also be used to restrict searches so as to reduce the computational cost and avoid overwhelming users with spurious information.

There are two types of interfaces for accessing books and documents organized in classification systems. The interfaces have been implemented in the X Window System using Motif widgets. The first interface is for the Dewey Decimal Classification (DDC). this uses the hierarchical organization to facilitate browsing and the presentation of book records. The second interface manages documents organized by a type of faceted classification system.

Electronic Book Interfaces

Several interfaces have been developed for accessing online book records. However, most Online Public Access Catalog (OPAC) interfaces are designed for ASCII terminals and do not have advantages, such as direct manipulation, associated with GUIs. Other OPACs provide extensive term searching but do not take advantage of the hierarchical organization. Book cataloging systems also provide access to the hierarchical classifications. However, these generally have only simple graphical interfaces and are not documented in the literature. Some prototype electronic catalogs introduce creative interfaces but may not scale well for large collections.

Many classification hierarchies have multiple components. These include faceted classifications, polyhierarchies, and multitrees. Faceted classifications are the most widely explored of these systems and they have been proposed as suitable for online retrieval by Godert; but electronic systems to manage these have not been previously described. Because documents may be included under several different nodes of a faceted classifications, the faceted classifications are a type of directed acyclic graph. On the other hand, any faceted classification can be expanded as a simple hierarchy.

Dewey Decimal Classification

The DDC probably is the most widely used international classification system. It is also one of the purest hierarchies of the major library classification systems. The DDC was designed for cataloging books, but it has been suggested as the basis for an interface to help the casual user. With the introduction of high-powered personal workstations and flexible GUIs, the accomplishment of this goal for the casual user is now feasible. The headings for a large part of the DDC were obtained and merged with the book records.

While the DDC, as with any classification system, is not suitable for all tasks, it is useful for a large range of tasks and is familiar to many users. In preparing the corpus, long call numbers were truncated to 4 decimal places. In a few cases, the hierarchy was not complete and filler headings were inserted. For instance, in the Classification immediately below the first-level node 000.0 Generalities is the third-level node 001.0 Knowledge. A second-level heading 000.0 General was created to match other second-level headings under 000.0 Generalities such as 010.0 Bibliography.

Book and document records numbered by the DDC were obtained from the Bellcore Technical Libraries. They covered approximately 50,000 books and technical reports. Each record included the shelf number, author, title, publisher, location, a subject field, and a list of the library locations where the book was held.

In a deep and wide hierarchy, such as the DDC, the contents of the expanding TOC would frequently scroll out of view. Although less information is presented in separate Subject Hierarchy and Current Node Lists than in an expanding TOC, these lists yield a more predictable display and are especially suitable for the DDC records where the shelf number provides an additional pointer into the hierarchy. Moreover, book-record hierarchies have looser semantic connections between nodes at the same level than the TOCs of most individual documents and books. Thus, displaying all choices at intermediate-level nodes would not be particularly informative.

Book Shelf and Book Display Widgets

The Book Shelf does not attempt to mimic a physical book shelf. Rather, it is a very long list of book records. The user, typically, has only a partial view of the list. The view of the Shelf is limited by the number of items that can be displayed on the screen at any time and by options that determine which book records and which attributes of those records are to be displayed. The selection of displayed attributes is determined in response to iterative queries that control a filter mask. Thus, the Book Shelf is "dynamic" in the same sense as the dynamic graphical query interface described in and as used in general purpose data viewers (e.g.,. Nodes in the classification system immediately above the selected books are also presented on the Shelf.

The Shelf shows nodes at different levels abutted one after the other. The default display for records on the Shelf shows titles. The user can select other attributes to be presented on the Shelf such as the author name, the length (number of paper pages), and the publisher. When the user clicks on a book title on the Shelf, a Book Display widget opens showing the full record for that book. Indeed, it is possible to browse the Shelf by selecting successive book titles to be displayed.

Fielded Search Widget

The Fielded Search widget generates searches on book record fields such as title, author, and subject descriptors. Three search algorithms are available: a Boolean OR of matched terms, term matches between the query and the document terms weighted by term frequencies, and Latent Semantic Indexing (LSI). For LSI searches, the LSI-value for a node is derived from the position of all the terms in the book titles and subject descriptions of all the books under that node. This is conceptually similar to the approaches of for other search algorithms. However, it meant that individual books were not able to be located with LSI. Moreover, because the LSI searches took considerable computational resources for matching vectors, the LSI space had to be precomputed.

Browsing

The interface can be used for browsing the DDC. The Current Node List displays items that allow the user to navigate deeper into the hierarchy. Initially, the current nodes are the top-level classification terms. When nodes lower in the hierarchy exist, the nodes above this are marked with an "=". The Subject Hierarchy List displays the hierarchy nodes above the books currently being displayed on the Book Shelf. Clicking on one of the higher-level nodes causes the immediate descendants of the selected node to be displayed in the Current Node List. In addition, the Shelf displays books at the selected node.

Searching

The hierarchical interface is most effective for comparing documents of relatively similar retrieval values because it does not easily display quantitative information about the matches. That is, unlike typical information retrieval (IR) systems that present items ranked by a similarity metric, the interface based on hierarchical structure does not readily show graded retrieval scores. The approach taken here is to set a threshold in the ranked-ordered list and to treat all items above that threshold as hits. Initially, a titration procedure was developed to select the threshold so that, not less than 5 titles and not more than 100 titles would be presented. However, informal user testing suggested that users often wanted to override the titration setting.

Restricting Shelf by Attributes

Attributes, such as library location, whether the document has been checked out, and the type of document, may be used to select subsets of books controlled by menus. By selecting various library locations it is possible to examine the virtual Shelf for any one location or any combination of locations of the Bellcore Technical Libraries.

Additional Shelf Traversal Modes

Two additional modes for skipping through search hits on the Book Shelf were implemented. It was possible to skip by Book and by search-algorithm-match order. Specifically, the UpBook and DownBook buttons allow the user to easily find book titles that match a search. The PreviousBookInOrder and NextBookInOrder buttons let the user examine books in the ranked order in which they matched the query. However, it is easy for the user to lose orientation because the books are not necessarily in order and the user viewing them may jump around the hierarchy. If the user requests NextBookInOrder after all the books in the initial set have been viewed, the set expands by relaxing the threshold.

Similar Books

An option for the Book Display allows the user to request Similar Books. It searches for books similar to the displayed book where similarity is determined by one of the retrieval algorithms rather than by shelf proximity. This option spawns a new search that, when it follows an initial search, is a type of relevance feedback. Because the book records are short, the Similar Book requests yield some spurious matches. As with the initial searches, posting similar-book hits against the Subject Hierarchy List allows the user to follow the classification semantics to identify relevant items. The Book Display also contains options for presenting other books by the same author. This links books across leaf nodes of the hierarchy.

For especially complex hierarchies, when a person using the browser reaches a terminal node they may not find exactly the information they are looking for but they may suspect they are close to it. Requesting a search for Similar Books would be one way to find other relevant sections of the hierarchy, but it is also possible to have precomputed lateral links between nodes (i.e., "distributed relatives"). A mechanism was implemented for this, in which a button was associated with each node and clicking on that button presented a list of other related nodes. At some point, these complex hierarchies would be better represented by faceted classification systems.

User Restricted Collections

In many cases, a user would be willing to restrict searches to certain segments of the classification hierarchy. This could improve computational efficiency and would focus the users attention. While that capability was not essential for the current prototype with about 50K book records on a powerful workstation, for a much larger collection (e.g., for the Library of Congress collection or for World-Wide Web (WWW) pages on the Internet) the user should be able to specify subsets of the records to search. For this system, users sub-selected nodes to include on a separate shelf and they could toggle back and forth to that shelf.

To show the context of the selected constraint labels, the parents of the constraints are displayed in parentheses on the Constraint List. The Shelf is updated with articles that match the constraints. Of course, the constraints propagate to all their descendants. Constraints can be dropped from the Constraint List by clicking on the "—" on the right side of the widget.

The interface allows the user either to take documents that match the union of the constraints (AND) or the intersection of the constraints (OR). For large collections, there are often far too many matches for the union. By switching to the AND display, the most relevant documents can be easily found. For the ACM CR collection, there is substantial variability in the number of categories assigned and the criteria for determining relevance of those categories.

Because most of the documents are assigned to several categories, a user could find a relevant node and then find other nodes that have similar classifications. The overlapping categories are presented in the current interface by selecting the "o" from the first vector on the right side of the Facet Menu widget.

Currently, term-frequency weighted searches are implemented in this interface. In one mode, it is possible to ask for all document titles to be included in the search. It is also possible to limit the search to those documents that match the constraints. Posting search hits against the hierarchy is more complicated in this case than for the simple hierarchical display because a single document can belong to several categories. The current system uses fractional category memberships when the hits are spread across categories. As noted above, the Book Shelf for the facet interface has no a priori order. Thus, there is no natural order to display search hits. On the other hand, a variety of other ad hoc organizations are possible. For instance, the categories might be ordered by the density of hits. A related problem is which facet hierarchy to pop-open after a search.

User Studies

While formal user studies have not been conducted on these interfaces, informal feedback from users of the hierarchical interface has been generally favorable. One major innovation here has been the introduction of a Book Shelf. Because this is the only full-scale system to include a Book Shelf (and hence the only system to allow browsing of books by shelf order), it is not clear what sort of evaluation is most reasonable. The greatest problem with these interfaces appears to be complex interactions among features. For instance, in the Hits Only mode there are often too few selections to fill the Shelf Display; thus, the UpBook and DownBook buttons have no effect. In addition, some test users have suggested that the elision in the Hits Only mode should apply to the TOC as well as the Book Shelf. Completely shifting context from one set of screens to another (e.g., with the similar books option) is also difficult.

Beyond the problems of the interface design, there are limitations inherent in this type of interface for hierarchical classification systems. A substantial concern is the user does not know how many books are included under each node. For parts of the hierarchy hierarchy, a user may know or may be able to take a good guess; however, the user may not be at all familiar with other parts of the hierarchy. The facet interface is probably harder to use than the simple hierarchical interface. This is because of the complexity of managing multiple facet hierarchies and the lack of a natural shelf order for the documents. Moreover, the facet interface described here has not been as well developed as the simple hierarchical interface. For instance, graphical displays might be especially useful for navigation of the facet hierarchies.

Integration with Information Systems

These interfaces could provide the basis for access to additional electronic information sources. Clearly, it would be possible to have the short document records pointing to the full text of the books and documents. Moreover, encyclopedia articles describing authors could easily be presented. Likewise, book reviews, citation statistics, circulation data, and user annotations could be included as part of the Book Display. Conversely, an electronic encyclopedia could access the OPAC for bibliographies.

Overall, these interfaces suggest that the structure of a classification system can be a useful aid for searching and navigating a digital library. Indeed, it may be worth exploring how digital library classifications can be extended to finding information in less structured domains such as for information in the WWW.

Envoi

Techniques such as the PreviousMatchNode/NextMatch-Node buttons and lateral linking show how search-based IR and structure-based Hypertext approaches can be combined. It is also worth noting that structure could be used to enhance a search-based OPAC. In any event, while the DDC provides links to related documents, there are many other dimensions of similarity (e.g., author, citations, publisher) that could be used for linking as well. It remains to be seen whether these dimensions can be coordinated into useful interfaces.

Preservation of Electronic Resources

The need to preserve electronic resources and continue to make them available has been recognized for years, but only recently have there been serious and broad-based efforts in this area. One reason is that many libraries now have experience with significant numbers of electronic journals and have started to consider whether they can truly afford both online and print subscriptions. The prospect of relying completely on electronic access to large numbers of journals or other resources raises a number of questions.

For example, if libraries rely completely on electronic access and have to cancel their electronic subscriptions in the future, or if the publisher goes out of business or discontinues access to older content, the library risks losing access to back issues. If the publisher provides libraries with electronic files in those eventualities, how are libraries to use them? Last, there is increasing awareness that electronic versions of journals may differ significantly from printed versions. Electronic versions may include video and sound clips, special-purpose data requiring specific software, and links to ephemeral Web sites that may be difficult or impossible to archive.

There seems to be a growing consensus that although publishers might be expected to provide archival access in the short term, libraries are the appropriate agencies to serve this function for posterity. Possible costs of long-term preservation could be substantial, if, for example, data must be frequently refreshed and migrated or if emulation software must be developed and maintained. Most libraries will have difficulty devoting substantial local funds to these activities.

Managing Electronic Resources

Electronic resource management systems vary in purpose and function, they have all been implemented to remedy perceived deficiencies in these institutions' online cataloging, acquisitions, or other systems. For example, some are used to generate alphabetical lists of databases and electronic journals or to keep track of important license terms. Some integrate the listing and license tracking functions; others focus on tracking acquisition status or organizing technical information. As these systems' similarities and common functions began to emerge, the value of a more thorough and systematic inventory became apparent. That is, if many libraries are trying to solve much the same problem, it might be possible to devise common functional and data definitions and standards that could be used as the basis for future design and implementation work—by libraries working individually or collectively or by vendors.

Several institutions record and display links to electronic versions of their licenses, and Penn State has initiated a special project to digitize and make its licenses available. As noted, libraries rely extensively on established online acquisitions systems for tracking and reporting financial details. Whether the complexities involved in e-journal pricing and their many permutations can be successfully captured in this way is open to some question, however. Interestingly, several libraries try to save key e-mail correspondence with vendors because they record important transaction details.

Where traditionally designed online acquisition systems appear to be least successful in supporting the purchase of electronic resources is in how they allow for coverage of "process" or status information. The importance of doing so is indicated by the fact that most of the electronic resource management systems incorporate some sort of "order status" information. However, the range of relevant system characteristics suggests that devising a standardized approach to process tracking may be difficult. One reason for this is that keeping track of a resource as it passes through the local acquisition process is likely to require steps that are highly specific to a given institution.

Several of the systems track and provide reports of upcoming renewals. This is important for two reasons. First, an unpaid invoice may result in the sudden interruption of an institution's access to an electronic resource. Second, as mentioned in the section on evaluation and usage information, several libraries and consortia conduct cyclical reviews of electronic resources prior to renewing them. It would be difficult to plan for and coordinate such reviews without being able to see which resources will be up for renewal at what time. A couple of institutions have also included a "follow-up needed" reporting function in their local e-resource management systems, which should help prevent staff from losing track of problems.

Bibliography

Andrews, Judith, and Derek Law, eds. *Digital Libraries: Policy, Planning and Practice.* Aldershot, England: Ashgate, 2004.

Arms, William Y. "Key Concepts in the Architecture of the Digital Library." *D-Lib Magazine* (July 1995).

Arms, William Y., Christophe Blanchi, Edward A. Overly. "An Architecture for Information in Digital Libraries." *D-Lib Magazine* (February 1997).

Atkinson, Ross. "Library Functions, Scholarly Communication, and the Foundation of the Digital Library: Laying Claim to the Control Zone." The Library Quarterly 66 (July 1996): 239-265.

Bailey, Charles W., Jr. "Integrated Public-Access Computer Systems: The Heart of the Electronic University." *In Advances in Library Automation and Networking, vol. 3,* ed. Joe A. Hewitt, 1-33. Greenwich, CT: JAI Press, 1989.

Bishop, Ann Peterson. "Document Structure and Digital Libraries: How Researchers Mobilize Information in Journal Articles." *Information Processing and Management* 35 (May 1999): 255-279.

Buttenfield, Barbara. "Usability Evaluation of Digital Libraries." *Science & Technology Libraries* 17, no. 3/4 (1999): 39-59.

Campbell, Debbie. "How the Use of Standards Is Transforming Australian Digital Libraries." Ariadne, no. 41 (2004).

Chowdhury, G.G., and Sudatta Chowdhury. "Digital Library Research: Major Issues and Trends." *Journal of Documentation* 55 (September 1999): 409-488.

Falk, Howard. "Developing Digital Libraries." *The Electronic Library* 21, no. 3 (2003): 258-261.

Fox, Edward A. "Digital Libraries Initiative (DLI) Projects 1994-1999." *Bulletin of the American Society for Information Science* 26 (October/November 1999): 7-11.

Graham, Peter S. "Requirements for the Digital Research Library." *College & Research Libraries* 56 (July 1995): 331-339.

Hamilton, Val. "Sustainability for Digital Libraries." *Library Review* 53, no. 8 (2004): 392-395.

Han, Yan. "Digital Content Management: The Search for a Content Management System." *Library Hi Tech* 22, no. 4 (2004): 355-365.

Harter, Stephen P. "Scholarly Communication and the Digital Library: Problems and Issues." *Journal of Digital Information*, 1, no. 1 (1997).

Janee, Greg, James Frew, and Linda L. Hill. "Issues in Georeferenced Digital Libraries." *D-Lib Magazine* 10, no. 5 (2004).

Liu, Ying, and Anita S. Coleman. "Communicating Digital Library Services to Scientific Communities." LIBRES 14, no. 1 (2004).

Logoze, Carl, and David Fielding. "Defining Collections in Distributed Digital Libraries." *D-Lib Magazine* (November 1998).

McCray, Alexa T., and Marie E, Gallagher. "Principles for Digital Library Development." *Communications of the ACM* 44 (May 2001): 49-54.

Reidy, Denis V. "The Electronic Icarus: Some Problems and Some Solutions in Digitisation." *Information Services & Use* 22, no. 4 (2002): 151-157.

Smith, Terence R "A Digital Library for Geographically Referenced Materials." Computer 29 (May 1996): 54-60.

Wilensky, Robert. "Toward Work-Centered Digital Information Services." Computer 29 (May 1996): 37-44.

Index